JACKSON'S TRACK

DARYL TONKIN was born in Essendon in 1918. When he was thirteen years old he followed his older brother, Harry, up to New South Wales to work on his uncle's station. Two years later he and Harry travelled the stock routes in Queensland, breaking and trading horses with the drovers. In 1937 they came south to settle in the great forests of West Gippsland where they established a timber business. Except for a short stint at Toora, Daryl has lived and worked at the original property at Jackson's Track ever since.

CAROLYN LANDON was born in the USA in 1945. She received a BA in Literature and Philosophy from Beloit College in Wisconsin. She came to Australia in 1968 as a traveller, hitchhiking by small aeroplane throughout the far north, stopping five weeks at Elcho Island Mission in Arnhem Land. She became English Coordinator at a private school in Ballarat, but in 1971 joined the Victorian state education system where she is still teaching Senior Literature, English and Journalism. With her husband, Larry Hills, she has written and published three musical plays.

JACKSON'S TRACK

MEMOIR OF A DREAMTIME PLACE

Carolyn Landon & Daryl Tonkin

VIKING

The authors and publisher would like to thank the Museum of Victoria for permission to reproduce fourteen photographs from the Richard Seeger Photographic Collection, which appear throughout this book.

Viking
Penguin Books Australia Ltd
487 Maroondah Highway, PO Box 257
Ringwood, Victoria 3134, Australia
Penguin Books Ltd
Harmondsworth, Middlesex, England
Penguin Putnam Inc.
375 Hudson Street, New York, New York 10014, USA
Penguin Books Canada Limited
10 Alcorn Avenue, Toronto, Ontario, Canada M4V 3B2
Penguin Books (NZ) Ltd
Cnr Rosedale and Airborne Roads, Albany, Auckland, New Zealand
Penguin Books (South Africa) (Pty) Ltd
5 Watkins Street, Denver Ext 4, 2094, South Africa
Penguin Books India (P) Ltd
11, Community Centre, Panchsheel Park, New Delhi 110 017, India

First published by Penguin Books Australia Ltd 1999

3 5 7 9 10 8 6 4

Copyright © Carolyn Landon and Daryl Tonkin 1999

Designed by Sandy Cull, Penguin Design Studio
Map on p. xix drawn by Juliette Kent
Typeset in 11.5/18 pt Berkeley Book by Post Pre-press Group, Brisbane
Printed in Australia by Australian Print Group, Maryborough, Victoria

National Library of Australia
Cataloguing-in-Publication data:

Landon, Carolyn, 1945– .
Jackson's Track.

ISBN 0 670 88332 8.

1. Tonkin, Daryl, 1918– . 2. Interracial marriage – Victoria – Gippsland. 3. Racism –
Victoria – Gippsland. 4. Loggers – Victoria – Gippsland – Biography. 5. Aborigines,
Australian – Victoria – Gippsland – History. I. Tonkin, Daryl, 1918– . II. Title.

306.846099456

www.penguin.com.au

I DEDICATE THIS BOOK TO EUPHIE,
WHO WAS AS GOOD A WIFE AND MOTHER OF OUR CHILDREN
AS ANYONE ON THIS EARTH.

GOD BLESS HER.

— Daryl Tonkin

CONTENTS

ACKNOWLEDGEMENTS

I acknowledge Pauline, my daughter who wanted our story written and who brought Carolyn home to hear and write it. My thanks go to Carol Fraser, a family friend, for her support. To my family, who gave me the encouragement I needed to tell our life story. To Richard, for the photos he took and developed of some of the people living on Jackson's Track.

DARYL TONKIN

Thank you to Pauline Mullett, who initiated and sustained this project; Venetia Somerset, who recognised the worth of this story and gave me a push; Stephen Johnson, who maintained his interest and encouragement throughout the long process of the writing; Nancy Mortimer, who opened the gates; and, of course, Larry Hills and our two sons, Damon and Julian, for their support.

CAROLYN LANDON

I decided to write this book because of my children. I believe they should know about the history of Jackson's Track, and their mother and father's life story. Euphie and I had kept silent for years but we knew the children should be told. We thought that if I wrote a book our children could hand it down to their children, and other people would be able to read about the problems between blacks and whites in Australia.

My daughter Pauline told me that she knew a school teacher who was interested in Aboriginal people and their culture. She said her name was Lyn Landon and she wanted to meet me, so Pauline brought her home to my place. I found her a down-to-earth person with a lot of knowledge, a person caring of what was happening to this country. I told her I was writing a book and could use some help with it. She told me she had some writing experience and would be happy to help me.

I would write down things I remembered about the early days on the Track. She would take what I had written back to her place and start putting it all together on her machine. Each week we would talk about what I had written, then she would ask questions and take notes. I found it hard to write about our private lives but she was encouraging and said the truth had to be told, even if it was about my own family. Week after week Lyn drew my story out of me.

I had lived with Aborigines for fifty years and have a deep feeling for them, as well as for the bush and living with nature. I know how the Aborigines have been treated by governments and the Australian people. I have endured a lot in my lifetime, living and mixing with Aborigines, seeing how the white people took over this country with no respect for nature and human rights.

Daryl Tonkin, September 1998

Daryl Tonkin and I wrote this book together. He is the teller of the story (and the one who lived it) and I am the writer. Let me explain how the biography of this astonishing bushman was written.

Five years ago, Daryl Tonkin's grandson and granddaughter walked into my Year 7 English class at Warragul High School in Victoria. They were two lively Aboriginal kids who seemed to be out of their element in the classroom. I didn't know what to do with them. So, on a hunch, I went to their mother and asked her what she wanted them to learn and what her hopes were for their future. She had no idea how to answer either part of the question, but she was so astonished that I had asked that she sat and talked to me. We talked as two mothers; I had my own lively Year 9 boy who was making his teachers' lives hell at another school.

What came out of our discussion was that Aboriginal kids loved to tell stories, but they didn't like to write. I decided to have these kids tell their stories to me while I sat at the computer and typed their words. I told them to read what I was writing on the monitor in case I made mistakes and didn't get the stories right. In the end, each child wrote and illustrated their own book of autobiographical incidents, Aboriginal ghost stories, family legends, sporting feats and thoughts on issues such as racism. Finally, these kids began typing the stories on the computer for themselves and reading them out to the whole class with confidence.

It was a success story and their mother, Pauline Mullett, and I became friends. One day Pauline came to me with twenty-six sheets of smudged handwritten paper. She said she had got her dad to write the history of Jackson's Track. I looked at the pages, which were written in a neat but fairly large and bold copperplate, the hand of a confident, still alert old person. I knew something about Jackson's Track; that it had been a saw mill, that Lionel Rose had been born there, that it was situated near Jindivick, north-west of Drouin. I didn't know that it was one of a handful of important Aboriginal settlements in Victoria, that every indigenous person in this area came from there, that members of the families of most of the Aborigines in this state had been there, worked there or lived there at one time or another. Most white people didn't know that.

'What would you like me to do, Pauline?' I asked.

'We want to get it published, you know, properly.'

By properly, I thought she meant something that could be spiral-bound and distributed to family. Pauline laughed and indicated that it might go wider than the immediate family. She thought she could get some money from the co-op to make it part of Aboriginal studies in the Warragul–Drouin area.

'We can do that, but the manuscript needs work,' I said.

She told me I would have to come out to the Track to see her dad; he wasn't coming in, okay?

'Oh, my dad's white, you know,' she said as she was leaving.

No, I didn't know that. A white man among Aborigines. A million questions leapt into my brain. What an opportunity,

I thought. What a privileged position Pauline has placed me in. I felt in my bones that this was more important than I knew. There were dimensions here to plumb.

When I finally met Daryl about three months later, I offered to be his editor and teacher to help him get his book under way. He insisted he wasn't going to write any more. Because of my experience with Pauline's kids, I asked if he would like to talk to me and let me go home to my computer to write up his story each week.

Yes, that would be okay. Why didn't I take my glasses off?

I didn't even consider asking him about using a tape-recorder. Besides, there was no electricity.

We made arrangements for me to return the following week. On the first working visit, Daryl was surprised that I began asking questions about his life. He thought he would be able to keep his distance from the story, that he would give me anecdotal information about Jackson's Track, that I would polish up his 'yarns' and that would be it. But I couldn't keep my curiosity about this man before me at bay. His very presence, his age, his silver-white hair, his clear blue eyes, his kind face, his laughter and close-to-the-surface tears posed too many questions. I was taken by his stature, his still well-muscled workman's body, his work clothes and Blundstone boots, the missing joints from the index and second fingers on his right hand. Who was this man?

'What do you want to know about me for?' he baulked. 'I'm just a fool, a villain in the eyes of most.'

No use telling him that he looked more like a hero to me than a fool. I was interested in the yarns connected with the Track, but what I really wanted to know was how Daryl had come to throw his lot in with the Aborigines. How come his attitude was different from his peers'? How come he was wise, generous, understanding way before his time? I wanted to know about Pauline's dad and how he had come to be the father of nine active, articulate Aboriginal children who were proud of representing their people in this country. I knew the central story of Jackson's Track was this white man's story, so I kept asking questions.

Daryl began to talk about things he had never told anyone. Within three weeks, I knew I was listening to an astonishing life story that embodied the whole of the Australian experience. And so I began collecting in earnest Daryl's thoughts, his experience, his pain, his joy and, most importantly, his language.

It was difficult for a man of eighty years to begin explaining his life in a way that he had never tried before. He was a bloke who knew how to tell yarns at the camp fire. These yarns were mostly about work, work skills, male competition. He knew how to tell me about fist fights that lasted all day long ('You don't see fights like that any more'), or champion axemen with bull necks and bulging shoulder muscles, or days of hunting in the Little Desert with the blackfellas, or dragging logs off Mount Fatigue. But he had never spoken before about his personal fight with racism, his love for his brother, Harry, his sense of himself as a man, his pride in his children, his guilt and grief over the inevitable tragedy that befell the blackfellas of Jackson's Track.

Memory.

Memory, of course, is about feelings, and a bushman is not used to talking about feelings.

'I don't like thinking back on all this sadness, but I guess I will if I have to,' he said. 'What do you want to know?'

With Pauline's blessing, I kept asking questions. Of course, the story didn't come out all at once. Daryl and I would have long conversations once a week. I encouraged him to write some things down himself, which he did, but he always expressed reluctance to do so. Nevertheless, he set his mind to it and most weeks for the first two months of our partnership, then less frequently later on, he would hand me pages of story, feelings, ideas, written in that same strong copperplate hand I had seen initially. He would say, 'Here, I wrote this, but I don't know if it's any good to you.' I eagerly accepted all of his offerings, aware of the pain some of it must have caused him as he toiled over it sitting at his kitchen table in front of the hearth with the ever burning fire. I loved Daryl's pieces and incorporated them into the larger narrative that was slowly building up through our conversations. Each week I would go home to turn his meandering talk and his writing into a story, which I would show him and read back to him the following week to see if I had got it right, asking him for authentication and approval, as it were.

'You know how to tell a good yarn,' was all he would say.

I became worried. Surely I wasn't getting everything right first go when I felt some of what I had written was guesswork. I began to realise that he was reluctant to change anything I had written because he thought the print-outs I was showing him were finished copy and that it would be too much trouble to correct. He was letting me hijack his story. It took some effort to fix that problem because the concept of how a word processor works is not easy to grasp if you've never seen one in use. Once he understood it was easy for me to change the copy, Daryl became a more active participator in the writing of the manuscript itself.

'Well, ya got one thing wrong here, I'll tell ya.'

'What?'

'There are no magpies in forests!'

Concrete details like magpies versus currawongs that I got wrong, and there were only a few, rankled with him. I guess he couldn't believe someone could be so ignorant. In addition to his other pieces, Daryl began writing down details he remembered during the week to show me when I arrived. He made notes on points he wanted clarified. I often asked him to make lists of items like bush tucker or the variety of trees or birthdays or names of children.

As we continued, getting the chronology right was difficult because, of course, no one tells stories about themselves from beginning to end. It was my job to shape what Daryl was telling me, to discover how one event caused another, to figure out motivating factors in the personalities of the characters that were developing, to define and describe relationships, to work out the historical context of events, but not let that intrude too obviously on the memory.

The most important thing was to find the voice, since what I was really trying to do was create an individual human being out of words, Daryl's words. His thoughts, his philosophy, his sense of self would not be authentic without the right set of words. The only way I was going to find the right voice was to spend time with him talking about all sorts of topics, not just focusing on the work at hand. I kept my pen ready at all times to write down unique remarks, phrases with flavour, words with texture and colour. As we talked about things as diverse as traffic in the city, fences going up everywhere, people not taking the time to talk to each other any more, how people have changed or, in the case of racism, not changed, how to cook damper and the qualities of different flours, alcoholism, good people as opposed to villains, the value of education, I would hear a certain, maybe almost archaic, construction in a sentence, smile and write it down. Daryl thought I was nuts, but he got used to it. Daryl used the verb 'to fall' whenever he talked about trees coming down. He told me all the old bushmen say they 'fall' a tree or they 'get a job as a faller'. He reckoned only educated people say 'fell'.

'To my mind, that's stupid,' he said.

My favourite expression in this book is Larry Dooley. To 'give someone Larry Dooley' means to give them a beating. I thought it was just Daryl's expression but, no, I found it in *The Macquarie Dictionary*. Daryl's family who have read the manuscript say they can hear the words coming right out of their dad's mouth.

'Yep. That's what he would say. I've heard it before.'

So we must have got it right.

In this book an individual human being has been created, a human being we can identify and recognise, but it's important to remember that it's not the entire human being. While I was in the process of mining Daryl's memory, I began to feel that in writing it down I was doing a disastrous thing. I worried that once I had finished the 'life' I was capturing I would have limited Daryl forever by defining him. I was concerned that I would have diminished his demons or unravelled the tapestry of his internal self. No, Daryl will never tell everything. In fact, there are many, many more stories in that wise head. As I have come to know Daryl better, I realise that he is alert enough to differentiate between my version of his life which I see as being filled with drama and his own version of a life he considers ordinary. I think Daryl has allowed me to write his story because he is ready to find a final version of himself to lock up and put away for posterity. He knows he will take the rest with him.

Carolyn Landon, September 1998

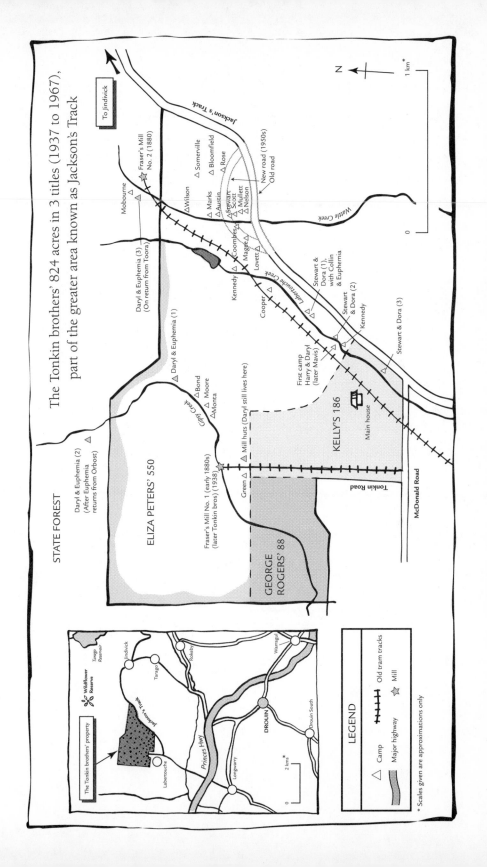

The Tonkin brothers' 824 acres in 3 titles (1937 to 1967), part of the greater area known as Jackson's Track

To Jindivick

N

1 km

0

Jackson's Track

Fraser's Mill No. 2 (1880)

Mobourne

Daryl & Euphemia (3)
(On return from Toora)

△ Wilson

△ Marks   △ Bloomfield
△ Austin   △ Rose
△ Somerville

Stewart △
Scott △
Mullett △
Nelson △

New road (1950s)
Old road

Wattle Creek

Coombes △
Magee △
Lovett △

Kennedy △

Cooper △

Stewart &
Dora (1),
with Collin
& Euphemia

Laberouche Creek

△ Stewart
& Dora (2)

△ Kennedy

Stewart & Dora (3) △

STATE FOREST

Daryl & Euphemia (2)
(After Euphemia
returns from Orbost) △

△ Daryl & Euphemia (1)

Gibson Creek

△ Bond
△ Moore
△ Monta

ELIZA PETERS' 550

△ Mill huts (Daryl still lives here)

First camp
Harry & Daryl
(later Mavis)

KELLY'S 186

Main house

Fraser's Mill No. 1 (early 1880s)
(later Tonkin bros) (1938) ☆

Green △

GEORGE
ROGERS' 88

Tonkin Road

McDonald Road

LEGEND

△ Camp

Major highway

┼┼┼ Old tram tracks

☆ Mill

* Scales given are approximations only

The Tonkin brothers' property

Wildflower
Reserve

Tanjo
Reservoir

Jindivick

Tanjo

Jackson's Track

Rokeby

Warragul

Princes Hwy

Longwarry

DROUIN

Drouin South

Laberouche

2 kms

Change

EVEN BEFORE WE CAME to this land it had already changed. Eighty years before us the hills had been colonised; the people with ancient knowledge had been hunted, massacred, infected with disease, scattered; the giant mountain ash trees had been falled; the primeval forest had been replaced with second-growth timber grown too high and too thick to penetrate. But it was still a place where a bushman could find mystery. In the sixty years since we first came here, the bush has continued to change and it will keep changing with time.

Nowhere is the bushman's camp to be found any more where we were always welcome and time was unimportant. The fires where we

Buddy Mullett fishing on the log bridge crossing Labertouche Creek

cooked damper no longer smoulder, nor do we take the time to listen to a well-told yarn at the end of the day. No longer are we comforted with the sound of bells through the night attached to cattle and horses' necks, nor do we hear the rattle of hobble chains on the horses grazing around the camp. The calls of the night birds are nearly all gone and the frogs no longer croak all night.

The pleasant sound of crosscut saws and axes is no longer heard. The voice of the teamster is silent, as is the creak of leather and the ringing of chains as animals strain in their work. Where is the crack of the stockwhip or the report of the hunter's gun signalling plenty of tucker to be shared around?

Where are the people who returned to their bush after we arrived and camped with their families along the creek beds, taking up the old ways? Where is the sound of their laughter, the chatter of their children, their dancing and music?

All that is heard in the bush nowadays is the roar of chainsaws and trucks and bulldozers. The men working in the bush today live in towns and have to pay for houses and machinery and cars to travel to work in. Although their work is done quickly, they have to make big money to pay for their modern lifestyle. Licences, laws, rules, restrictions take away the freedom and independence we once knew. Today's bushmen are soured by their burdens and have become like the machines they use.

Bushmen have changed, like the bush.

This is the story of my brother and me, some of the bushmen and the Aborigines who lived and worked in the Jackson's Track area from 1936 until 1975.

Eliza Peters' 550

CHRISTMAS 1936, at the height of the Depression, my brother, Harry, and I had just finished breaking a string of horses at a station on the Gilbert River in the Gulf Country in far-north Queensland. We thought it might be a good time to take a long slow trip down the coast to Melbourne to see our family and look over the country down there since we'd heard there were some blocks opening up for selection.

Our outfit was a sulky, a horse to pull it, two hacks and a heap of harness we used in the horse-breaking business. We drove that sulky into Cape York and over to the coast, but when we got there,

Daryl Tonkin on Sadie

we found the country rough and loaded with ticks, which bothered the horses, and, on top of that, the grass was sour. We kept plodding along, even though our horses were losing condition, until we got just past Ingham.

We camped for the night along a railway easement where the poor grass seemed to have some length to it. We hobbled the horses, as usual, so they could wander some distance to find feed. Of course, we belled them so we could find them in the morning easily enough. But during the night, one of them wandered onto the tracks and in the morning we found it in pieces all along the banks. We had no idea that's what a freight train could do to a horse. A fella came along and helped us clean up the mess. He told us we'd better move along before the inspector discovered whose horse had got in the way of the train. We didn't want a fine so we made a dash for Townsville.

Losing a horse that way kind of knocked the stuffing out of us. We weren't sure what we wanted to do. We crated up all of our harness and sent it by rail to our parents' place in Essendon. Then we worked our way slowly inland until we got to Ayr where we met a bloke who wanted us to go with him to find gold. We were almost ready to go along with him until he told us his method for finding gold.

'My hand'll turn when we see it!' he said.

Harry and I didn't know exactly what he meant but to us it sounded like mumbo jumbo and we knew we didn't want any part of it. We told him we wouldn't go with him, but we would sell him our outfit at a low price. He was happy.

Now, we had nothing to travel on except our own two legs. So, we went and bought two bicycles – not motorbikes, push-bikes. We rode them the 1600 miles to Melbourne. We managed about 100 miles a day, so it didn't take us long. Nevertheless, by the time we got down south, there were no selections left. No worries. We were so confident in our good luck, nothing would stop us for a moment. We decided to head east from Melbourne, curious to see the great forests in Gippsland. I was seventeen and Harry was twenty-two.

We had it in our minds that if we saw something good, we might stop and try to make a go of it. So before we left Melbourne, we asked our father to help us find a sound second-hand wagon. Father had a nose for these things as he was a haulage contractor who worked out of Essendon. He never drove anything but a wagon pulled by teams of horses. He hated motor vehicles, which he said would be the ruination of Australia, and I guess his influence rubbed off on us, on me especially. He was, of course, a good judge of horse flesh, and found us two fine horses to pull the wagon.

We loaded the four-wheel lorry with farm tools (plough, harrows, a seed bag of oats and a seed bag of barley, axes, crosscut saw, hammer and chains) and with setting-up tools (lantern, camp oven, billy, tin cups and plates, thick blue blankets) and with supplies (kerosene, sugar, flour, rice, tea, a few bags of stock feed, a few chooks in a crate). The last thing we loaded onto the lorry was a house cow. She stood at the back of the load, docile as could be inside her makeshift stock crate, just gazing around her and chewing on her cud as if she owned the place. And she stayed like that as we drove the wagon right through heavy Melbourne traffic, heading for Caulfield and eventually Dandenong. Of course, we were getting in the way of cars and trucks who wanted to pass us, but there were plenty of other horse-drawn vehicles still in the city in those days and those that were petrol-driven just had to put up with us. I would say we were the only overloaded vehicle being supervised by a cow, however. We must have looked a treat.

As we topped the long gentle hill into Oakleigh, the city suddenly turned into country, with paddocks and farm sheds as far as the eye could see, and we hadn't even got to Dandenong. There were still cars and trucks on the road, but suddenly things slowed down. I remember just outside of Oakleigh we had to stop for an old woman who was walking her cattle across the Princes Highway, cursing and screeching at the motor cars that came upon her too quickly. She was a rough nut all right, untidy and unconcerned about what people thought of her. I liked her straight away because she was a battler, and there were plenty of other battlers along the road in the 1930s. I guess Harry and I looked like battlers, too, but we were young and felt that we were on the way to our future rather than battling the odds as others felt.

We stayed on the Princes Highway until we reached Berwick. Those of you who drive your fast cars along the Princes Highway these days most likely don't even notice that there is a long, steep hill going into Berwick, but if you were in an old fourteen-foot wagon creaking along under a heavy load, you would be all too aware of it. Our horses just couldn't pull that load up the hill. Their hooves kept slipping on the bitumen and we were going backwards faster than we were going forward.

Finally, we had to turn around and go back, turn off the high-way, and try to find our way around the Berwick hill. After a long haul we got back onto the highway and stayed on till Pakenham, then continued along the back roads, going through the Koo Wee Rup swamp. We turned off the old coach road from Melbourne to Sale at the Robin Hood Inn and headed up Old Telegraph Road until we hit Jackson's Track, where we knew the biggest trees in the world were still standing.

It had taken us two days to make the hundred-mile journey.

We had a job driving our lorry along the Track, which wound around tall, spindly timber and ploughed through the bracken and ferns and scrub. The Track was gouged out in deep ravines by the big floods in '34, and there were plenty of boggy patches which had to be avoided – sometimes we would come upon a pothole big enough to bury a cow in. We would have been all right with just horses, but the lorry and cow made it rough. So it was slow going, just the right pace for having a good look around and a good think about what we were seeing.

In early 1937 we found ourselves looking at mostly second-growth timber with only the odd giant blue gum looming through the thick bush now and again. Before the old saw mills first started cutting trees out of this country in the 1880s, the forest was fairly open as the trees were the original growth and never had big bush-fires through them. But after the mills had finished their work, the floor of the forest was thick with the heads of the fallen trees, and when the big fire of February 12, 1898 came through, it changed the bush as the hot fire germinated the seeds and a dense mass of saplings came up, making a second-growth forest so thick it was almost impossible to penetrate.

As we looked through this country, we had a mind we could work it. A lot of the scrub on the south side of the Track was farm-land that had been deserted and had all gone back to bush. We knew it could be bought at a cheap price. We came across old George Rogers, the only person left out here on the Track. George was a funny and interesting old-timer who loved to talk. He could talk to you all day long without taking a breath. He loved the forest where he lived and wanted to tell us all about it: about the blocks in the district, who owned what, who worked it and who abandoned it. He gave us many cups of tea in old cracked china teacups while he explained about the bearings of the country. His memory went right back to the old mills and the original forest.

It was George who first told us about Eliza Peters' property, 550 acres of heavily timbered country bordering the Track. We wanted to see it, and so we left our gear at George's place and rode our horses out to have a look. It had thirty acres of red hill good for spuds, which we could see had once been cleared but was now half gone back to scrub and covered with young twelve-foot saplings. But it wouldn't be hard to clear it, farm it, make room for the horses, put up a shed and build a homestead. The rest of the acreage was criss-crossed with flowing creeks and covered with timber: tall silver-tops, mainly, and thick-barked messmates, stringy-barks, grey gums, iron-barks. Beautiful and thick with tall trees.

The acres and acres of timber, the plentiful running water and, across the Track, the added bonus of the 2000 acres of deserted farms where there looked to be the promise of good hunting made it seem, to us, a likely spot to live. George Rogers had told us the cattle deal-ers and local farmers were in the habit of putting fires through the scrub on the deserted farms on suitable days so as to burn the bush and bring up new growth for stock to stop on while the feed was fresh. Of course, he had said, the bush animals also followed the burns for the sweet feed and were easy prey for hungry bushmen in the clearer going. Harry and I sat on our horses for a while just breathing the air and getting a feel for the place. Finally we looked at each other and nodded in agreement. Yes, we were sold. We turned back and made our way to George to ask him where we could find the owner.

'You interested in starting up here, then?' he asked.

'We could make a go of it, where others couldn't,' we said, full of the confidence of the young. When you're young, you think you're smart and have plenty of spirit. Sometimes that's all it takes.

'I knew it! I knew you two young bucks'd see the beauty of this place. I knew it!' old George crowed. From then on we were his fast friends right up until he died.

My brother, Harry, was pretty smart and negotiated a price of thirty shillings an acre for Eliza Peters' 550 acres. Later we bought George Rogers' last eighty acres for ten shillings an acre and another 200 acres adjoining our place for eighteen shillings an acre. Of course, we didn't pay cash. It was the Depression. We didn't have the money. We were going to work it off.

Here we were, a couple of roaming stockmen and bushworkers from Queensland, with 800 rich acres to settle on and work. We thought it was great to own our own land and be our own boss. Harry and I had the makings of a good partnership. He was clever and a good businessman. He was good with people and enjoyed mixing with the neighbours and yarning with them. He was good at finding out this and that and keeping his ear to the ground for business.

I, on the other hand, liked to put my head down and get to work. I liked work. Up in New South Wales and Queensland, I had been working like a man since I was thirteen years old. I started out on my uncle's station by being the cow boy, which meant I had to milk the house cows, but they were not dairy cows. They were beef cattle brought in off the scrub with their calves to be milked. And they were brutes who used all their cunning not to get rounded up each evening because they must have known I was going to separate their calves from them all night so they would have milk for me to get in the morning. Those brutes would bellow and kick and head-butt me every morning to try to keep me from milking them. It was quite an initiation. I was then apprenticed to a chap on the station who specialised in fencing and yard making. He taught me to be a good axeman, that what makes a good axeman is being able to 'do up' an axe properly, as we did on the sandstone grinder wheel. You can't be any good if you haven't a sharp axe. I was only fourteen, but I was fully grown and strong as two men. I used to have races with him to see who could finish cutting a hundred fence posts first. If he wasn't there, I'd race against myself: I'd cut a hundred posts one day, bore a hundred post holes the next, and stand up a hundred posts on the third day.

At our new property, I was a quiet type who kept to myself. So, while Harry was off doing business in the neighbourhood, I liked being off on my own amongst the tall trees, chopping with the axe and being good with the saws. I liked working with the horses, clearing away the scrub or dragging logs out of the bush. I especially liked going out riding my best mare after hours, exploring the forest and discovering the history of my new home. I used to ride all through the bush on horseback. Whenever I saw something interesting I'd chase it up. I saw the old tramlines the first timber mills used to haul logs to the mills and then sawn timber to the railhead at Longwarry. They used tramlines then instead of roads, which could never be made good enough to carry heavy loads of timber through this country. The tramlines were built with sleepers laid about three feet apart and wooden rails cut at the mill dogged down to the sleepers. Then trolleys were put on to carry the timber. These were pulled by horses. Even though it was half covered with scrub, I could see all of this: the sleepers, the rails, the horse tracks. My horse and I followed them along. After the '39 fire all trace of the tramlines was burnt away, except you could still see the beds along which they ran. Now they have completely disappeared under new growth, but I remember where they are. There is something satisfying knowing the history of hard work and skill that went before you in a country.

There is also something mysterious about being in the bush on your own. I was always aware of the ancient history that happened well before the ring of steel on hardwood was ever heard in this forest. Not long after my brother and I came here, a bushman found an ancient axe made of stone, proof that people had been walking through these hills forever. I thought about where the people could have roamed and camped and how the bush had changed. I wondered about their way of life and wished I knew what they knew. There were none of those people here now, just second-growth timber and ruins of the old, original mills.

The Tonkin Brothers

THE FIRST THREE MONTHS on our new land was spent clearing the thirty acres of red soil. We planted only two acres of potato that first year and left the rest to the horses and the house cow. We built a shack to live in at the bottom of the hill. Harry had found a good deal on second-hand tin and we used it for the roof, walls and fireplace of our shack. The floor was dirt and the windows were covered over with hessian. It was comfortable enough.

For cash, we started cutting firewood which we delivered to Longwarry. Harry began looking through the papers to find workers to help us. Men were easy to find in 1937 because of the Depression.

Daryl and Harry

I would say that we were dead lucky to have a Finnish bloke named George Klinksbourne sign on with us almost from the first.

George was an excellent axeman and he could use a saw, too, but really he was a jack-of-all-trades. He was easygoing and not at all interested in money; he did things because he wanted to learn how to do them. Before he came to us, he had been a miner, then he had learned about the timber industry. It was George who talked us into setting up the mill. He knew all about saw mills, knew about operating the engines, knew how to build tramlines, knew how to size up a good tree, knew how to cut logs into timber.

Harry was convinced. He had heard about a mill in Drouin South worked by two brothers, Bill and Arthur Alan. The mill was run by a steam engine. Harry, who was a champion talker, had a yarn with the Alans and managed to talk them into selling him the steam plant as well as working it for us until we got the hang of it.

George knew exactly where the mill should go. He had been scouting around the ruins on a site just over the cleared thirty-acre hill from our shack. There wasn't much left of it except an old pitsaw and a big sawdust heap with a deep track going into a pit that ran beneath where the rip bench and breaking-down bench had been. But it was a good site because there was a nice fall line for the log yard; it was near the creek for water; and the area was already levelled off for the engine, benches and blades.

And so it was that Harry and I built our first mill on the old Gipsy Creek site where Fraser had built the very first mill in 1881 about a half-mile west of Jackson's Track. In Fraser's time, about thirty men were employed on this site. The trees then were fallen with axes and crosscut saws, just as they still would be in our day. Before the tramlines were established, the fallen logs had been hauled into the mill with bullocks. The original mill had eventually had a tramline built running about one mile into the forest, but that was all over-grown now. We would be using a team of horses to pull the logs into the yard from our acreage.

It took a whole day to cart the Alan brothers' steam engine the twenty miles out to the mill site from Drouin along Jackson's Track. It was brought out by truck. By this time we had done a fair bit of work to make the Track passable by piling split wood into every hole we could find, then corduroying the rest of it by laying logs side by side. You can't beat the corduroy, but it was rough as anything. At the mill site the engine was lowered off the tray of the truck and pulled into position with horses.

Once the engine was put in place, we had to make strong wooden benches to hold the blades and equally strong bench trolleys to carry the logs to the saws. For this we cut logs out of the bush and bolted them together with long bolts, made them smooth and mounted them on axles and wheels. George made a beautiful hand windlass out of wood which was to be used to pull the truck carrying a cut log through to the breaking-down saw. We dug out the sawdust pit beneath the benches deep enough for a man and wheelbarrow to go down there and cart out the dust as it filled up. We repaired the path from the pit to the sawdust heap to make it easy going for the carter.

George and I, under George's instruction, dug the creek out into the bank and worked it along to the mill for the steam engine. It takes a bit of know-how and bush engineering to bring water across a hill, keep it running slowly and gradually coax it to creep up the hill along the fall. That George was a clever man and I was his eager student. It was great to watch his mind tick over while he nutted out how to make things work perfectly. I had much admiration for this bushman, who never lived inside but camped out near the creek the whole time he was with us.

It took us a month of hard work to set up the mill. The only things we bought were saws, spindles, engine, axles and wheels for the bench trolleys. Everything else was handmade. As we stood back to look over our work, we all felt we had made a good job of it. We were proud.

Harry and I had our future set before us. We were the Tonkin brothers.

The Mill Work

OPERATING A SAW MILL is not an easy thing. It is strong work, tiring work, but you've got to be alert all the while or you may put yourself and your work mates at risk. It can be dangerous work.

Each man working at our mill knew his task. We had two men at the breaking-down bench, four on the ripping bench, two working with the sawyer pulling out from the blade, one operating the gauge and turning the handle on the rollers, one wheeling out the sawdust in a wheelbarrow. We also had an engine driver who kept the engine going and sharpened the blades. On top of this, there were the log cutters falling the trees and barking them out in the bush and the

Worker falling trees for the mill on Gipsy Creek

sniggers who hauled the cut logs into the yard and lined them up ready to roll onto the trolley.

It worked like this.

The axemen falled the logs in the bush, either by axe or with crosscut saw. Sometimes a tree had wide root spurs so the axeman had to work off boards where the trunk straightened out above the spur. It took a man of skill to put boards in a big tree and work off them. First of all he had to be a straight cutter and be able to put a scarf in the trunk with two or three swings and only six inches deep. This wasn't so difficult when you were working from the ground, but often the spurry butts rose several yards before the trunk straightened out and the axeman had to put a few boards in before he could work on falling the tree. So he would have to stand sometimes four metres above the ground and swing straight at shoulder height from a springy board, trim the new board to fit the scarf, then pound the board in tight.

We had one champion axeman working for us named Snowy Kerslake who showed his skill by putting a board in a big tree next to the mill every night until he was up about fifty feet. It was a pleasure to watch a good man working. I could do it, but you'd never catch me more than one board up. The height scared me. These men were artists.

The axemen needed to know the dangers of falling a tree. They would look up the tree to see if it was straight or leaning so they could work out how to place it to clear the other trees or it would get hung up. They didn't want to break the limbs of other trees on the way down either because that often left 'free swingers' overhead that could fall at any time. If the bush was thick with scrub, a track would always be cleared so if the limbs of the tree flew back as it was falling, a quick getaway could be made. Falling a tree with a saw tended to be slow business and if the tree was a 'free-splitter', it could split up when the saw was about halfway through it, especially if it was a windy day. If this happened and the top of the tree broke off, the tree would jump back and fall behind the stump.

Once cut, the fallers had to trim the trees, take the bark off them and cut them into suitable lengths – about eighteen to twenty-five feet – before the snigger could cart them to the yard at the mill along what we called snig tracks. A freshly barked log was easy to pull because it was 'greasy' with sap which allowed it to slip along. It was also important to bark the tree so the grit that lodged between the wood and bark didn't ruin the saw.

We called the bloke who pulled the logs to the yard the snigger. I was chief snigger at our operation because I was good with the horses. It was only a few years earlier, as late as 1934, that everyone used bullocks to snig the logs. I was glad that tradition had fallen away because, to my mind, working with horses is a pleasure. The horses were chained one before the other so they could pull in single file along the narrow tracks. The log dragged behind the last horse, attached to a heavy chain with a swivel in it and connected to two heavy spikes or 'dogs' belted into the log evenly on each side. If trees were falled across hills, they had to be chocked on the bottom side before being cut off to stop them from rolling, and the snigger always worked on the top side of a log, but as soon as the horses began moving the log, it would roll and the horses would have to brace themselves against being dragged down with it. We always controlled the horses by voice, yelling, 'Gee!' to make them go forward, 'Gee off!' to the right, 'Come here!' to the left, and, of course, 'Whoa!' to make them stop. If necessary, the voice would be accompanied by the crack of a stockwhip, which echoed in a wonderful way throughout the trees. It's not easy getting a log out through the twisting tracks. If the head of the log hits a stump, for instance, it may jump back and snap the chains. The snigger has to be able to depend on a smart lead horse that will respond quickly to commands. I've handled some wonderful animals in my time and I feel I could trust some of them better than I could ever trust a man, especially a white man.

There was another snigger on our place named Dick Bones, who was a champion axeman but preferred working with the horses, so he helped me out when I got behind. His lead horse was a beautiful and smart animal which could be sent anywhere through the bush by voice alone. Dick used to take his wagon and team into Bunyip to get the horses shod. He would swing by the grain store to load up the wagon with chaff and oats before he stopped at the blacksmith's where he would leave the horses for the day. Then he went to the pub to wait out the hours. He was a wine drinker. He would head for home at closing time, but be in such a state that he would rely on the lead horse to get him home without mishap. He would approach home in the early hours of the morning drunk and singing along the road. His dogs would hear him from a long way off and go mad barking and howling, giving him a good welcome home.

As the sniggers, we worked long hours, keeping pace with the fallers and making sure the yard on the top side of the mill was full enough to keep the saws going without let-up.

Once the logs were in the yard, they were rolled onto the first bench trolley which lined them up for the breaking-down saw. That would then cut the log into sections, called flitches, which could be handled by the ripping saw to be turned into timber. The mill workers were adept at handling the wood: rolling the logs, lining them up, throwing the flitches onto the skids, pulling the timber out, sending unfinished flitches back to the sawyer. They were all alert at all times. Even though the engine driver was responsible for maintaining the pressure and watching the belts on the saws, everyone always had their eye out for something to go wrong.

One day as I was pulling a log into the yard, I heard a big noise from the mill, and a huge cloud of steam burst from the engine.

'She's gonna blow, boys! Run for your lives!'

Everyone came shooting out of the vicinity as if their pants were on fire and they dived for cover. There was still someone shouting down at the mill. Then a large splash, a hiss, another puff of steam, then nothing. Finally the engine driver stumbled into view.

'No worries, boys, I put the fire out.'

While the sawyer had been ripping an especially difficult flitch the boys pulling out had put too much pressure on the blade. This had loosened the belt that was driving the saw, and caused the belt to fly off with such force that when it hit the side of the boiler it had broken a tap off, allowing the steam to escape and frightening every man near to death. The engine driver had had his wits about him and managed to throw water on the boiler fire, thus saving the boiler and the backsides of all our men.

I have to say, my horses appeared to think nothing of the whole event, except to wonder why I was standing with my mouth agape and not getting on with the job.

That night, at supper, there was a fair bit of laughing and retelling of the tale.

Characters of the Bush

LOTS OF MEN came and went on Jackson's Track. Some worked for us, some set up their own operations, some did contract work for the government, working out of the state forest that backed onto our place. They cut firewood, or fence posts, or pulp, or palings, or poles for the SEC or for the wharves.

Sometimes on a weekend we would find ourselves sitting around a fire swapping yarns. Usually the talk was about trees, axes, terrain, or who could cut the most, go the highest, fall the straight-est, work the hardest. There was a fair bit of competition amongst us and a fair bit of admiration for those who were skilled.

Jamesie Scott, who lived on Wattle Creek, cooking a kangaroo

Of course, we had Snowy to skite about, but the best woodcutter we ever had on our place was Dick Young, a man of fifty who had cut wood for a living all his life. He was as honest as the sun and worked from dawn till dusk. His wood was always the right length and all split to the right size. He cut seven tons of wood every day and didn't boast about it. He often beat champion axemen like our imported Tasmanian, Dick Bones, who used to enter the local woodchops. Bones would spend days sharpening his axes and would rather race at the woodchops than cut wood all day. On one day he would cut more wood than anyone and then the following day he would not cut any, nor was he too worried about splitting logs to the right size.

I have to admit I have never seen a man as good as Charlie Ekhart, who worked for a contractor named Bickerdike. He was over six feet tall and his hands used to brush his knees as he walked along. He was a champion faller and usually went up two or three boards high to get away from the spurry butts of the trees. He could fall a tree and split eighty to a hundred posts in one day, and anyone will tell you it takes a good man to do that.

One time Charlie's boss, Bickerdike, who had a small paling mill, had a special order for ten eighty-foot poles which had to be thirty-eight inches in diameter at the butt and seventeen inches at the head. Charlie falled the trees and barked them and left them to Bickerdike to pull them out of the forest. It could be a real problem getting something that long out of the bush. Firstly, the weight alone was more than my team of horses could shift. Bickerdike asked the owner of a team of bullocks to see what he could do, but twelve beasts working in tandem found it impossible to move the long poles so they gave it away. He asked us if we could move them with the crawler tractor we had acquired. Well, the tractor could move them all right and so that was the weight problem licked, but getting a straight and rigid eighty-foot length of wood out along the snig tracks which twisted through the forest was the second major problem, and a dangerous one at that.

The danger in moving such a long pole is in the way it swings and roles as it's being pulled. If the path isn't straight enough, the front end of the log may glance off a standing tree and that will send the back end of the pole sliding mightily across the track and slamming into whatever stands in its way. My brother, Harry, suffered a broken collarbone from the end of a long pole whacking into a tree which then dropped a sizeable branch onto him.

We managed to haul those ten poles out but we had to straighten out the whole track to do it. It was a mighty feat. We all worked together on it, and told the story of it over and over until it became legend.

Not long after that, Bickerdike was killed by his own truck, which was a 'well-used' vehicle. It had a bashed-in cabin where the logs had smashed into it while they were being loaded. It had a cracked windscreen and at the end it had no doors on it at all. It was known that Bickerdike, who was built like a barrel, used to drink a lot of beer, but no one knew for sure whether the grog contributed to his death. One day while working at his mill, he drove his truck over a log in the yard. The bump threw him out the door and he fell under the wheels.

There were others who died early on the Track. Jack Vandam used to visit us when he was a famous bike rider. He was a good one! Before breakfast he would ride to our place and back to his place, which was forty miles away. When he gave up his bike career, he bought a log truck and started carting logs around the Jackson's Track area. He worked the same way as he rode his bike – speed was the name of the game as he was always in a hurry. One day he had an offsider with him loading logs and didn't take the time to get heavy skids but used the light ones which were at hand. The light skids broke while they were rolling a log up to the truck tray and the log fell down, breaking his mate's leg. That didn't teach him, though. Later, when he had taken a job as foreman at the Noojee Mill, he was hurrying to stack logs and one got away and crushed and killed him.

The maddest bloke who ever worked on the Track was employed by us. His name was Matheson and he said he had been in asylums, but we could see he knew how to use an axe so we put him on to cut pulpwood. We told him the logs had to be six feet long, but he must have had a voice in his head that told him otherwise because his wood was all lengths and he couldn't be corrected. He used to curse the chips that he cut from the logs and he would stop to pick them up and throw them away as he said they were making trouble.

We could tell stories about Matheson all day long. Some days he would sing operatic songs at the top of his voice while he was working away in the bush. It was a wonderful sound echoing through the trees but you could never quite tell what he was singing. He would carry a billycan to work and fill it up with witchetty grubs, which he cut out of the trees he falled. He took them home to eat. To me that was the sanest thing he ever did. Roasted witchetty grubs are wonderful.

Some mornings, while going to work past our house with his axe on his shoulder, he would turn in, open the door without knocking, walk in without saying a word, sit down, lay his axe on the floor at his feet, pick up a newspaper if one was lying about and start reading it out loud. He was well educated, having been to college. After a while he would stop, fold the paper, slam it on the table, pick up his axe and walk out, never having acknowledged our presence. Harry and I would just stand there gawking at him.

One morning, on the way to work, instead of coming inside, he stopped at a big dry tree three feet thick about fifty feet from the house, swung his axe off his shoulder, chopped it down, swung his axe back on his shoulder and went on his way.

Some days he was crazier than others, but he always gave us fair warning on his mad days by wearing a felt hat with the brim cut off all the way around. On good days he went hatless. One day, with his hat on, he decided to walk across country to his brother's farm in South Drouin. On his return, at about two in the morning, he walked through Lloyd Menck's racehorse farm. Lloyd and his stablehands were still up playing cards when Matheson, carrying a twenty-two calibre rifle, came upon the house. He looked in the window, raised his rifle, took aim, shot Lloyd through the arm, and took off. No one was game to go near him, but the next morning we saw him from afar, still with his hat on, going to work as usual.

About ten o'clock in the morning, his brother and a police officer came along and Matheson quietly went away with them. He never came back so I suppose he must have been sent back to the asylum.

We had lots of interesting personalities working for us, but we never had a row with any of them. I believe you've got to mind your own business when it comes to others. People should be allowed to live their lives as they see fit or as they are able. As you sow, you reap.

I suppose the person I enjoyed knowing and being around most on the Track in the early days was old George Rogers, who first showed us the area in 1937. He was a bushman and lived a truly independent life. He lived on his own on one of the deserted farms, a property right next to ours which his father, who had been the schoolteacher at Labertouche from 1890 to 1899, had first selected in the 1890s.

George was crippled with rheumatism and on the pension. He had worked in the bush all his life but now had to get around with the help of two walking sticks that he had made from tea-tree with the root for a handle.

He had a lovely grey pony who was honest and loved his master. He never wandered far from the house even though there were no fences on the property. George used to put burns through the bush to get fresh sweet feed for the pony which quietly grazed among the trees. On pension days George would call out to the pony and it would come running. He would give him a handful of oats then harness him up to the sulky and drive to Longwarry to pick up his pension check. He would then spend the rest of the day at the hotel and get so drunk he had to be helped into the sulky, but the pony would faithfully take him home at the jog trot through hard-to-negotiate bush tracks and stop at the doorway.

I used to visit George one night a week and have a yarn about old times – when Fraser's mills were still running, when the trams were still shifting timber from mill to railhead, when they were using bullocks to pull the logs out of the forest and the place rang with the sharp crack of the stockwhip. I told him about the discoveries I made riding my little chestnut mare out in the forest and, of course, he'd remember it like it was originally. He had possums living in his shack and they used to crawl all over him and play with his beard as he sat near his fire. He loved the native animals. Kangaroos and wallabies used to feed right up to his door, showing no fear of him. He bred kelpie sheepdogs that took out prizes in the local shows, but they were well trained and never chased native game or rabbits.

Fleas used to give him Larry Dooley. It used to make me laugh to see the fleas chasing each other around the brim of his hat while he was talking to me. He would always be scratching away. On fine days he invariably had his blankets hanging on the line to try to get rid of his fleas. I don't think he was ever free of them.

I truly enjoyed the company of that old codger. Finally, he got too old and crippled to care for himself and was shifted into Longwarry where he died not long after. Before he left, he sold me the eighty acres where he was born and lived all his days.

Fire of '39

IT WAS CERTAINLY a man's world on Jackson's Track in the early days. We had no women living there to look after us or mother us or love us. There were dances at the Jindivick Hall where it was possible to mix with women, but I don't know, I wasn't interested in going just to stand there gawking and shuffling my feet and never dancing with anyone or even speaking to anyone. None of the hands from the mill were much interested either. I suppose we were a bit wild and lived a bit rough, but that's how I liked it. I didn't want to worry about getting along with women just yet. I was only twenty years old and didn't want to worry about anything but

Forest before the fire

developing my skills as a bushman and keeping our business together.

Harry was naturally the boss, him being five years older, but we were equal partners in ownership and responsibility. We never stopped. We were up at daylight and worked until dark.

We awoke with the sound of currawongs calling through the trees as the sky began to lighten, but it would be about an hour before we saw the sun. My job was to locate the cow and bring her in to be milked. Trudging through the damp grass on the red hill of a morning, I listened for her cowbell. Often mist was hanging in the trees at the edge of the paddock and bellbirds punctuated the early morning silence with their distinctive ringing call. Something about the bush early in the morning is that you can see thousands and thousands of cobwebs covered in dew in the grass. Smoke would rise from the tin chimney of our shack where Harry was setting a fire to cook damper. On a still morning the smoke would spread along the ground and the smell would mingle with that of damp bark, eucalyptus oil, fresh grass, mud and dung. Smells of the bush. I loved the early mornings.

Once I had milked the cow, I would carry the bucket full of warm milk to the house, stopping to check the chooks for eggs along the way. In the kitchen – actually, it was the kitchen while we were cooking, the dining room while we were eating, the lounge while we were relaxing, the office while we were tallying the books, the bedroom while we were sleeping – I poured the milk into the billy and put it on a grate over the fire to boil so we could skim the scalded cream off the top. By that time Harry had the damper cooking and, if I had been lucky enough to find a few, the eggs were on the boil as well.

For breakfast we would have half the fresh cooked damper, scalded cream and jam washed down with tea. Then I would wrap up the remaining damper and the eggs to take with us over the hill to the mill for dinner at midday. We didn't ever eat much meat in those days. We basically lived on damper and tea.

We didn't need much to satisfy us. Once a week we went to the general store in Jindivick to pick up basic supplies: flour, sugar, tea, matches, soap, kerosene, petrol. The kerosene came two tins to a case and those tins and wooden boxes were very handy: to sit on, to build shelves out of, to store things in. Did I say it was rough? Rough as bags, but it all worked very well. We didn't have to spend much time thinking about cooking or cleaning, and that gave us time to get on with our work.

We began our work at the mill about eight o'clock and stopped for dinner at midday. We always lit a fire and boiled a billy then. The engine driver was responsible for that. We all ate together, usually about eight of us. That's when we would hear some stories, usually about the brawls that had gone on in Drouin on the weekend, or funny stories about mishaps. Maybe there would be some talk about prices and good deals on equipment, or perhaps a discussion on how to make something work better. Often we didn't say much at all, but ate and had a doze to conserve our energy for the next hours of hard physical work. I was developing hard muscle by then: the thick arms and broad shoulders of an axeman, the strong back of a crosscut sawyer, the callused thick-fingered hands of a snigger used to man-handling logs and tightening chains. It was hard work, but satisfying.

We knocked off at five o'clock, partly because it was getting dark by then in the winter time, but mostly because the horses had had enough. The horses always knocked off at five, summer or winter. We had to look after our animals or the whole operation would come to a halt. In fact the whole operation did come to a halt in the late summer of 1939.

It had been a bushfire summer. Dry and hot. We don't seem to have the kind of heat now that we had then. Weeks and weeks of dry heat. The leaves on the trees were curled up and grey with heat and dust. The bark on the ground was tinder dry and crackling. The birds and other wildlife retreated from the heat, making the bush quiet. Snakes and blue-tongues were about.

We were on the lookout for fires and finally word came that one was burning, but well back in the bush. The days were still and unbearably hot, but we continued to work, going out every morning into the forest alert and wondering, aware that the fire had not been brought under control. After several days, we began to smell the smoke, faintly at first but stronger and stronger. Still, the days were absolutely quiet, no breeze, no sound except the echo of the axe, the scrape of the crosscut saw, the intermittent screaming of the big blades at the mill.

We knew no one was in there fighting that fire and we knew, in spite of the stillness, that the fire was creating its own storm as the flames sucked in the already overheated air to feed itself. We knew the fire would reach us eventually.

We kept working.

With nothing to blow it away, the smoke became thick. It hung in the timber by the mill, it swirled around our legs as we walked, it slid over the logs and through the trees. It became so thick we could only see five yards in front of us and the day became like an eerie twilight and finally almost like night. The axemen had to stop entering the forest for the thick smoke was as disorienting as a heavy fog, the kind of fog that makes a person drive off the side of a road they know like the back of their hand. No good wandering lost in a forest with a fire coming.

We had no idea how close it was, but we could hear explosions far off in the distance as if there was a war going on. The sound fright-ened everyone. The booming blasts came from trees so consumed with heat that they would explode even before the flames reached them. The heat was drying the gas out of the trees and exploding them about forty feet ahead of the fire. The blasts would send out fireballs as far as a mile and set off spot fires, almost like advanced scouts making way for a fierce army to follow.

We told the boys to knock off and clear out to safety in Drouin. Almost everybody on the Track was making their way out of the bush by then, but Harry and I stayed and waited. We were responsible for the horses: my beautiful chestnut mare, the trusted lead horse and the rest of the team. There was no way we could leave them. We knew when we felt the first breeze and then the wind finally begin-ning to pick up that it was time to head for the middle of the thirty-acre clearing on the hill with the stock. It was thirty acres of newly ploughed red soil and we thought we would be safe enough, but it's no use saying we weren't worried. That oven-baked wind was blowing the fire straight towards us. The temperature was 114 and there was no hope of saving anything. We waited and watched.

We could see the huge billowing cloud rising from the fire, and at last the fire itself. We could hear a roar of heat and loud explosions still in the distance, but the first flames were advancing towards us more quickly than we would have believed. The flames were running fast through the scrub, burning it down to the ground as they spread from tree to tree, but ahead of the flames were two old swaggies, a man and a woman, running up towards us from the Track, panting and groaning, crazy with fear. Where had they come from?

'We're on the move. Our barrow and swag are down there!'

'The fire's got it for sure!'

'We were almost burned ourselves.'

'Thank goodness we saw you and a way out!'

They were trembling and crying, shaken by their close encounter and not sure if they were actually any safer now. We were calm enough and so was our stock; surely that must have been an indication that we would be all right, but we felt sorry for those people.

The four of us, along with the six horses and the cow, watched in amazement as the fire proceeded around us. The fire crackled and fizzed, sang and whistled at a great rate. Suddenly a gas jet would scream out of a tree before it burst into flames. Flaming bark flew overhead and ignited the waiting tinder across the paddock. It was so quick. I would be looking at a bush and suddenly it would explode. I watched fire move around us before the wind, flames like gas burners, flying along, but burning evenly. All round us, as it reached the clearing, it would fizzle out as if in disgust, then turn and go on to find something more to burn.

In a matter of twenty minutes, it was gone. All around us was black and smoking, but there were no flames. We began to realise that it wasn't the main fire that came through; the main fire had missed us and, as we later found out, was heading towards Noojee and Neerim where it burned fiercely and ruthlessly.

We were safe. We ventured off the red hill, a bit dazed, to see the aftermath. Nothing was the same. The mill was gone, the timber and logs turned to charcoal, the great saws on their sides, the engine a carcass. Our shack was a pile of twisted and blackened corrugated iron lying on a bed of ash. The trees in the forest were black and leafless, but we knew all but the mountain ash were still alive and would soon thrive. Because the scrub had been burnt to the ground, the forest looked empty, cleaned out and colourless. And there was no sound, no life anywhere, except the occasional hiss and crackle.

We found the ash of the barrow that belonged to the two swaggies.

We could still identify the wheel, but that was all. They stopped the night. We scratched out some potatoes at the edge of the field for tea and cooked them in the coals.

We also had potatoes for breakfast. Then we sat down in the middle of that clearing and did some thinking. All our work had gone up in smoke, but it was no use being upset. We just had to put up with it and save what we could. We knew we still had our health and strength and we could start again.

We didn't know about the old couple, though. What did they have? They had the road, I suppose, and wanted to keep moving. We gave them some more potatoes and watched them move off and kept watching until they disappeared down that blackened, empty Track.

Rebuilding

AND SO WE DID start again!

In the soot and ash we managed to locate enough bark to erect a shack near our clearing. We didn't mind the rough conditions. Harry and I never minded the weather, rain or shine. Since we had been stockmen and boundary riders on the big stations in Queensland we were used to sleeping under the stars, or under the clouds for that matter. I could sleep the night through anywhere I laid my head, no matter how hard it might be raining or blowing, as long as I had a wool blanket over me. A bark hut, a camp fire, a few stumps to sit on was all we needed to get going again.

Snig horses just finished pulling logs into the mill

We cut blackened saplings and near the hut we built yards for the horses. We fed the working horses there and turned out all the other stock to find grass as they could.

The only usable equipment we had left after the fire was our axes and our horses.

Harry managed to buy a Bedford truck.

I fashioned a sled made out of a forked tree, even on both sides, not too heavy and not too wide to navigate the burnt-out snig tracks, big enough to hold a sizeable load of chopped wood, but not too big to be pulled by one horse.

We set to cutting firewood for the Longwarry Butter Factory.

George Klinksbourne returned to us with three other workers. Each man cut four tons of wood each day. I pulled the wood out of the bush to Jackson's Track where Harry loaded it onto the truck to cart it to the butter factory. He could take eight tons at a time so that was two trips to Longwarry a day to keep pace with the cutters.

Jackson's Track, the only road from our place to Longwarry, was still just that: a track. Even though the shire kept the track in fair order up to our property by forever filling up the potholes which formed pretty quickly and spreading ever more gravel, it was still not an all-weather road. On rainy days truck traffic was prohibited so Harry's side of our little operation came to a halt often. But even as Harry's truck stood idle, the axemen kept cutting and I kept dragging the chopped wood to the siding. Sometimes this build-up would go on for three days before the Track was finally reopened. Then Harry and I had to work late into the night carting load after load, as many as six loads of firewood, forty tons, to catch up with the cutters.

We didn't have time to think about much but work, but we knew we weren't going to keep cutting firewood forever. We had to expand. We had no tall mountain ash trees on our property, but there were still some in the state forest. We knew that contractors had gone into the burnt forest to drag out the dead ash, which were the only trees actually killed by the fire. They made beautiful timber, but it was important to get to them quickly after a burn before they began to rot. We would have got them ourselves, if we'd had the equipment. It galled us to see others, who hadn't been burnt out, profiting from the bushfire while we were scraping through to get going again. We needed cash in hand to set up an operation to handle trees of that size.

So we kept chopping and carting.

The charred grey gums, stringy-barks, messmates, silver-tops, ironbarks began to sprout green leaves all up and down their trunks. New leaves appearing after a forest has been attacked by wildfire are the brightest and greenest green you'll ever see. They seem to dance with life on what had only days before looked like towering black ruins. With the sprouting leaves come the birds. Grass begins to appear and burnt-out scrub magically takes on a green hue. The forest awakens. A bushfire does a forest a lot of good. It takes a fire to liven it up a bit. It makes me laugh these days when I hear on the radio how many acres were 'destroyed' in this and that fire. A forest needs a fire.

It's a magical thing but we didn't have time enough to stop and appreciate it as we should. We were still chopping and carting – and running schemes through our heads which would help us expand.

We heard that the Australian Paper Mill at Maryvale was letting out contracts for the supply of pulpwood and we decided to take up a contract with them. We had a neighbour named George Bellman who was already cutting pulp for APM and doing well. He had set up his own operation, building most of it himself, and invited us to look it over so we could have some idea how to plan our own operation.

George had put in a swing saw at the foot of a hill covered with a thick forest of sixty-foot saplings that were very free-splitting trees. He was clever the way he had cut into the hillside to enable his truck to back in below the cutting bench so that as he docked the saplings into six-foot pulp lengths they fell directly into the truck. He needed only two people for his whole operation.

George introduced us to Stewart Hood, a very smart full-blooded Aborigine working for him. George would fall the trees and bark them while Stewart hooked the chain onto the falled logs and a well-schooled two-horse team pulled them into the mill. When the yard was full, Stewart would roll the log onto the docking bench and sling a wire rope onto it, which would allow George to pull it along and dock it with the swing saw.

George and Stewart seemed to be a good team, but we knew that George was a hard man. He didn't live out at his mill but went home to Drouin every night where he had a wife and children. Jackson's Track wound tightly through the forest over creeks and around the trees in those days, and George's truck had barked many of those trees along the way as he sped to and from Drouin each day.

Out in the bush he kept a clean operation where no rubbish or bark was allowed in the log yard and his snig tracks were always kept clear. The horses were well looked after and everything was kept up to scratch with his gear. In Drouin it was a different story. His house and garden were never tidy, but nobody would be game enough to say anything to him as he would soon give them a hiding. He was a beer drinker and was always looking for a fight or a wrestle. He was of stocky build with thick, strong legs and couldn't be beaten. He had no fear and seemed to get away with a bad temper and dangerous activity. It was clear that Stewart had a lot to do with the smooth operation of the mill. While George was fighting and drinking in town, Stewart would organise the place for the next day's work.

After he met us, Stewart would often come over to our camp looking for company and ready to tell a few yarns and listen to a few. We began to understand that Stewart felt George was a hard man to work for. He was wild and dangerous and would drive Stewart to do things too fast, risking injury. We often heard George's voice echoing through the forest as he swore and cursed at Stewart and the horses. It was enough to frighten anyone.

We knew that George probably cared more for his horses than he did for Stewart as we had seen men with this attitude before when we were in Queensland. It made no sense to Harry and me. We had both mixed with Aborigines most of our lives. I had been working with them since I was thirteen on our uncle's station. I had always got on well with them and enjoyed their yarns. I enjoyed living like they did when I, too, became a stockman like Harry and we were all working together on a muster or riding the boundary fences.

I was keen to hear them tell about the old life in the wild and curious about their way of life. A bushman has something in common with a blackfella and you can always learn a bit from them whenever you're around them. They have a kind of wisdom, but the especial thing about them is their sense of humour. There is always laughter when blackfellas are around. People might have said that Harry and I were innocents, at least that I was an innocent, the way normal whitefella ideas about blacks had never really rubbed off on us. We took no notice of a bloke's skin colour. It was his attitude that worried us. Harry and I always treated people as we found them. Anybody decent will treat a man well and give him a fair go.

Stewart Hood had a good attitude. He was easygoing, sensible and honest. He wanted to help people, not take advantage of them. He would put in a good day's work, but he wouldn't push himself into a bad temper the way George did. He believed that you've got to be able to enjoy life, that it's better to be happy than miserable. He was not worried about money, but about the way he lived. He was most satisfied with bush life. I admired his values and much later watched him teach these values to his children. He taught them to be tolerant, generous, giving and not greedy; to be happy and satisfied with a simple, clean life; not to drink and not to steal.

We realised that Stewart would like to get away from George, but being George's neighbours, we were not in a good position to offer him work unless George fired him first, which didn't seem likely. The thing about Stewart was that he did not drink at all and so he was reliable and very valuable to a fiery bloke like George.

One night, about a fortnight after we had first met him, Stewart came over to us and said he had quit working for George, that George was pulling up stakes and moving his operation deeper into the forest. Stewart said he would like to work for us. It didn't take us long to decide to take him on.

He helped us set up and work a pulp plant much the same as the one George worked. It was also at the foot of a hill which had a good stand of trees on it. We also used two horses to pull the logs – one good smart lead horse, with another coupled behind. We had long poles in the log yard leading on to a set of steel rails with a bench trolley. When the yard was full, we would start cutting the logs which were skidded, one at a time, one end onto the trolley and the other end onto a roller. Then the trolley was pushed by hand up to the swing saw and the log was docked into six-foot lengths, one man doing the docking and another stacking the lengths ready for carting. Another man split any lengths that were too thick, for six-foot lengths had to be no bigger than eleven inches thick. The pulpwood then had to be loaded into railway trucks at Longwarry and sent to the pulp mill at Maryvale.

Everybody at our place liked Stewart. His easygoing humour seemed to loosen all of us up so the atmosphere around our camp somehow seemed lighter, even though we were working just as hard, maybe even harder than before he came to work with us. We were glad to have given him a job.

Little did we know that he would change our lives forever.

Stewart Hood

STEWART HOOD became a great friend of ours. Almost immediately he and Harry struck up a firm friendship. I guess they were pretty much alike: both were champion talkers who could keep a company of men rapt with their yarns, both were proud and honest men.

We spent a fair bit of time with Stewart, at first helping him build a bark hut. He positioned his camp along Labertouche Creek at the Jackson's Track end of our property where it was heavily wooded and had a sense of wildness about it. He wanted his hut to be of a good size because he had it in his mind to have his family around him, although we were unaware of this plan at that point. He wanted

Stewart and Dora Hood

to be near the creek for the water, the fish and bird life. He wanted to be in the heavy tea-tree scrub for privacy as well as for the game he might find in there. Stewart knew how to live off the land and, of course, he would take up the old ways of his people if he could. He sensed that we were generous enough to let him live as he pleased.

He was right. I, especially, was interested in his way of life. All my life I had somehow felt chafed and hemmed in by the white man's civilised ways and always felt more comfortable with bush living. Here was a bloke living on our property who was brought up to natural living and I had a lot to learn from him. It wasn't as if we were living much differently to Stewart ourselves at the time, with our own bark hut for shelter, but he had natural skills that were razor sharp, skills I wanted to learn.

I admired his eyesight. He could see things in the bush, minutes before I could. When we went hunting, he could follow a track that I couldn't see and pick up the slightest clues as if by instinct. Later, when I watched the children and grandchildren playing in the forest, I saw how they learned to track, always playing at hunting, always carrying their small spears and bundies, always practising their throwing until they could throw straight. They played with great energy and humour and noise, but their playing was serious for it was sharpening their skills. In the thick tea-tree scrub along the creek, the possums used to build nests and the boys would find them and shake the trees until the possums ran out, and then the chase would be on, possum scrambling through the bush between trees, kids squealing, leaping and diving. Bandicoots and bushrats lived in holes under the tea-tree and they were fun to track and catch. In the creek were fish to spear and freshwater crays to trap. The girls would hunt along the creek bed and collect the freshwater mussels. I have seen the children knock a goanna with a bundy, which is a kind of wooden club, about twenty feet up a tree and take it home for a meal. Stewart had played like this when he was child. He knew where to look and he knew what was good. I watched and learned.

Stewart told us stories about his life. He grew up on the Albert River at Yarram, but in 1919, for some reason, the government made a decision to move all the blackfellas they could find to Lake Tyers Mission Station over at the Gippsland Lakes. Stewart's family was moved by force. He said they were put in a small weatherboard house just like all the other houses that were lined up in row along a dusty track. Each house had a couple of small rooms with basic furniture: a table, some chairs, a stove for cooking. If there were beds, they were often dragged outside for sleeping and lounging about on. Better to sleep outside.

Stewart wasn't popular with the manager of the station, just as his father hadn't been. His father, Collin, had agitated for land rights, or possibly just basic human rights, and Stewart had followed in his footsteps. He had a strong personality, was respected by his people and would speak up for his rights. He ended up riling the manager enough so that he was banned from living at the station, banned from setting foot on the place. By this time he was married with five children, but the manager paid no heed to that. Stewart, whose life had been disrupted before by representatives of the government, had to go out to find work for himself, but he would sneak back to his family at night. He was caught more than once and the manager not only punished him but his family as well by reducing their rations whenever he realised they had been disobeying him. Finally, Stewart left altogether to try to find a place where he could settle and eventually bring his family to be with him.

Harry and I, who by this time had learned to admire many things about Stewart, were disgusted by these stories. Stewart's posture would become dejected as he told them. He was not a tall man, but a strongly built, almost stocky man and it was terrible to see him slumped over in sadness. His face had the classic features of his people, with the wide smile and quick, alert eyes, but when he told us these stories, there was not much smiling to be seen. He would run his hands through his thick wavy hair and look away. We realised the only decent thing to do was to go to Lake Tyers and fetch Stewart's family to live here at Jackson's Track. When we suggested the idea to him, his brilliant smile flashed across his face and we knew immediately that it had been his idea all along. We all laughed together. As I say, there is a lot to admire about Stewart Hood, not the least his way of getting round a man.

Two days later, Harry and I were rattling along the Princes Highway in the Bedford truck, headed for Lake Tyers just past Lakes Entrance. Along the way, we didn't say much. Neither of us was too sure what obstacles we might have to overcome once we got to the reserve. We didn't know if we would face locked gates and high fences or an irate manager. We didn't know if we needed any paperwork, but we sure weren't going to worry about that end of things. To our mind, the government had no right to interfere and no one was going to sign anything. People in this wide country should be free to go where they please and live in peace the way they want to. There should be no fences anywhere, no locks, no chains, no papers or documents laying down the law restricting people's movements. We believed that then and I believe it now. Our faces were set and our jaws were working. We were determined.

The Princes Highway wasn't what it is now and it took us at least three hours of rattle and bounce in that noisy truck, gears cranking and brakes working, before we got to the entrance of the mission station. The gates were open! We just drove on through. Just as Stewart said, it was a dusty track which continued along for about six miles before we came upon any sign of human habitation. We slowed down and crept along. There was the line of wooden shacks. People came pouring out of them, the children running and laughing, to surround us and find out who we were and what we wanted. They showed a gentle, accepting kind of curiosity, not a suspicious one. There was no manager in sight.

Kids jumped on the running boards of the cabin and clamoured onto the tray at the back to guide us to Stewart Hood's family. They all looked happy and energetic, but also skinny and faded somehow, with raggedy but clean clothes, dusty skin, and short hair blonding at the tips. It seemed Stewart was right about the rations. The people looked underfed, or at least undernourished, on a mission diet of white flour, white sugar and tea. They also got sago, rice, split peas, meat, jam and soap. Even so, there seemed not to be enough of it and conditions looked difficult.

The Hood family came out of a house like all the rest of the houses. Somehow they knew we were coming, although no one had rung the mission or sent a letter. That didn't surprise us, however, because we were well acquainted with the 'bush telegraph' that gets blackfella news around quicker than any modern device. Stewart's wife, Dora, wasn't afraid of us at all. She was a lovely looking woman who seemed to command respect. She stood on the verandah, calmly gazing at us, sizing us up. She was surrounded by her family: three girls, two boys, and one grandchild, Buddy. They all stood and looked at us. These sorts of people are naturally trustful, but they know immediately if you're genuine or not and you can't fool them. If a whitefella were to come up to them with a bottle of beer, they would not trust him because they would know he was up to no good. The womenfolk were especially aware of that.

We got out of the truck and stood in front of it so Dora could see us and make her decision. Finally she smiled and invited us in for a cup of tea.

'C'mon in and have a cuppa. Ya gotta be thirsty, hey!'

Her children immediately went to work getting their gear together to leave with us. They didn't have much: some blankets and a few clothes. We sat in one of the small rooms, a bit awkwardly, drinking our tea while all around us was much excited chattering and movement, from all except Dora, who was gracious and calm. Soon everyone was ready. They said their goodbyes and climbed onto the back of the truck and waited for us to get going. We gulped down our tea and handed the cups to Dora, who put them into her bundle and with real dignity climbed onto the back of the truck with her family. Harry and I got into the red cab of that Bedford, started her up and left Lake Tyers Mission Station without a backward glance. We never did see the manager.

Three hours later Stewart was reunited with his family. He moved them into his camp on the edge of our property and that's where they stayed until 1962.

Mavis Tonkin

Mavis

ABOUT THIS TIME our sister, Mavis, began to take an interest in us and proposed that she come stay with us and cook for us.

'What do you reckon, Daryl?'

'It doesn't bother me. I don't know why she thinks we need her to cook for us.'

To be honest, I wasn't so sure about having her here. I had left home when I was only thirteen years old to go work on the station up in New South Wales with Harry and that was the last time I had ever had anything to do with women. Every couple of months, Harry and I managed to get to Essendon to visit our parents, who still lived in the house where we grew up, but that wasn't the same as living with them. I remember how it was with my mother and my four sisters when I was a lad. The girls seemed to overwhelm my two brothers and me – especially me, since I was the youngest in the whole family. I remember I didn't spend much time in the house with them. I would make an excuse and go out with my billycart to gather firewood or catch the cow in the small paddock next door and milk her or feed the poultry or play with my father's kelpies, anything to stay out of the house where all those girls were. Lucky for me, I had a small bay pony I could ride anywhere and everywhere around the small paddocks and market gardens that were still part of Essendon in those days. So I never had to go home at all if I didn't want to. If I was like that then, I wondered, how would it be with Mavis now that I was a man? This was a place of hard work, rough living – a man's world. It seemed to me that it was no place for a woman, at least a woman like Mavis.

I didn't know what effect her influence would have on all of us. Stewart's wife and daughters were the only women who had ever been here, but their gentle presence didn't interfere with the way we conducted our lives. There was a communication between us. We were all living rough in bark shacks, all equal. On the other hand, I had a pretty good idea Mavis wasn't going to fit in with us; rather, we were going to have to fit in with her.

And I was right.

'You know, we can't have Mavis living in this hut.'

'What's wrong with it?'

'She wouldn't stand for it. She's been living in Sydney, after all.'

Mavis had been working in Newcastle as the head buyer in a department store. We knew that much. She had the bad luck to break her back in a surfing accident while she was up there. She landed in hospital for a long time and was told she would never get right again. Of course, she lost her job and had to come down to Melbourne to live with our mother and father while she got better. And she did get better, in spite of the doctors. Then she became restless and decided we needed her.

Harry's mind was ticking over: 'We'll get in a load of sawn timber and take time off to build her a small cottage.'

'You mean a shack!'

'With a good fireplace.'

'Hmmmph.'

We built it right next to our bark hut. It was just one large room and it did have a good fireplace. We bought a good cooking stove and set up our bark hut as the kitchen with Harry's and my bedroom coming off that. We got a good table with chairs and a dresser to keep crockery and glasses and knives and forks. She wasn't even here yet and I could feel her influence weighing on us.

I wondered if all she was going to do was cook for us. She was older than Harry and me, and I seemed to remember she had a bossy streak. Harry said she had a very good head for business. In fact while she was convalescing in Melbourne she met an old Jewish man in St Kilda who was an SP bookmaker and she convinced him to take her on as a partner. She worked with him on weekends and made a packet of money. It was during the week when she had nothing to do that she wanted to come stay with us.

So she came and we started having three-course meals every evening. She served up soup first, then probably a roast, followed usually by a rice pudding. And I'll say I didn't really appreciate it. She would tell you that, too, if she were still here: that I didn't appreciate it and that she didn't know why she bothered. What I didn't appreciate was that she put too much salt in the food and she put bicarbonate of soda in the peas to make them green and she used white sugar and white rice and white flour, and she served us jellies and cakes and too much meat and too much fat. I was a very fussy bloke and I would rather have had my own meals, what I was used to. I didn't think her food was so healthy.

She was fussy about setting the table and we would have to sit up properly, conversing about the day's activities and all our business plans and the like while we ate. She made us have some manners, 'Use your knife and fork', which I guess was good for us. Anyway we put up with it.

Well, she didn't get everything her own way. Our tools eventually found their way into the dresser next to the cutlery and she couldn't do anything about that.

It was clear that Mavis wasn't going to stick to cooking. She was an energetic woman with a restless mind. She had all sorts of ideas about expanding our business. It was her idea for us to sell flowers.

Wild flowers and gum tips were abundant around Jackson's Track. The most popular flower was boronia, which blossoms in October and lasts to December, but there were also maiden's blush, mulga, orchids, tree ferns and sphagnum moss. For years a group of about six families had been coming up in the spring to pick the flowers which they took back to the Victoria Market each day. They were a wild lot who were used to battling for a living, mostly from the slums of Fitzroy, but they were hard workers. They competed with each other to get in first and get the best position. They would often get bogged in their light trucks and we'd have to pull them out with our horses. One year, one of the young lads in their group must have done something seriously wrong for they deserted him out in the bush and never returned to collect him. He found his way out of the forest and was taken in by one of the neighbours who put him to work clearing some land. He did this until he joined the army and was later killed in action in the war.

As Mavis watched the flower people come and go, she knew she was looking at a good thing. She also had an idea how to outdo them. When she was in town on the weekends, she began doing the rounds of shops, trying to open a market for bunches of flowers rather than just dumping them in bulk into Vic Market. She went into the Coles stores and talked them into buying our flowers. She could talk herself into anything.

Well, now that she had a market, all she needed was someone to cut the flowers and bunch them up for her.

As I have said, Mavis was bossy. She was a very determined woman and whatever was on her mind she would get to happen. If it didn't, she showed her terrible temper, stamping her tiny foot with rage, and making her big silly brothers agree to almost anything.

It was Harry and I who picked those flowers for Mavis. We would each cut a 'rope' of flowers, which amounted to a total of about fifteen dozen bunches of flowers. To tell the truth, I loved going out into the bush to pick those flowers. The smell of boronia is the smell of the bush to me. It's hard to describe: a kind of lemon, musk, bitter-sweet smell. The flowers come in whites and pinks and we'd make sure we picked a combination. The boronia wasn't the only thing we picked. At that time of year, the silver-top has beautiful new leaves that are a deep-red colour that look marvellous shooting out of the old green. Real smell of eucalyptus sprang from them as they were picked. And we would get the yellow mulga, too. Springtime in the forest is a time of colour, gentle warmth and deep heavy perfumes. I used to love knocking off at dinnertime and, after drinking my tea, just lying back and breathing it all in: the hops, the grey-gum shoots, the blanketwood, the ferns, the bottlebrush, the clematis. It was enough to make you dizzy. We'd tramp home late in the afternoon laden with flowers.

And Mavis managed to make sure it was Harry and I who would make those flowers into bunches, too. The flowers were easy to pick but hard for thick axemen's fingers to put into bunches. We bundled up the flowers in the bark hut at night in front of the fire. Mavis would have made arrangements to deliver them to Coles on a Friday, so on Thursdays we would work through the night. It must have been quite a sight: two awkward bushmen making bunches of flowers with their tiny, quick-witted sister watching over them, planning and calculating. I didn't mind the work. I never mind the work. And those nights were good, just the three of us. Mavis was as good as gold if you went her way. She was a good talker and she and Harry kept up a steady stream of conversation with me listening mainly and having a good laugh when the story called for it. I guess we were a family then.

We made good money out of those flowers. Mavis bought herself a car and helped us expand our business even further, especially the milling. She became our travelling salesman, negotiating with firms in Melbourne for our timber. But I'm getting ahead of myself here.

Plenty of Work

AFTER STEWART AND HIS FAMILY settled and Mavis had established herself, lots of things seemed to be happening at once.

The war had started by this time, but neither Harry nor I felt it our duty to fight for a government. I'd say we were true-blue Aussies, but we were bushmen, and bush people and governments don't mix so well. It's my opinion that governments and councils have ruined Australia with their laws and I didn't want them telling me who I had to fight and when. I was pretty sure that I couldn't be bothered being ordered around. At this time I'd only just met Mavis again, and wasn't fully aware of how much ordering around

Poppa Dodge Moffat and Stewart Hood

I would be experiencing in the near future.

I did get a conscription notice that informed me I was expected to get on a train at eight o'clock the next morning. I think it said, 'bring a toothbrush', but I took no notice and that was that. I knew they'd come and get me if they really wanted me, but I also knew they would have a job to find me. The trouble with me is I do what I want to do. If I think something's right, I do it, and the fact is, I always think I'm right. How would a bushman like me survive in the army?

I still think wars are more for city people. Many people thought it was a great idea to get into the army and escape overseas, but not Harry and me. We were doing our bit by cutting pulpwood for APM to use in the making of explosives, and growing potatoes, which we sold directly to the army for the soldiers.

We planned to plant thirty acres of potatoes on the red hill where we had sheltered from the bushfire. Harry had signed a contract with the army to grow the potatoes at twenty-two pounds and ten shillings a ton. We had the cleared land for it, but we had no seed so Harry organised a deal with a large landowner and potato grower in the swamp near Koo Wee Rup to go fifty-fifty with him on bags of spuds if we dug out the paddock for him. Of course, it was me who had to camp out there on that paddock in the swamp all alone for about six weeks and spend every waking hour digging and bagging potatoes.

If it weren't for the only accessible water being some brackish muck brought up out of a well by a windmill, I would have had no complaints. I didn't really mind the solitude and I didn't mind the work. A bushman never minds the hard work. In fact, it's a point of pride how much hard work he'll put up with. It's easier if you have a goal and my goal was to get enough spuds to seed our thirty acres as quickly as I could.

About three weeks into the task an old chap came along look-ing for work so I paid him three shillings and six pence a bag, but he wasn't real quick. We dug the whole paddock with forks. I could dig twenty bags a day – dig the spuds, bag them, and sew the bags, that is. Eventually we dug six hundred bags and I kept three hundred of them. I was a bit sly because while I was working I noticed that the landowner had left two different-sized bags for me to fill. Of course, I managed to take three hundred of the larger bags home with me!

Back home we ploughed the ground with our horses and planted all that seed. Then, while the spuds were growing, we got back to work cutting pulp, and we sent George Klinksbourne back to the original mill site to re-establish our timber mill. We hired a truck driver and two more men to help Stewart with the pulp so Harry and I could build the shed to house the mill while George designed the saw mill itself and built all the benches. Everything was ready for the new suction engine we had bought, but that would have to wait because it was time to harvest the spuds.

We had a good crop, about eight tons to the acre. We employed Stewart's family to help us dig them, as they had experience with potato digging. We carted the crop with our truck to the Bunyip rail-way platform where the load had to be passed by a government inspector before it was then off-loaded into a railway truck. These spuds went directly to the soldiers. I wondered: if I had gone into the army, would I be peeling those spuds? Some poor soldier would be. My hands were better suited to an axe than a paring knife!

When we finished the crop we went back to work on the saw mill and took about six months to set the new engine ready to drive the mill. Harry had found this twin-cylinder suction engine that had formerly been used in a coolstore in Ringwood. We had to go down there and dismantle it to bring it home a bit at a time. It had one cylinder on each side with a flywheel in the middle. Each cylinder weighed 30 hundredweight while the flywheel was five ton and split in half with eight huge bolts holding it together on the crankshaft which weighed 30 hundredweight itself. There were also scrubbers which were ten feet high and three feet across, a boiler, seven by twelve feet with an air compressor and two air cylinders to turn the engine over for starting. It took us a fortnight to dismantle the engine and cart it home.

Back at the mill, George and the boys were digging a hole fourteen feet wide and four feet deep to fill with cement and stone and iron reinforcement. Nothing less would support that huge engine. Eventually the engine was bolted down to this platform with twelve four-foot-long bolts.

Finally the mill was ready for action. It was Harry who got the engine going. He was a smart fellow, smart and stubborn. He could pull an engine down, put in rings and bearings, tinker with it until it purred like a cat. He was self-taught, like every bushman. I was lucky to be in partnership with him for I would have nothing to do with engines and machinery. Machinery is different from tools. I love a good tool, know how to keep an axe and a saw sharp – there is a bit of an art to that. I love cleaning and oiling the harness for the horses as well as the hunting rifles, but I am not, and never was, interested in bolts and gears and pistons and cylinders the way Harry was.

Even though he loved horses as much as I did, if he could, Harry would use machinery for everything we did on the Track. He had made friends with the Weatherhead brothers from Tynong North, who were as mad about engines, especially steam engines, as he was. They were from an old pioneering family and lived on the same property they were born on. They had a paddock full of traction engines, steam engines, old parts to any kind of machine you'd care to name.

Harry would go over there and look and talk and scheme and invent. He bought a steamroller from them which drove a winch erected between the back wheels. He figured he would use it instead of the Trewella horse winch we had to clear the already logged areas on our place and make productive farmland. He had to drive the thing home from the Weatherheads' and it took him three days to do the twenty-mile trip! But Harry reckoned it was a handy thing to have as it was cheap to run since it worked on wood and water and only needed a little oil for the moving parts. Myself, I thought the horse winch was doing fine and would keep working with it instead of coping with the noisy and dangerous steam engine. But Harry loved that sort of thing.

With the huge suction engine going at the mill, the saws began to buzz and we were back in business. Once again, George Klinksbourne could stand back and admire his handiwork. This time, however, he had set himself up in a more substantial way than before, by putting in a huge vegetable garden next to a new bark hut he had built along Gipsy Creek just above the mill. In his clever way he had put in a race and built a water wheel so he could irrigate the garden. No matter how hard we were working, I still had time to admire that old bloke.

The timber industry was booming and it was impossible to keep up the supply. On top of our mill work, and the pulpwood for APM, we had organised a contract to supply two-foot wood to be stacked in the railway yard at Longwarry to be used to fire the steam engines, and another contract to supply five-foot green wood for the boilers at the Longwarry and Drouin butter factories. We were also cutting fence posts and palings.

We needed more men to work for us. We needed anyone who was able-bodied and anyone who could swing an axe.

Making Camp

STEWART SENT WORD to his oldest son, Collin, that there was plenty of work at Jackson's Track and to come as soon as he could. Along with him came his wife, Mavis, and her two brothers, Dickie and Sammy Kennedy. They had all been working down on the swamp, picking up spuds and living in a clapped-out farmhouse down near the Bunyip River. Collin's sister, Euphemia, was also living there with them. She decided to come to Jackson's Track, too.

Harry and I knew all these people and were happy to have them on our place. We knew Collin and Dickie and Sammy to be good workers. Euphemia was a bit of a mystery to us, however. We knew

Stewart Hood's hut next to the smaller hut of his son, Collin

that she had been living up on the river bank near Dimboola where Dora's people came from, that she was called Mrs Mullett even though she was quite young, that she seemed to have no man to look after her and that she was the mother of Dora's two young grandsons, Gary and Buddy. Buddy came with us on the back of the truck from Lake Tyers. Stewart and the boys built a good bark hut for her and her two youngsters to live in about twenty yards away, and then they built another hut for the rest of the newcomers about another twenty yards away from that, turning Stewart's camp into a nice triangular compound. The three women – Dora, Mavis and Euphemia – kept that camp as tidy as you please.

Soon word got around what a good place Jackson's Track was, with plenty of work, good water and firewood, plenty of wild game to be had. Blackfellas from all over the country began turning up. Most of the people actually came from Lake Tyers. Just like Stewart and his family, they had been forced to go there in the 1920s but they still identified with their original place. Stewart's family had always been in Gippsland and had sought the protection of Lake Tyers Mission now and again before 1919, but until then they were Port Albert people. From the Western District of Victoria came the Austins, Roses, Lovetts and Wilsons, while from up north came the Coopers, Coombeses, Nelsons and Bloomfields, and from Gippsland came the Hayeses, Stewarts, Tregonings, Mobournes, Scotts, Hoods, Montas, Bulls, Moffats and Mulletts.

They all came in dribs and drabs over about two years. During the war, we heard a new policy had been decreed that the Aborigines should be allowed to take on work wherever there was work if they were able-bodied and capable of doing it, since the war effort was creating more jobs than there were people to take them. The Aborigines had to be allowed to live away from the missions. So the blackfellas began to build their camps all over the country and were free to roam about anywhere. It seemed at last that they could live their own lives where they wished.

There were always blacks travelling through and they were welcome to stop with us as long as they liked. Stewart and Dora often had visitors. Many of them were old fellows, the kind of dignified blackfella you used to see all the time. I remember, in particular, a fella we called Poppa Dodge used to stop with Stewart on a regular basis. He was Stewart's cobber from Lake Tyers. The two of them had some yarns to tell, with plenty of laughter in the telling. Dora's brother with the hoppy leg used to visit from Dimboola, and Stewart's brother, Jack, used to turn up. Several womenfolk, Dora's relatives from the camps around Dimboola, used to stop over for months at a time. At times there were as many as one hundred and fifty blacks on the Track.

We used to cut and stack all the good bark off the stringy-bark trees so if anyone wanted to build, there was plenty of bark for them. Stewart used to pass over our bark and get his own. He reckoned the only way to get it was by prising it off with a stick rather than giving it two or three slaps with an axe. It would take him forever. Actually the best way to prise off the bark was with a special barking bar which was about four feet long and had a flattened end like a blade about three inches wide and curved to go around the log. You could get any amount of bark off you wanted in as much as thirty-foot lengths. It was better than using an axe because sometimes the axe handle could split from pulling at it the way it wasn't designed to be pulled at.

Another thing Stewart reckoned was that you had to fire the bark to strengthen it and straighten it before you used it. He used to spend a lot of time and energy pulling the bark over a fire and then laying it out and rolling it flat. When I first saw him doing this I thought it might be something mysterious he was doing to smoke out the spirits in the wood, for he was deadly serious about what he was doing, but when it was clear he was just trying to straighten the bark I had a good laugh at him for wasting his time.

'My father did it this way,' he insisted. 'This is the blackfella way!'

I shook my head. Every other blackfella used the bark that had already been straightened by being stacked up with logs on it to weigh it down. They didn't know what Stewart was on about either, but he never changed his habit and he used up a lot of extra time to do it.

The people liked living in the bark huts because they were easy to extend or rebuild or add onto whenever they wanted a change. All it took to build a bark hut was six strong and straight poles – four short ones and two longer ones – with forks in them, a shovel for digging a trench, and plenty of bark. They lined up the bark vertically, the rough side out to put off the snakes, beginning at one side of the tin fireplace and going right around – leaving space for a door – until they got to the other side of the fireplace. The huts came down and went up continuously. They could burn bits of it when they needed to. Every summer, the huts would be opened out, walls knocked away, to be like large verandahs, and in the winter they'd be closed in and cosy and there is nothing warmer. A bark hut is an economical abode.

There were two older men, Jackie Coombes and Wagga Cooper, who seemed to command respect but built their camp a bit separate from the rest on the Labertouche Creek. They could talk in their own language and they preferred to live in the old way. They wouldn't live in a bark hut, but built themselves a mia-mia, which was the traditional dwelling. It was made with tree forks leaning into each other and then covered thickly with brush tea-tree which was thatched together to run off the rain. Over this were placed eucalyptus boughs, starting at the top with the leaves drooping down towards the ground.

The entrance was narrow and we had to part the leaves to find a way in. A fireplace made out of iron with an iron door next to it which allowed wood to be carted in for the fire was built on one side. Jackie knew the scrub in the bush that was used for a fire stick to start a fire, knew where to find it and knew how to use it. He and Wagga cooked all their food in the coals of their fire. They snared wild game and made a beautiful fish trap which they lowered into the creek. They were healthy and well fed.

I was especially interested in these two old men and found a way to visit them often of a night-time. They had a lot of know-how, a lot of experience got from drifting across the country working in all sorts of jobs: from producing eucalyptus oil in large vats, to threshing sunflower seeds, to surviving some of the roughest shearing sheds in the country. They told some great stories, but their stories weren't just yarns about life in the white world. These two blackfellas were elders who had knowledge of the Law and an ancient spirit world that makes the whitefellas' understanding of things seem small. At first they didn't tell me much, but right from the beginning they filled me with wonder. I did understand one thing straight away: compared to the blackfella, the white man has no Law. Maybe that's why we can act so cruelly sometimes without even being aware of it.

We supplied every man who wanted one with an axe. Some of the blackfellas worked on the mill, some on the pulpwood, some on the clearing, but mostly it suited them to cut firewood because they could do it at their own pace. It was interesting to see how Stewart became an organisation man. Once he got all his people around him, he never actually did much work himself, but acted as a headman, getting others to do the work. The people seemed satisfied with that arrangement.

We never fired a blackfella the whole time they were on the Track, never even had an argument with any of them. Their work was all contract work. Maybe we were a bit lenient with them as workers because we didn't mind when they worked or how long they worked. Each Friday, we walked around the bush to measure up all the stacks and paid everyone for their cut. We kept an account for each cutter. After they were paid, they often knocked off and played cards. I know they had a two-up game on Sundays. We wouldn't see them again with an axe in their hands until maybe Tuesday. It didn't worry us. It was a good arrangement all around: the more they liked working for us, the more workers we had.

And they brought their families, same as Stewart did. Well, they all seemed to be related to each other one way or another. Over the twenty years that those people stayed at the Track there were many marriages that happened and children who were born. The women kept the camps in order and the children wandered and played first in one hut, then another. They were welcome anywhere and they were safe anywhere. At first they didn't go to school, but later, when there were more children about, Jimmy Bond, one of the finest fellows I've ever worked with, made it his duty to lead the kids to school of a morning and then be there in the afternoon to make sure they got home all right.

These people never really wanted much. They were honest and overflowing with good humour. Stewart himself was a good-natured man who loved having his family around him living in the bush. They wanted good water and food, their own kind of shelter and the freedom to go where they wanted to when they got the urge. They went where they were welcome and where they would find family who would care for them. We were always happy to have them and they could stay as long as they liked. We were sorry to see them go and looked forward to their next visit.

Euphemia

As I HAVE SAID, Harry loved machinery and he was always scheming to bring more of it to the Track. I don't know how he knew it was there, but just toward the end of the war he located a boiler at the Orbost butter factory, which was closing down. He thought he could use it to make the suction engine more efficient, and so he enlisted me to travel the two hundred miles east along the Princes Highway with him to dismantle that thing and bring it home. I told you he was a champion talker and could talk anybody into anything, including himself. I won't begin to explain what Mavis thought of the project.

We were on our way home with a very heavy load on the back

Euphemia Mullett

of the Bedford when we passed the Lake Tyers Mission Station, and there on the side of the road were Euphemia and Gina Hood waiting for us. Harry was amazed.

'You think they knew we were coming this way?'

'Seems like it.'

'I didn't even know they were here. I thought they were still on the Track.'

'No, Euphemia hasn't been at her camp for a couple of weeks. Her kids are stopping at Stewart's.'

'You know a lot.'

'Hmmmph.'

Our noisy Bedford was struggling along very slowly under the weight of the boiler and ground to an even slower halt. We were having trouble with the clutch. The two women walked up to the cabin of the truck to look at us. They were grinning. I tossed my head to indicate they should climb aboard and sit on the tray with their backs against the cabin to keep warm, there being no room inside. As they turned to throw their bags up before them, I saw that Euphemia had a black eye swollen almost shut.

We slowly, and with some difficulty, ground through the gears to get going again. Neither Harry nor I said much. The noise in the cabin and the bounce along the old road prevented talk. I thought about Euphie. Did she know we were coming or was it just good luck? I thought about her black eye. I wondered who would hit a woman like that.

'You see Euphie's eye?'

'Yes.'

'Shame to see a woman with a black eye.'

'Having some kind of row, I guess.'

'That's her business. You'd never ask her.'

'Course not!'

When Euphemia came to Jackson's Track to be near her parents and her two children, Buddy, a toddler, and Gary, still in arms, she was married to Dave Mullett, who everyone called Crockett, but I never saw her with him and he had never been to the Track. I had heard stories of rows between them, but I never thought much about it until now. Maybe she had come across him again at Lake Tyers. None of my business anyway.

The Highway in those days was still tree-lined and kind of wild. It grew dark. There were no lights anywhere except the lights of our truck inching along, straining up the grades, grinding with more and more difficulty through the gears. Our clutch was giving us real trouble. It began to rain, which made things slippery and affected the clutch further, so we made the decision to stop and camp the night along the road. The women, riding on the back, were grateful for that decision.

Nowadays, people can always stop at a milk bar or a fish shop if they get hungry on the road so they never think to carry a billy and the makings of a meal and a camp with them. Back then, everybody carried their own supplies: a billy, a waterbag, tea, sometimes flour and some blankets. So making the decision to stop along the road for the night was nothing extraordinary. We soon had a big roaring fire going, since there was plenty of dry wood about and all of us were handy with setting a fire. Some water was on the boil for tea and some damper laid in the coals. It was still raining but we were warm next to the fire and covered in wool blankets so we weren't bothered.

The two sisters were at ease with us and now that we knew there was no hope of getting home before the next day, we settled back and enjoyed our tea which we drank out of tin cups held lightly in our hands, steaming warmth rising in our faces. Nothing like a cup of tea out in the open, sitting warm by a good fire. We told stories and laughed. There was lots of talk about family. The girls set us straight on who was related to who, where people were from, where one person had gone, when another had returned. Gina told us she was keen on Roy Rose, who was cutting wood at the Track while Gina was doing housework on a dairy farm in Drouin. Very soon, in fact, they would be married, even though Gina's mum reckoned at eighteen she was a bit young for Roy Rose. One year later they had Lionel, born right on the Track.

Euphemia chatted on as fast as Gina, but she never said anything about her black eye. No one asked. I could see that Euphie was a good-looking woman. I had never noticed that before. It was her I looked at, not Gina. She was not tall, but well built like her father, Stewart, with plenty of meat on her bones. She was easy to talk to and quick to smile. She seemed like a nice person to know.

Eventually we all wound up in our blankets and lay down to sleep through the night right where we were, next to the fire in the rain.

I don't remember the rest of the trip home, but I remember that Euphie was in my thoughts from that day on, although it would be another three or four years before I made up my mind to do anything about it. I was a working man and didn't think of myself as anything else for a long time.

Life settled into a routine on Jackson's Track. Mavis, with her head for business, found some good outlets for our sawn timber, the most important being with Luxford's in Oakleigh, so the mill was going full-time. I spent my time falling trees and pulling the logs into the mill. Our 800 acres of forest was still thick with trees, but the snig tracks were lined with stumps now and it was possible to peer into the bush a short distance. Some patches had been logged out and we were clearing it with the winches, pulling the stumps out and dragging them with the toppings into huge piles to burn. We had it in our minds that this would be a working farm one day, with clean, rich paddocks. It was what we were working for, but it was a distant thought. Now I wonder whether we had any idea of what we wanted or what the consequences would be. We weren't philosophical. We just worked.

The blackfellas worked cutting firewood from their huts outwards, clearing the trees from around the camps so there would be no danger from falling limbs, but they were still nestled deep in the tea-tree so there was a strong sense of a never-ending bush around them. Even though the huts were not far from each other, it was difficult to see one from the other. The huts were scattered over an area of about a half-mile. The people living in them all visited each other to check how they were and spread news if they had any. They were always busy and had plenty to do on top of cutting firewood for us. Every morning they walked around their snares or traps and fishing lines. They also gathered the abundant native tucker that was growing in our bush: grubs, wild tomatoes, sour cherries, tubers, and more that I hadn't had time to learn about yet. They carted water to the huts and picked up firewood for their own use. And they looked out for each other, sharing food, caring for anyone who was sick, watching the children; for that was their code, to help each other and to stick together.

I enjoyed having the children around. Euphie's son Buddy, Stewart's son Jewel, and their mate Axel Harrison were a tight trio of little boys who used to follow me around all day as I worked. They would help out sometimes, but usually spent their time playing just out of harm's way. Their constant chatter was amusing and comforting. They used to love it when a tree went down. They'd play amongst the branches until they were told to clear out while we cut them away. They waited until the log was barked, clean and 'greasy' and fresh, then they would pick up a woodchip with a sharp edge on it and scrape it along the log to pick up the sap which they loved to eat, but it always made them sick. I never tried it myself so I can't say what the attraction was.

Buddy used to show up on his own over at our place. He was a quiet, sensible boy. I'd give him a feed because you know kids always want something. Every once in a while, I would accompany him back to his mother's place and have a cup of tea. I always felt relaxed with Euphie and liked her company. She kept a very clean camp, with everything tidy and put away, the dirt floor swept with a branch of leaves. Every time I was there there were clean clothes hanging on a line or carefully folded, and she was usually mending something: trousers, a shirt, a dress. I liked the looks of Euphemia, but it took me a long time to realise I fancied her. I never thought of myself in connection with a woman. I was young and strong and some say good to look at myself, but I didn't know that.

There was always too much to do. With the mill going full bore, we had full-time mill-hands working there to house. We were also sick of Mavis's complaints about her 'shack', so we employed a builder to put up two small 'mill houses', as we called them, one just above Gipsy Creek for the workers, and a larger house on the other side of the red hill to replace Mavis's shack and our bark hut. They were built out of our own timber.

We listened to Mavis and realised that of course she was right when she insisted we put in a telephone. We bought copper wire and erected a line two and a half miles through the bush from the mill to the Jindivick West Road where the Department's line went to Jindivick. The saddle horses got plenty of work then, as sticks used to fall from the trees and lie across the wire, or boughs would snap off in the wind and break the wire altogether. It was a constant battle. We made quite a track from the horses' hooves treading up and down that line.

The only time we took off from working flat out was on Fridays when we walked around the bush to measure the stacks of wood cut by the blackfellas for the week.

It was a busy place, our forest, with blacks and whites working together. It's true that we never thought about whether we were black or whether we were white. We were workers, we were bushmen. We all lived together on the same bit of land and we all got on, gave each other room, accepted one another.

Except Mavis. She was aware of who owned things and who didn't, who worked hard and who didn't, who was white and who wasn't.

People Talk

MAVIS DIDN'T REALLY have enough to do to keep herself occupied on the Track so every day she used to climb into her little blue Austin, which she had bought new with the flower money, and go into Drouin to do the rounds of the shops, picking up groceries for her cooking, and expanding her SP bookmaking business. She knew lots of business people, people who were the big punters. Her final stop was always the pub, where she never drank any alcohol but relied on people who did to do business with her. Apart from the 'business' she spent her time, as far as I could tell, gossiping till she was blue in the face.

She loved mixing with people. She used to come home and tell

Mavis Tonkin ready for town

us how popular she was, who she knew, who she liked and who she didn't like. I guess it was true that people waited for her to come around, because, if they are honest, everyone will admit to being interested in news about their neighbours, especially if it's a little bit scandalous. And a country town is the worst place for 'news'. I imagine that Mavis, the good talker that she was, probably managed to tell all the town about every detail of life at Jackson's Track.

People's response was to shake their heads and commiserate with her about having brothers who hired blacks to work for them. She would come home and tell us that all the blacks were giving us – she meant herself – a bad name, that we shouldn't employ so many of them.

'We'd be better off without them!' she would complain – I'll never forget that shrill voice of hers. 'They're lazy and they're taking advantage of us.'

When she would start on someone in particular, I'd leave the house and let her talk to the walls. It got on my nerves how she was always on about the way people were talking about us. There seemed to be no decency in her world.

She would invite her special friend, Mrs Brew, who she was very thick with, over for afternoon tea and you could hear the two of them complaining and moaning about things you wouldn't ordinarily think to consider. I always felt uncomfortable about entering the house when the two of them were there. Those two women could pick fault with anyone, and I avoided them so they wouldn't pick fault with me, within my hearing at least.

Mavis let the blacks know she didn't approve of them, by being bossy with them, ordering them around and not being friendly. She put them out in the woodheap, so to speak. There was one fellow she warmed to, though – she couldn't help liking Jimmy Bond.

Jimmy was the finest man you could find anywhere. He came from up the coast in New South Wales, Wallagah Lake near Bermagui. He was honest and always ready to lend a hand to help anyone. He loved his people and spent a lot of time looking after them. Before starting work each morning, he used to walk the children two miles through the bush track on their way to school and then meet them on their way back and bring them home, often carrying the littlest ones if they were too tired.

Jimmy lived at the mill and worked with me in the bush. He was my partner on the crosscut saw. It's not easy to find a good sawing partner. Some men hold onto it just too long so you have to drag it back with their weight still pulling on it. Others push it back at you too early. A good partnership means the saw is always light in the hands and a natural rhythm is established so there's no strain and no competition. Jimmy was my perfect partner.

I suppose the reason Mavis took to him was because, without ever being asked, he began bringing dry wood to the house every day for her stove. She invited him to have his evening meals with us. He was the only one, black or white, who ever came to eat with us. Neither Harry nor I would dare ask anyone into the house unless Mavis wanted them in.

Jimmy was a good addition to our table for he was an alert and bright character who was always on for a joke. Mavis was relaxed with him and spoke to him kindly. She allowed him to become one of the family. She thought he was a hard worker and deserved her generosity, unlike the others who she thought were lazy and deserved nothing but her disregard.

Harry and Jimmy and I used to escape to the blackfellas' camp now and again after tea, especially when Roy Rose was prepared to give a concert. Roy was married to Gina by this time and they had already begun their large family. Roy was a very good guitar player and singer. He played and sang songs he had composed about the bush he loved. Most nights everybody made tracks to Stewart's place, where there would be a big log fire and, when they weren't swapping yarns about their experiences around the country, Roy Rose would sing and get everybody to sing along with him. It was fine those nights at Stewart's.

There was nothing Mavis could say about our going there of a night. The mill-hands used to join us and George Klinksbourne, too. Maybe if Mavis had joined us as well, she would have stopped listening to the way people talk and her life would have been filled with more happiness.

Seasons

DURING THE WAR we planted potatoes for three years but did not do well enough out of them to keep going. The first year was good, but the second was a dry year and the crop was poor; the third year we had a bumper crop but the price was so low we couldn't afford to harvest it. Instead we bought pigs and turned them out on the red hill to fatten them up while they snorted and wallowed their way through the crop. The blackfellas also made the most of it, digging the free spuds all day every day until they had enough.

While the wheels at the saw mill kept turning, it brought in a steady income and kept us out of trouble. Our lives continued in an

Front to back: Gary Mullett, Buddy Mullett, Norman Coombes, Cecil Coombes

ordinary fashion with only occasional reminders that a war was still being fought all around the world. Our neighbour often had American servicemen out to this 'wild' part of Victoria to hunt deer. He had a pack of beagle hounds that would regularly raise their howling throughout the forest. I might be out barking a log or getting the horses lined up to haul one into the mill yard when the howling would begin and I'd know there was a hunting party up from the city and the dogs had caught the scent of a deer. I'd stand and listen, following the path of the quarry by the echoing plaintive sound of the dogs through the bush. I could never see anything through the thickness. I knew every bush noise around me would go silent as if the forest had come to attention until a shot rang out and the baying turned into excited yapping. Then usually everything went back to normal.

One day a big buck charged out of the thick bush right next to me with the dogs on its heels. It found itself up against a large tree and turned to face its attackers. I had nothing but an axe, which I raised, but that only made the buck notice me and, in panic, it dashed off. The pack swarmed after it and I followed, ducking and weaving through the trees, but as the buck leapt over Labertouche Creek a shot rang out and it fell in a heap. Dead. It had a beautiful set of antlers. The American who shot it said he would keep them and take them back to the States after the war.

We heard about the bomb being dropped on the Japanese and about the war being over, but it made little difference to our lives. The blackfellas stayed on, came and went, married, had children; built up their camps, moved them, extended their huts, pulled them down, rebuilt them. There was no end to activity. Children played and chattered, laughing or crying, showing up in the most unlikely places. Axes rang throughout the forest. Men called out jokes and filled the forest with laughter. Sometimes the singing rhythm of their original language was an accompaniment to our work.

Out in the forest, I never had a row with anyone. I was good at what I did and easy and relaxed with my skills. Some said to me I should go in the woodchops at the shows, I was that good with an axe, but I never did. I'm not a sportsman, not interested in sport. I knew what I could do and I couldn't see any reason to chop wood for no practical purpose except to win something. The blackfellas were the same, although I wonder now if it's because they felt they wouldn't be accepted on an equal level. I wonder, too, if maybe I had ventured out and become known off the Track, then people would have better accepted my way of life later. You never know.

Back then I had no sense of things to come. Harry and I were the Tonkin Brothers and satisfied with our effort and the way life was on the Track. I felt lucky to be Harry's brother. We were close; we never fought and we respected each other. I not only respected my older brother, but I admired him.

It had always been that way. The reason I left my parents' place and went up to work on my uncle's station in the New South Wales outback when I was so young was because I wanted to follow my big brother up there. Then, after I had learned how to do a man's work, I followed my brother into the horse-trading business, dealing with the drovers along the stock routes that went from the Gulf Country right through to Homebush in Sydney, or if they branched off at Cooper's Creek, right on down to Adelaide.

That was a good life. At the height of the season, the mobs of cattle would be about one-thousand-head strong. One mob would follow another with about a mile between them and they had to keep going, covering ten miles a day. We knew all the drovers along the way and we had a reputation for handling horses and dealing honestly.

We had a sulky and usually three hacks in tow at a time. We would break the horses on the road and sell them. Of course, they were rough and ready, just like everyone was in those days.

I loved being with my brother on the stock routes. Sometimes it was so quiet we wouldn't see anyone for days, but we knew where all the waterholes were. We would stop at one and eventually a mob would pull in. We'd have a time talking to the drovers at night around the fire, with the horses hobbled and the mob settled. All the talk was about water and feed.

'What's the country like?'

'Much feed up ahead?'

'How's the water holding?'

Sometimes we'd move off the stock routes and go on to the stations to do some horse breaking or fence contracting or even shearing. We could do everything: shearing, crutching, killing, skinning, butchering. We could handle cattle, branding and marking a fair mob each year. We even hunted wild pig and I was a dab hand at skinning them, but just about the only thing I never learned to do on the stations was to plait. So I had to get someone else to make my bridles and whips for me.

Although Harry and I were both known for our ability to handle horses, and even though I was the one who had the most to do with them on the Track, Harry was the better horseman. He had no fear and could stick to a bucking horse no matter how it twisted and jolted in an attempt to 'plant' its rider.

When we came to the Track our reputations were soon made and people would sometimes bring us their rough hacks for us to knock some sense into. I remember that the Woodalls of Labertouche, who used to supply us with chaff for our own working horses, challenged Harry that he couldn't tame one of their horses.

Well, Harry would always accept a challenge, but what he didn't know was they had kept this horse stabled and fed him up on oats for two weeks before they brought him over. By the time we got him, this horse was feeling his oats and ready to burst out of his own skin.

As we led him into a small yard we could see he was excited, all lathered up with nerves and tension. I got on him first, muggins that I am. Within ten seconds I was face down and bum up in the dirt. The horse pranced around me, triumphant, but when Harry approached him he propped on four straight legs, put his head down and stared, snorting and rolling his eyes. Harry lunged for the rein, pulled the brute's head right around so his nose was almost to the girth, and sprang into the saddle before he had any notion of Harry's intention. With his head pulled around, this mongrel could do nothing but spin in circles, faster and faster until he fell, but Harry didn't budge in the saddle.

With the horse still down under him, Harry called, 'Open the gate!' and gave him his head. The horse sprang to his feet, aiming for the treetops. He twisted towards the gate in mid-air and hit the ground at full gallop, charging through the gate like something demented. Harry dug his heels in and sent that creature flying though the bush, bending around trees, jumping logs, avoiding stumps, until he and Harry disappeared. We could hear Harry laughing at the horse at the top of his voice for some time, but then there was nothing.

Two hours later they returned, the horse exhausted and placid, Harry grinning broadly. He dismounted.

'There you are,' was all he said as he handed the reins to the owner.

'Thanks.'

Later Harry said to me that the horse might have been placid, but it wasn't beaten. It was mad and should be sent to a circus.

He waited with interest to hear what happened when one of the Woodalls tried to ride their newly tamed horse. I couldn't help admiring Harry all over again. We had a firm partnership.

So the Tonkin Brothers kept at it. We were doing well enough to extend the mill. Around 1948 we bought a new diesel engine to run it. We put on another team of mill workers. Later we closed down the suction gas engine that had taken us so long to put in place and used only the new engine to run everything.

By this time George Klinksbourne, who was already an old man when he first came to work for us, began to slow down. He had always worked in the mill, but that mill work is fast and dangerous. It's hard on your back and joints to keep hauling timber back and forth. He preferred to be out in the forest cutting where the pace was slower. He loved being out amongst our great trees. The trees were that big that, now, I think it would have been better if we had left it for forest. The pioneers who had come in before us had ringbarked most of the trees hereabouts, but they had skipped our acres for some reason. Ours was a good green forest and George loved being out in it. Back then it seemed like it would never disappear, even though at that point that was our goal.

George was very experienced with the crosscut saw and I believe that the reason he remained active and healthy for so long was because the saw kept him fit. It wasn't hard on your back, it kept you moving and you could pace it the way you wanted it. More and more often, though, George would stop to sharpen his tools. He was a skilled sharpener and many men would rely on him, but, finally, he had to decide to be honest with himself and call it quits.

We never told him to retire; he told himself. We told him we were happy to have him living down by the mill, tending his garden, sharing the vegetables he grew with all of us, but he bought himself a small property on the other side of Drouin. We helped him build a two-room cottage to live in. He established another much bigger garden and that's how he lived until he died about three years later when he was seventy. I reckon that old man was one of my most important teachers and I still miss him.

The flower people from Fitzroy continued coming every year to pick the boronia. Three of them made friends with the blackfellas and asked them to pick their loads of flowers for them and have them ready to put on the trucks three days a week. Jimmy Bond, Dave Moore and Jack Kennedy were more than willing since it was easy work and they were supplied with plenty of food and some drink. Those three men who worked the boronia season felt privileged and were always sorry when the season ended.

Seasons came and went. Harry and I were friends with everyone on our place. We always had a mixed workforce and there were never any rows amongst us. I know that's because we were all bushmen who had a respect for the bush and for people who had the skills to work and live in the bush. Whenever we went down to some of the old people's camps we were always welcome. All of us who lived and worked here looked after each other, did the decent thing by each other. Everything about life on the Track was good.

Except for Mavis. She pushed and bossed and challenged us all the time.

Moving Out

'WHY DO YOU keep putting these blacks on when you should be hiring whites?' Mavis asked continually.

Of course, she was thinking of the talk from the town. And there was a lot of talk, but people only talked amongst themselves and never faced us directly. They spoke to Mavis and put negative thoughts in her head. Then she put pressure on us.

'People don't want so many Abos around this district. They come to town and they're dirty,' she'd growl at us.

Harry and I took no notice.

Daryl and Bob

'They're lazy. You're letting them take advantage of you,' she would complain.

We began to resent her.

She was a very good woman if you were on the right side of her, but she wanted things her own way whatever. She was a good businesswoman and helped us by keeping the books and finding outlets for our timber, but no matter how determined she was, she was not the boss and they weren't her decisions that were final. Regardless, she still felt she had the right to say something.

'We'd be better off without them!' she insisted.

Harry ignored her. He was as stubborn as she was and could get the better of her. She would give in to him, but she never let up trying to boss me around. Even though I didn't like it, it went against my grain to row with her. I have never rowed with anybody and no matter how terrible her temper, she couldn't get me to fight and neither could she always get me to do what she wanted. That doesn't mean she didn't make me fret: I worried about her temper; I worried about her comments; I worried about her claim on me and her interfering with me.

'You're not going down there again tonight, are you? It's not right for you to mix with Abos so much.' She scolded me in the presence of Jimmy Bond with disregard for anything he might feel about her comments. I had no preference between black and white. I went where I was welcome.

'She's always at me and I'm sick of it,' I said to myself at last.

I began to avoid her if I could. I noticed while George Klinksbourne was still at the Track, he avoided her, too.

'I am not overly concerned with business; I am not a gossiper nor am I a gambler on the horses. I'm just a bushwhacker and I'll keep to myself where your sister is concerned,' he once told me.

Now, I admired that old man and I agreed with his attitude, but it took me a while to reach the conclusion that the best way for me to keep to myself where my sister was concerned was to move out. Move out of my own home, which didn't feel like my own home any more. Besides, I was almost twenty-nine years old and it was time for me to live away from my older brother and sister.

By 'away', I meant that I would build my own camp somewhere on the property separate from Mavis and Harry. I wouldn't leave the Track nor stop working even for a moment. I began to scout around for a good spot and found one near the boundary with the state forest where the trees were tall and the light was dim, where there was a feeling of solitude and peace. Peace. It would be good to have some peace.

Once I found the spot, I started planning in my mind how the camp would be. I would build a bark hut with two rooms, a couple of yards for my working horses and my hack, with a shelter for them and a storage place for their feed, harness and tack. I would carve out a track, more or less the size of a snig track, to the spot for easy access. I would have a big tin fireplace.

I would also ask Euphemia to come and live with me.

My mind was working overtime. Once I realised it was possible to move out, I began dreaming of the best possible life for myself, and every vision I came up with always had Euphemia in it.

I had been visiting Euphie for years. Her camp wasn't so far away from the main house. I often had work to do around the house when it was first built, clearing dangerous timber away from it, dragging logs and burning out stumps. If I looked over across the creek, which I have to admit I did quite a lot, I could see Euphie in her camp doing the laundry or sweeping out the yard around her bark hut with a tea-tree broom. Pretty soon after noticing her, I would convince myself I needed a break and walk over the creek for a cup of tea.

It was always the same when I went over there. I'd go inside and sit by the fire on a four-gallon drum. The billy would be just on the boil, hanging over a low greenwood fire on a wire hook in the fireplace. Euphie would take up an iron hook to protect her hand before she reached over to lift the billy off the fire and pour a bit of hot water into her chipped blue enamel teapot. She'd swirl the water around and then toss it in the fire, causing a small burst of steam. Good sound, means the tea's almost ready. She would take a handful of tea leaves and dump it in the warm teapot, then pour the hot water out of the billy into the pot. That's another good sound, the boiling water hitting the sides of the tin billy before it pours into the pot and hits the leaves. I don't know, I watched Euphie do it so many times, I just liked it.

While the tea steeped she would put two or three teaspoons of sugar into her own cup and give my cup a rinse with hot water. I didn't take sugar, still don't. She served her tea in the bush tradition, in used tins with the lid bent back and the sharp metal of the lid folded under to make a comfortable handle.

Once the tea was served she'd sit down on another drum and we'd have a yarn. I don't know why having a yarn with Euphie was different to having a yarn with other people. Maybe it was because I cared for her. We had the same interests, the same idea of how to live. Well, she must have felt the same as me, otherwise why would she always seem to know I was coming over and have the billy on the boil? If we didn't have something in common, she'd tell me to get going, wouldn't she?

We became great friends.

I knew there was nothing left at all between her and Crockett Mullett. He had even lived here on the Track for some time, but they never spoke or even acknowledged each other. My guess is they had once had a terrible row that they never got over. She was friendly with Johnny Rose for a while and her third child, Dorothy, who, at the time my plan to have Euphie come live with me was taking shape, was still a babe in arms, was a result of that relationship, but Johnny was gone and not about to return. I didn't think Euphemia was sorry to see the back of him either. I never asked Euphemia about her past relationships and she wasn't interested in telling me. I knew she was on her own; I knew she was honest, kind and generous; I knew she was a good mother; I knew I liked her and that I wanted her to share my camp with me. That was good enough for me. It didn't occur to me to use the word love then, but I know now that I loved her.

I was planning all kinds of things in my head, not telling any-body. I was still eating dinner at Mavis's table every night, talking business with Harry, and wandering down to Stewart's camp of an evening. Finally, one night, instead of dropping off at Stewart's I continued on over to Euphemia's camp. Now, I'm not a sentimental fellow or a smooth-talking bloke, so after she handed me a cup of tea I just told her what was on my mind.

'I'm setting up my own camp. How would you like to live with me?'

She looked straight at me, didn't smile, didn't hesitate.

'That will be all right,' she said.

I just sat there looking at her and she looked at me. I knew she would have told me 'No', if she'd wanted to. She wasn't frightened of my being white or even being the boss at the Track. In fact, her father, Stewart, had told me long before that I was considered a white black-fella by most of them. I don't think she was considering my colour at all right then, neither was she considering whether I would improve her life because she knew I liked to live rough. She was considering whether she would have a stable life with me and she knew she would. Yes, she could have said no, but she didn't. I finished my tea and put the cup down on her clean table. I rubbed my hands on my thighs.

'Well, I better get to work on that bark hut, then. Two rooms all right with you?'

She nodded. I stood up and nodded back at her.

'I'll come and get you in a week.'

I turned and left.

Walking through that dark forest, I had such a grin on my face. Well, she must have some attraction for me if she was willing to move away from her hut near her father and especially her mother, Dora, who she was very close with. She could have said no, but she didn't! I don't know if I laughed out loud or danced a jig, but I should have.

A week is too short when you have too much to do, but it is an eternity when you are waiting for your life to begin. I knew I could build a good camp in a week, but I didn't know if I could do it and not let on while keeping up with the mill work, so I was worried I had taken on too much of a burden when I told Euphemia I'd be back for her in a week. At the same time, I counted every hour that passed, and each hour seemed like a day, while I waited for the moment to go fetch her.

In the evenings, after we knocked off at the mill, I went over to my site and worked on the hut. During the day, I managed to arrange it so the logs I was collecting for the mill were somewhere in the vicinity of my site so I could haul bark there and stack it to straighten it, and so I could locate the appropriate poles for the frame of the hut, cut them and haul them to the site without wasting time.

On the first evening, I pegged out the size of the hut. It would have two rooms about twelve foot by twelve foot, so I stepped out four long paces by eight long paces and put a stake in the ground every four paces to mark where the outside poles would go. I pulled a string tight between the stakes to make sure it was square and the line was straight and to give me a guide where to dig the trench.

After I pegged out the hut, the next thing I had to do was dig a trench about ten inches deep all around. It's this trench that would eventually keep the walls in place. Ten inches doesn't seem very deep and a ten-inch trench all around doesn't seem like it would be much work. And it isn't, if you're digging in sand, but the ground of a forest isn't sand. There are rocks and, more importantly, roots which get in your way. When you're digging a trench in the forest, you need a spade with a sharpened blade that will cut through the roots of the trees when you come down heavy on them. I had worked up quite a sweat digging that trench on the first evening and getting it finished in time to get home to Mavis's cooking.

By knock-off time of the second day, I had accumulated fifteen good straight poles with strong forks at one end to be the uprights for the hut. I intended to have them all in place before I finished in time for dinner. I began work on the post holes with a long thin shovel strong enough to withstand any rocks I might strike, sharp enough to get through the tree roots. Sometimes I had to ram the sharp end of a long tamping bar into the hole to break up the rock or smash through a root before resuming with the shovel. Each hole had to be two feet deep or as long as half the length of my arm. By meal time, I had the holes dug and the poles in them, but I had yet to ram the earth in around the bottom of them to make them secure. I would do that the next day, as well as start fashioning a fireplace out of tin I already had stacked ready for use.

That week at home with Mavis and Harry was both easy and difficult. My mind was off in another place, planning and dreaming, so Mavis's complaints and sharp words ran off me without making an impression. At the same time I was becoming more and more impatient with her and showing her a kind of boldness I had never dared to before because I knew I wouldn't have to put up with it much longer. I think it surprised her when I came close to arguing with her once or twice, but she didn't take the time to wonder about it. On the other hand, when Harry wasn't getting much sense out of me about the business, I could feel he was perplexed and watching me a bit more closely than usual. During meals, he kept looking over at Jimmy, as if checking for clues to some mystery. Of course, Jimmy knew I was building a hut on the other end of the property since he was with me a large part of the day. I imagined he knew about Euphemia, too, since the blackfellas seem to know everything, but he kept it all to himself.

The more tense it got at home, the harder I worked. Soon I had all the posts firmly in the ground and the fireplace and chimney in place. Next I had to find three long poles to lay in the forks of the posts. These would make the frame upon which the roof would rest. I put in a frame for the door at the end opposite the fireplace, but left no place for windows. There are never windows in a bark hut.

I was ready to put up the walls. No matter how much you work to flatten bark, it will still retain its curved shape somewhat. But this is used to advantage because as you line the bark up you overlap the first piece with the second and the curved edge keeps the first piece in position by locking into it. I began at the fireplace, putting the bottom edge of the length of bark in the trench, rough bark side out, and raising it up vertically until the other end leant against the pole at the roof line. Then I put the next piece in place, overlapping its neighbour until I got around to the door. Next step was to shovel the dirt back into the trench, filling it up around the bottom of the bark and tamping it down to make it firm. Then I started placing the bark on the other side of the fireplace again until I got to the door and once more filled in and tamped down the dirt in the trench. There, the walls were on!

Jimmy volunteered to help me with the roof. Even though I was able to do it alone, I was glad of his company and help as time was passing too fast, and at the same time not fast enough. The roof is always put on rough side out to let the rain run off it efficiently. It is put on like roofing iron, vertically, running from the gable down to the eaves, and, just like the walls, one piece overlaps another. Along the ridge at the top pole line we put one long, fairly curved piece of bark to hold the roof in place and make it watertight at the top seam. The weight of the roof holds the walls in place, so there are no nails or wires used at all in the construction, except in the last step where logs are lifted onto the roof to hold it in place. These logs are wired on to add weight to the bark on the roof in the face of high winds.

Well, there it was! Walls, roof, fireplace and three days to go! But I wasn't finished. I wanted a proper swinging door on my hut so I found some good splitting wood and made palings for a solid, fine-looking door with a latch on it. I made a table by digging posts in the ground and laying new palings over it. I brought in drums for chairs. I put in hooks over the fire for cooking and had a good camp oven and some iron pots ready. I had knives and forks, enamel plates and cups, and stacked kerosene tins to put them all in. I made a bed the same as the table, but instead of palings I used bark to lay across the poles. Bark makes a good bed.

I was liking the look of this place. It felt like home, like the good years when Harry and I were just starting out, when the forest was all round us and we felt a natural part of it.

I still had the yards to build, and the shed and shelter for the horses. I also meant to clear away any trees that were too close and looked like being a danger to the camp. And I wanted to get the track into the place more passable. And maybe we would have chooks which would need a shed . . .

But, for now, it was time to get Euphemia.

Confrontation

WHEN I FIRST brought Euphie to the camp I made out I was not
worried about what she thought, but I was heart-thumping anxious,
if you must know. At first she just stood there hanging onto her few
belongings which were tucked up under her left arm. She looked
around and I hoped she thought the hut looked well built. She
looked up and noticed there were no overhanging branches on the
tall trees to threaten the roof. She looked away and I saw her men-
tally thinking that Gipsy Creek was the right distance for easy carting
of water.

She didn't look at me but went inside and peered at the fireplace

Daryl and Euphie with Sadie at their first camp

where I had a fire burning and she took in how well the chimney drew. She saw the camp oven, the billy and the cauldron for heating water. She walked around the room, picked up a spoon then put it back in its place in the kerosene-tin shelf. She inspected a tin cup with a bent-wire handle lined up with three others just like it on the table. She ran the fingers of her right hand over the newly split and smoothed palings of the table. She noticed the dirt floor that I had raked and tamped down to make hard as concrete. She wandered into the other room. Did she smile when she inspected the bed I had made? She put her swag down on the left-hand side of the bed.

Then she turned and finally looked at me! I could tell by the tiniest smile that Euphie was pleased with my camp, and I knew she was here to stay.

Euphie and I were alone at the camp for starters. Her mother, Dora, was looking after the three kids, Buddy, Gary and Dorothy. What I remember about those first days was that there was no shyness. We were good mates from the beginning, and we immediately swung into a routine that never changed for thirty years.

In the mornings, as soon as I awoke I lit the fire for the day. We always let the fire burn out at night. No use wasting wood while you're asleep; besides, there is nothing worse than sleeping in a hot house. You've got to let the fire go out to give yourself some air. I would always collect the kindling and small sticks, which I call 'morning wood', in the evening and have it ready to lay the fire when I awoke.

Once I lit the fire I would go outside to make sure there was enough wood split and piled up for the day. Even though Euphie was a good woodcutter and could swing an axe all right, I always did it for her. And I wouldn't let her light the fire, either. I would never let a woman light a fire. To my way of thinking, that's a man's job.

Euphie would be up with me. She never stopped in bed waiting for me to bring her a cup of tea, which I would have done if she'd let me. She would be out the door with two tin buckets, heading down to the creek to fetch water before I could turn around. Euphie was a great user of water because she was the cleanest woman I ever knew. She felt it was her job to keep things clean, to wash the dishes and the clothes, to scrub down the table and wipe over every surface that could collect dust every single day. She needed lots of water to be so clean so it was a good thing I chose my camp only thirty yards from Gipsy Creek!

As soon as Euphie returned with fresh water, she would put the billy on. I would get my own breakfast, probably because I had the habits of a bachelor that wouldn't change. We had no cow at that bush camp, so there was no milking to do. I always made damper, as I had been doing all my life and as I will do until the day I die. It would be cooked by about the same time the billy came to the boil, and so, as always, I would have tea and damper with jam for breakfast. Euphie only had tea with plenty of sugar. She would sit there and roll herself a cigarette while I had my damper. That was the only vice Euphie had: she smoked two ounces of fine-cut tobacco a week. That item was always on the list for the weekly shopping trip to Jindivick without fail.

When I left the table to go outside to harness the horses for work, Euphie would be stoking the fire and putting more water on to heat for washing up.

On the second day, when I returned to the camp after work, Euphie had Dorothy with her. She was still a babe and on the breast so she couldn't stop with her grandmother for long. She was a quiet, happy baby and I was glad to have her around. Several days later, Buddy and Gary came to see what it was like. They only stayed on for about three days because it was too quiet for them way off in the bush away from the others. They went back to Dora and that's where they stayed. Dora was a wonderful woman who loved children and could never have too many stopping at her camp, so it was a good arrangement. The blackfellas are happy to accept arrangements like that, too, because they believe the children belong to everybody. If you think about it, you'll never see a homeless Aboriginal child. They always have somewhere to go.

Stewart's camp was the centre of activity because he liked to have his people living close around him so they could share the food together and share their lives with each other. The boys liked that. Euphie, on the other hand, was like me. She was a homebody who didn't need lots of company. She was a loyal woman who believed in a settled relationship. She only needed one person and that was me.

I was with Euphemia for two full and happy weeks before either Harry or Mavis acknowledged that a change had taken place in the living arrangements at Jackson's Track. At first they accepted that I had built myself a camp out in the bush and wanted to look after myself, but that was before they discovered Euphemia was with me. Then there was an almighty row!

Harry stopped me while I was in the middle of using the back end of my axe to knock some dog spikes out of the logs I had just dragged in. I halted mid-swing and looked at him.

'Come up to the house when we knock off. We've some things to discuss,' he said.

I stared into his face for a minute, then continued to swing at the spike. Harry walked back down to the mill.

After I put up my horses in the new corral at my camp, I told Euphie I wouldn't be stopping for tea and turned in the direction of the main house. It was a beautiful evening, with red, late summer sunlight filtering through the trees. I walked past the mill and the hands were sitting outside the mill houses with their feet up. I could smell their meals cooking. I walked across the red hill with a setting sun hot on my back throwing my shadow long across the ground before me now that I was out of the trees.

I had an idea what was coming once I reached that house. A few days ago, when I had stopped in at Stewart and Dora's camp to see how things were going, Dora and I had a long talk over several cups of tea. She said she was glad that Euphemia had someone like me to look after her. She said that Euphie was a good girl and deserved happiness. She also felt she had to warn me. She said now that Euphie and I were together and people knew about it, we would not be able to avoid trouble. She said she did not know where the trouble would raise its ugly head, but that it would and we would have to face it. She said that we would face it all of our lives together and she prayed we were strong enough. She said she thought Euphie was. She said she loved us.

I knew, then, as I approached the house, that I was about to face trouble, and I felt strong enough.

Jimmy was stacking wood by the kitchen door. He looked up and waved, stepped back from the wood, turned and walked away from the house rather than into it as he usually would do. I took a deep breath and went on inside. Mavis and Harry were sitting at the table waiting for me. I didn't sit down with them, but preferred to stand at the end of the table. Mavis started.

'Do you have any idea what you're doing?'

I looked straight at her but didn't answer.

'No brother of mine is going to live with a black woman!' she shrilled.

'What's wrong with it?' I asked quietly.

Mavis looked at Harry in exasperation.

'Daryl,' said Harry in a more reasonable tone than Mavis, 'it's not natural. A white man cannot live with a native woman.'

'How do you expect to be able to hold your head up and look people in the eye?' Mavis spat out, impatient with Harry.

'What people do you have in mind?' I asked.

'Decent people!' she shouted, spoiling for a fight that I was determined not to give her. The thing about Mavis was that when she got wild her face would go white with rage, the opposite of most people. I could see the blood was draining out of her face and I didn't like it. Harry could see it, too, and he knew just as well as I did that she could be a terror.

'Daryl,' Harry said, 'you can't live with her. It's against our religion. It's against God.'

That stumped me. How could the happiness Euphemia and I have be against God? What God?

'Well, I guess I have my own religion.'

Mavis hissed.

'It's unnatural,' Harry repeated quickly, putting his hand up to keep Mavis quiet. 'You can't keep her there with you. You must send her back to her people.'

'I didn't order her to come and stay with me. And I won't order her to leave. She is free to do as she pleases. It's up to her what she does.'

'You'll be an outcast with your people, with your family, with all white people!' said Mavis.

'I'm sorry about that. People are entitled to their opinion, but I will live life the way I like and I don't care about other people. I never have,' I answered.

'You're a fool!' she shrieked.

'It's fine to have blackfellas working for us, but it is against the law to live with them,' said Harry, trying to sound calm and reasonable.

'What if there are children?' said Mavis with a look of horror on her drained, by now almost blue, face.

'It's not our way, Daryl,' said Harry.

I stood there looking at them both, one after the other. It was a stand-off. Nothing more to say, but Mavis couldn't have me so calm.

'What have you got to say?' she screamed.

We all jumped at the tone of her voice. I took a deep breath.

'You've got your way. I've got mine.'

Mavis rose up.

'You'll finish up with absolutely nothing! I'll see to that! I'll never have anything more to do with you!'

Harry put a hand on her arm to stop her haranguing, but I had had enough. I turned and walked out. Neither of them followed. I had known this would come and I had not cared. When I had asked Euphie to come live with me, I hadn't been interested in thinking about the complicated social issues, and I still wasn't interested in thinking too hard about them then.

I walked back over the red hill facing the angry red sun full on. The sun had hardly moved in the sky since I had entered the house. Very little time had passed. It seems that it takes no time to cross from one world into another. I passed the mill, I re-entered the forest and . disappeared from view.

Taken

THE TALL TREES closed in around me and the air became cool. I walked the snig track back to my camp, gum leaves and twigs crackling underfoot in the sudden dusk. The currawongs stirred the air with their wings in the treetops above me as they moved from branch to branch sorting out their settling spots for the night. Their calling was constant but gentle. I kept a lookout for snakes beginning to make a move as the heat of the day receded. I took a deep breath, filling my lungs and limbs and head and heart with the deep forest aroma. As I breathed out, the forest seemed to sigh with me. I had found comfort here and would never venture from this place if I could help it.

Mavis, Harry and Dora might have been right in what they said,

Dora Hood and grandchild

but I didn't care, nor did I think about it much when I was working amongst my trees and around my camp. There was little call for me to leave the Track, so eventually I put all their thoughts behind me and had real satisfaction in my life with Euphemia.

I found Euphie was just as I thought she would be. I had got used to coming home to a meal after work, but, more importantly, I liked having some company, and it was nice to have someone to come home to who didn't growl.

Euphie was a good cook. I don't know how she came to know it, but right from the beginning she cooked what I liked. She was a great pasty maker and that's usually what I had for lunch now that I was with her. I couldn't get enough of those delicious pasties. She was, above all, a bush cook and made lovely possum soup with rice and vegetables in it. She also knew how to cook goannas, wallabies, rabbits. Sometimes I caught this game for her, but usually it was supplied by the boys, her cousins and uncles. They would bring something around and often stop for a meal so there was usually company and laughter at our table of an evening. Often Buddy and Gary would stop with us, too, depending on how interesting the company was, but they travelled backwards and forwards and normally stayed with their grandparents because both Stewart and Dora loved having the grandchildren around.

Euphie made wonderful johnnycakes and steamed puddings and damper. We always had damper. I never bought bread in my life until recently. Then we would wash it all down with tea, of course. I drank mine black – still do – made straight in the cup, but Euphie stewed hers and liked plenty of sugar and some powdered milk in it. She would always roll a cigarette and quietly smoke it with her tea after a meal. She'd sit over by the fire smoking while she listened to the talk of those of us still around the table, but pushed back from it and spread out to give ourselves room to digest her good food. She would smile and chuckle at us, satisfied.

Euphie was marvellous at keeping the camp clean and tidy, just as I knew she would be. And I didn't mind keeping my things in order to please her. I never put tools in with the spoons to rile her like I did with Mavis. With Euphie everything seemed to have a natural place, so it was no trouble keeping tidy. Just like in a tool shed, things seemed to belong where they fitted and were always within reach just as you needed them. You couldn't ask for more.

With Euphie, I had the cleanest clothes, beautifully folded and with the most perfect patches. She proved to be an expert at sewing with the needle and later with a treadle Singer sewing machine. It was her pride to keep her family well clothed. It was my pride, too.

I kept adding onto the camp and turned it into a real homestead. I extended the yards for the five working horses and my hack, and I finished the shelter and shed for them. I had a marvellous thoroughbred mare for riding now. She was quiet enough until you mounted her, then there would be a few kicks and some rearing up before she settled. She was a beautiful chestnut I had bought at the sale yards. She had been raced, but, as happens to so many racers, had gone a bit mad in the head. She had never been properly mouthed and was trained to run the minute you landed on her back, so I had my work cut out with her, but she came good and I loved her. I had several wonderful foals out of her. I think Euphie liked to see me on her, but she wouldn't come near her herself.

I built a chook shed and Euphie tended the chooks.

I also built a garage. I knew I had to buy my own car since I was finished with relying on Mavis forever. I was being practical, as well, thinking that a man needs a car if he is going to have a family. So I bought myself a brand-new cream-coloured Ford van. It didn't stay new and shiny for long, however, since it had to negotiate Jackson's Track and then the unmade track to my camp. That track wasn't much to speak of. I had filled up holes with logs and boggy spots with iron-bark, but whenever it rained it was still impassable. But I was satisfied. I only drove once a week and that was to the Jindivick store to get the week's supplies: flour, rice, tea, jam, powdered milk, sugar, matches and, of course, two ounces of fine-cut tobacco for Euphie.

Life seemed to be good. Harry and I continued to work together. But some things changed. Harry and I had always taken time to visit our parents in Essendon now and again. They were both getting on and appreciated knowing about our lives in the bush. But after the row, I began making the trip to the city on my own so I wouldn't have to meet up with Mavis.

One day when I arrived, Mother met me at the door and instead of inviting me in she just stood looking at me, shaking her head and muttering, 'Daryl, Daryl, Daryl . . .', every once in a while sucking in her breath as if she were trying to keep from crying.

'What's wrong?' I said.

'Mavis has told us that you have taken up with a bad woman.'

'Mavis only knows how to tell lies,' I said as I moved past her into the kitchen. Father was there having a cup of tea and he gave me a sly nod when he saw me and looked as if he were trying not to laugh.

'We all know our Mavis, don't we, son?' he grinned.

'And what's more you're living with her, Daryl!' said Mother with tears in her eyes. 'Oh, the pain of such disgrace,' she went on as she sat down at the kitchen table with her hand over her heart.

I was forlorn. Was there going to be a fight here, too? I stood looking at Mother and then at my father, whose expression had become serious. He shifted his gaze from my mother to me.

'In my opinion, Daryl, if you've fallen for her, she must be a good woman, not a bad one. You're no fool. And in my opinion, colour has nothing to do with it,' he said. Then he looked hard at Mother and continued. 'That is the end of this subject in this house now and forever.'

And that was it. I sat down and had a cup of tea as if nothing had passed. I never told Harry how his attitude differed from that of our father. Maybe I should have, but I didn't.

Back home, I could tell Harry was getting an earful from Mavis from time to time, because some days you could cut the tension with a knife. I wondered if Harry was having a battle with himself over Euphie and me. I guessed it wouldn't be easy for him living at the main house without me there to take the bulk of Mavis's grumpiness. I don't think he had any real idea of how happy I was, probably because Mavis wasn't letting him relax or know any real happiness himself. There was a bit of friction between us, but no bitterness. We had no rows. I was sorry he felt the way he did. I had always respected my brother, relied on him and was proud to be in partnership with him. We were both practical men and this situation should never have put a wedge between us. I thought, with time, things would heal, if Mavis would just let up.

I spent my days mainly pulling poles into the mill. I helped fall and bark the trees and oversaw the firewood cutters as well. Axes were ringing out everywhere in the forest, mingled with the duller sound of the crosscut saws and pierced by the call of 'Timber!' and the big trees crashing to the ground. Still there seemed to be no end to trees. The forest seemed eternally thick and mighty. We worked hard and believed this life would never end.

One night, late autumn, when I arrived home, I found the camp in darkness.

There was still laundry hanging on the line in the damp evening air, some clothes were folded on the table inside, but most were piled in an untidy bundle.

The fire was out – cold. A burnt, but now cold, damper was in the camp oven hanging over the ashes.

The place was deserted, and it was clear Euphie had left in a hurry.

I saddled my mare and rode over to Stewart's to find out what was wrong. Something must have happened, for Euphie wouldn't leave the camp like that for no good reason. Little Dorothy was crawling by now. Was it snake bite? No, too late in the year for snakes. Redback? Scalding? Wood burn? One of the elders sick? Someone die? I rode into Stewart's camp feeling anxious and perplexed. Dora met me. She had Dot balanced on her hip.

'Where's Euphie?' I called out before I reached her.

Dora had been waiting for me to turn up. 'Harry's taken her,' she said.

'What do you mean?' I dismounted and led the mare into the camp.

'He stopped by here and told us he was taking Euphie away from here and he didn't want her back.'

'He took her away?'

'He said we should never ask her to come back. She's not wanted here.'

'Where did he take her?' I asked. I must have looked like a stunned mullet because I couldn't take in what she was telling me. I had been ready to hear of some kind of accident, but not this.

'He wouldn't tell us.'

'He just took her?'

'He brought her over here to leave Dot, and then he put her in the truck and drove off. He wouldn't look at us.'

'He put her in the truck? Did she fight him?'

'She wouldn't fight Harry, Daryl.'

'Which way did they go?'

Dora shook her head.

Stewart came up and put his hand on my shoulder. 'Daryl, you'll work something out.'

He seemed sure of this, but I could hardly take in that she had gone, let alone see a way to get her back. Where had he taken her? How could he do it? Harry was my brother, my partner. How could he do it? I wanted to go after them, but which way should I go? Where had he taken her? My mind was circling.

Without another word, I turned, mounted my mare and rode out. I wouldn't go to the main house. My pride wouldn't be able to take the triumphant look I knew would be on Mavis's face. I didn't stop at my dark camp either, for the emptiness there was shocking. I rode out into the bush, past our boundary deep into the state forest, where I knew, when night fell, the starry sky would be completely blotted out by the treetops and the night amongst the tall trees would be still and as dark as pitch.

Found

I RODE UNTIL it became too dark to move on before I dismounted, unsaddled and hobbled the mare, letting her go to scrounge what feed she could in the scrub. For a long time I sat very still in the dark.

Finally, I moved to build a fire.

I had some thinking to do, but I wanted to let the fire empty my mind first. A fire is the best company you can have when your mind is overheated and amazed at the folly of men. It's not a bad occupation, poking at a fire, getting the logs just right, watching the flames climb and then die, for it calms the senses while you patiently wait for the coals to blaze and fall away, shift and rearrange themselves

Daryl and Euphie together in East Gippsland

into complicated patterns. Your eye searches for the very centre of the fire, the core of heat where the colour is pure and most brilliant.

In spite of the fire, or because of it, my mind raced. I knew Harry would not hurt Euphie, but I couldn't think where he had taken her. I was feeling angry with Harry, but I could understand his point of view about Euphie and me and I wasn't sure he was wrong, in spite of what Father might have said.

Maybe it isn't right, maybe it is unnatural for us to be together. Maybe Euphie let him take her because she has had enough herself and wants to leave. Maybe she agrees with Harry. Oh, no. Don't think that!

I put some more sticks on the fire and poked at it for a while, listening to it crackle, feeling its heat on my face.

Harry is trying to put one over on me. He is trying to straighten things between us. Perhaps he thinks if he parted Euphie and me, I would forget her and things would return to normal with no more friction between us. Well, he's made a miscalculation. There will be no going back to the way things used to be. How can I look him in the face after this? I will never work with him again!

I could hear my mare snuffling at the ground nearby, the thump of her hoof, the quiet jangle of the hobble chains. A mopoke called and tiny feet scurried.

Mavis did this. Harry wouldn't have thought of it himself. Why has he given in to her? Harry is a bushman and respects blackfellas as equals. He has never shown them any disrespect before this. Harry seems to be going against his own nature doing this to me and Euphie. Mavis is his problem; a big problem. Because she is not a bush person, she doesn't understand what is right and natural. Bush people are busy doing their job in the forest and accept each other for what they do, not what they say. Mavis lets the neighbours talk her into bad values. They tell her I am bad and make her feel ashamed.

But they don't know me! If I went to the pub and got drunk every weekend and kicked up a row in the streets, I'd be one of the boys and people would accept me. But here's me, quiet as a mouse, working all weekend instead of drinking and I am the pariah!

More sticks on the fire. The coals flamed up and reflected a tiny pair of eyes watching me. I sat still and they moved on into the cover of darkness.

Harry is a religious man. For him to do this, he must think it's against his religion to allow Euphie and me to stay together. But he's wrong! I think he knows he's wrong, too. He must be sorry he's got this moral standard, sorry these values exist in the world. I know he is sure these views cannot be challenged without causing deep suffering. I guess he is right on that score. I am suffering. Euphie is suffering. Is the suffering proof that what I am doing is sinful? I have always classed myself as a religious man, too, but I don't believe in church so much as knowing right from wrong. Being loyal and faithful is as good as church in my book. I have learned my values from nature and the animals. I trust animals because they are predictable and act according to their nature. They don't chop and change. They don't spread rumours, they don't lie, they don't try to change you. In this way I am like an animal. I'm natural. I guess that's my sin.

Suddenly a shower of sparks rose from the fire as one log fell against another and broke it. The sound of one pair of wings thrashed about overhead and flew away.

I have brought the wrath of my brother down upon me and even that won't stop me. Even if it makes me a sinner, I must find Euphie. I know she is happy with me. I know she depends on me. I know I will never forget her.

I lay down and slept right there next to the fire, a deep dreamless sleep, my horse standing a short distance from me asleep as well.

I awoke at dawn as I heard the mare begin to move and the curra-wongs stirring. I was hungry and aching. I caught the mare and rode back through the bush to my camp, lit a fire, put on the billy, made some damper. I shifted the unfolded clothes off the table onto the bed and sat to eat my usual breakfast. Nothing else to do but go back to work and wait to hear from Euphie.

I had done enough thinking, and work would keep me occupied until I knew what to do. I was sure I would hear from Euphie sooner or later. I decided to let her make the first contact, just to be sure it's what she wanted, to come back to me. I didn't let myself think she mightn't want to. Well, I didn't let myself think it very often because I didn't give myself time to think about much at all that week. I worked like a demon and I never once saw Harry, nor did I try to see him. What was the point of seeing him, anyway? What was done was done. I didn't see anyone, not even Stewart and Dora, although I took heart from Stewart's confidence in me and was determined that Mavis and Harry would never win this war with me.

So I waited and hoped and worked. I expected to hear word from someone, expected that Euphie would tell someone to tell me where she was, but I was wrong. Instead I got a letter from her about a week after she had gone. Jimmy Bond found me amongst the trees and handed it to me. Euphie had learned to read and write at Lake Tyers but this was the first time I had seen any more than a list written by her. It was written in her own hand and was about a page long. I wish I had kept that letter. I wish I could read it now. Even though I received it almost fifty years ago, I read it that often that I can see it in my hands and I can see the colour of the paper and ink and the fold lines in it and I can still remember some of it: *Dear Daryl, Harry's dumped me at Orbost. I'm at the sleeper cutters' camp about five miles out of town, staying with my aunty at Newmerella.*

Well, I don't know if that's how she worded it, but I know the letter told me exactly where she was. The words I remember for sure were the ones that I was waiting to hear, and they are etched on my heart: *I belong to you and nobody else and I am waiting for you to come get me.*

My spirit soared at those words. *I belong to you.* I felt ashamed to think I hadn't been confident she felt that way. But if I hadn't waited for her to get word to me, I never would have heard those words. *I belong to you.* Yes, and I belong to you, Euphie!

I should have known Harry would take her to Orbost. He knows Orbost and would have been aware of the sleeper cutters working there and that Euphie would find some of her own people. I had thought maybe he had taken her to Dimboola, where her grandmother and many cousins lived, but I should have realised he hadn't been gone long enough to take her all the way up there. I had thought of Lake Tyers also, but Harry didn't like the idea of blackfellas being stuck on mission stations. At least he stuck to his principles there. So she was in Orbost. Maybe Harry thought she would pick up with a young 'buck' and not want to come back, but that's proof that he didn't know Euphie very well. She's a proud and loyal woman.

She's loyal all right. She said, *I belong to you . . . come get me*!

In no time I was bumping along the Track in my Ford panel van. I don't know if Mavis or Harry saw me go, or if they would have known where I was going, had they seen me. I did know that when I returned to Jackson's Track everything would be changed for me.

I found Euphie just where she said she would be, in a woodcutters' camp about five miles out of Orbost on the Snowy River where her aunty was staying. She was glad to see me. She said she had never been worried, that she knew I would turn up to fetch her. She said

Harry's actions hadn't worried her either because she knew all along it was a waste of his time. She knew she'd get back to me. In fact, that seemed to be the attitude of all the blackfellas this whole last week. They seemed to have infinite patience, as if they had a deep knowledge of their own strength and of human nature. They seemed to know that Harry's wrong-headedness would be defeated in the end, that Euphie would be found, that life would go on. It was almost as if they enjoyed watching the developments unfold. 'Something's bound to come up,' they said over and over, sitting back, waiting, watching with interest.

Euphie said she didn't fight with Harry about leaving the Track because there was no point in being disrespectful to him, knowing as she did that she would be back. She was a bit surprised was all. She didn't know he felt strongly enough to act the way he did towards her. She reckoned she might have changed her mind about him a bit, but that she still believed he was mostly a fair and honest man. And, no, he didn't touch her or speak harshly towards her. He didn't speak much at all, but what he said was well mannered. He knew an uncle of Euphie's, Dingo Hood, had a camp in Orbost. There used to be many camps along the Snowy at that time. So Harry made sure she was with her people before he left her. She had found her way out to her aunty's on her own.

I shook my head, amazed at her wisdom. I guess patience is a kind of wisdom. Even though I was ten years older than she was, I had a lot to learn from her.

Well, I thought, I'm not ready to go home yet. I've still got a lot to take in and sort out before we go back to the Track.

'How about we drive up through the mountains and go to the Tumbarumba Buckjump Championships?'

'That'll be all right.'

'Just you and me.'

She grinned at me.

'We'll take it slow.'

And so it was that we went away into the mountains. We went up through Bombala and Cooma. We had the bare necessities with us. We saw no one at all and it was good to get away from everybody.

We camped about along the beautiful creeks and Euphie swam in the clear water and dried herself in the sun on the rocks. She was beautiful. The nights were cool and we enjoyed good big fires under the stars, drinking smoky tea boiled with a gumleaf in the billy for good measure, speaking now and again. I admired my wife's strong and beautiful face in the firelight.

It was good to be with a natural person. That was the beauty of her. No matter how rough it was, she loved it. Being in the bush was what I liked and she was a marvellous person in the bush. She was an ideal companion. A jewel.

Forest

FINALLY IT WAS TIME to turn towards Jackson's Track and make our way back there through Omeo. I spilled out my thoughts and plans to Euphie as we travelled home. Home? It was still half my property, but was it my home any more?

'Harry cannot stop us living together.'

Euphie agreed.

'But, I think he is within his rights to keep you from living at Jackson's Track. I know Harry. He's a stubborn man whose decisions are always right. He won't change his mind. If he says you're not wanted back, then that's the law on our place.'

Euphie with Dot and Bob

'What are we going to do?'

I had been thinking and thinking, but I kept hitting snags. I thought of going to Harry to talk things over, but I knew it would end up looking like I was asking his permission.

'I won't beg. I would never beg.'

I wanted to find a solution so I could live with Euphie, still work on my own property and not aggravate the situation any more than it already was. And I didn't want to put Euphie through such an occurrence ever again. It was degrading for her. Painful.

'Moving off the property into the state forest is the safest move.'

Euphie nodded slowly, probably thinking through the meaning of that plan. She'd be even further away from Stewart and Dora, but at least it wasn't Orbost or Dimboola. She knew it meant we would have to start from scratch, build yet another bark hut, establish another camp.

'We would still be on Gipsy Creek,' I said, 'only just over the boundary, half a mile at the most.'

'The bush is thick there.'

'That's the beauty of it. I know an out-of-the-way spot where no one could ever get to, well back off the Track where it's scrubby and pretty wild. We'll be in the trees, a bit away from the creek. I'll cut a path through the scrub to it. There will be plenty of game.'

'Not much sunlight in those trees,' she said. 'It'll be damp and cold.'

'But no wind! I know the spot. In a gully. There's only a bridle path to it. We'll be safe.'

Fancy having to go into hiding from my own brother on my own property. Maybe I was being a fool. Maybe I was taking the easy way out, but it was the only way I could see to go. I was as stubborn as Harry. I would go my own way and nothing would stop me.

We arrived back at the Track at night and I took Euphie straight to her parents' place and told her to stay out of sight until I came to get her. It's easy to hide in the blackfellas' camp. A refugee doesn't cause a ripple, especially when she belongs there in the first place.

I avoided the main house, went straight to my camp and fell into a deep sleep. At dawn, I began gathering my gear to shift it to the new camp. Since the only path to it was a bridle path, I packed work horses, strung them together, mounted my red mare and led them along single file. It took me two days to establish a rough camp, fit enough for Euphie to stop at while I built a new hut and new yards. I cleared a place for a good fire and cut a path through to the creek, then went and got her late in the evening.

It didn't take us long to re-establish ourselves. I built a hut and a small yard where I kept only three of my work horses and my mare. All the blackfellas knew what Euphie and I were up to, but I was sure neither Harry nor Mavis had a clue. Jimmy, or JB as we all began calling him, turned up to help me with the new hut and yards. He would stop over now and again. The Kennedy boys often came around and, of course, Dora and the littlies came regularly to see Euphie.

I parked the van about a quarter of a mile off and would have to walk into the camp from there. I would go into town once a week for supplies, and we lived well. There was plentiful native food that was growing throughout the bush. All the blackfellas could identify it and knew how it tasted. Euphie was no exception. She knew how to use it. There was cumbungi (a lily-like vegetable) for salads; the small seed from nutgrass for seasoning; ribbon reeds which grew at the edge of the creek and in the swamps and was delicious raw for filler; bracken roots, all white and starchy, for thickener. She sometimes used wattle gum mixed with water to make a jelly that was good for diarrhoea if anyone got sick. But we didn't live on this tucker. It just added a taste to our table whenever any of us came across something while we were working. Euphie did make a habit of picking berries in season. Any children around went with her, but they usually ate all that they picked. They would soon get a bellyfull, but Euphie would have to work to pick enough for a feed for a bushman. She was good to me, though. I especially liked cherry ballart, a tiny wild cherry with a sharp, wonderful taste.

We ate a marvellous variety of food. Of course, witchetty grubs were everywhere and easy to collect as they fell out of the logs we were splitting. Every once in a while I would bring a shirtful home. They were a special treat, cooked in the coals of the fire. We also ate crayfish and mussels from the creek. Goanna was my favourite and, of course, possum soup. I tried a snake once, but couldn't come at the smell of it. It had a stink that put me off my food, not like possum which made your mouth water when you smelled it cooking. We ate game whenever it came our way, but those of us that were working never had much time to spend hunting it. The children caught lots of tucker and dragged it home to the different camps for the adults to cook up for a feed. I enjoyed our out-of-the-way life in amongst the tall trees, feeling more and more like a true bushman and becoming ever more appreciative of the blackfellas' way of life.

But I had to decide what to do about work. I had gone back to work at the mill, but I felt the strain there in the log yard after being away. Of course, Harry had soon realised that Euphie was living in the forest with me. I believe he accepted it as a fair solution between us since I was respecting his 'law' and he knew in all fairness that he had to accept my rights. There was an unspoken truce between us, but I knew the mill-hands were talking behind my back. So I told Harry I was giving the mill away and that I would work on my own.

'I won't be snigging any more logs into the mill, Harry.'

He just looked at me, waiting to hear what I had to say next. He didn't look surprised or angry, just resigned. He knew as well as I did that my presence at the mill was a strain to the harmony of all.

'I'll keep the two draughthorses, and I'll take the cart.'

He nodded, and so I began my own fence post cutting business. I still worked from our property. I would snig the logs to a landing and then cut the posts there. I made several landings and cut tracks to them so a carrier could get in. I hired carriers to cart the posts as I was too busy falling to cart, and I wasn't interested in leaving the forest to drive all over the countryside delivering posts. I always made the landings as far in as I could to make the snig work easier on man and horse.

One of the beauties of our property was that we had no fences at all. Harry and I both hate fences, and I personally think that fences have meant the ruination of this country because they stop you from being free to go wherever you want to go or need to go. So I cut logs from both the state forest and our place without worrying about boundaries. I guess it's funny my establishing a business out of the makings for fences when I disliked them so much, but there was a big call for posts.

I found my own contracts by advertising in the local papers. I got lots of orders that way, but I also answered 'fence posts wanted' ads. I had a standing order from one firm down in Box Hill and another for Fisher's in Korumburra, but most of my posts went down to the swamp near Koo Wee Rup, where the finishing of the canals made farming viable and the land was being developed at a rate of knots.

I didn't really have to rely on workers to help me, but I had three or four blackfellas working with me. JB became my main man. Sid Austin joined us, too, and became a good friend. He had a lovely wife and a wonderful family. He was a great worker, a hard worker.

He'd work solid all week, but on the weekend he would drink till he dropped. He had a strong constitution and would always be on deck on Monday morning and he wouldn't touch a drop all week. Both men were champion axemen, but I could beat them because I could work just as well left-handed as right-handed, which meant I never had to walk around the tree to fall it. We all competed with each other in good humour and the work went quickly that way.

Of course, Harry knew what I was doing, and how I was doing, and I believe he accepted it. We helped each other if the need arose. If we came across each other in the forest, we would stop and have a yarn about the weather, trees, machinery, horses, but never about Euphie, never about Mavis, never about anything but business, as if nothing else was going on. Mostly we stayed out of each other's way and tolerated our differences.

At that point I chose to forget about Mavis, as long as Harry and I were content to acknowledge our differences and remain cooperative. But I should have realised that my doing well in the fence post business was driving her mad. She was a businesswoman and hard as nails. She must have seen my business as competition and every time she saw one of my advertisements in the paper, anger must have pierced her heart. But I was unaware of all that then. As long as Harry and I were at peace, that's all I worried about.

I went on working in my beloved forest.

The air in the forest is as pure as the water ploughing in the creeks. No matter what the season, it's the finest place in the world to be. In the winter, it is the warmest place to live and work because it is sheltered from the wind and no matter how cold the temperature is you can always get a sweat up working. In the spring, the buds of the wild flowers open up, giving the bush a sweet smell, and sometimes you just have to stop in your tracks and concentrate on the heady aromas that send you dizzy with pleasure. The bees work over-time and the birds whistle about, getting ready for mating. As it gets warmer, the lizards and snakes, moving very slowly, slither out onto rocks to bask in the sun and then get about looking for food after their long winter fast. The ground dries out underfoot with the onset of summer, but also the insects and flies become a nuisance and keep the bushworker moving. Some bushmen work only until summer, then give it away until after the autumn rains finish and the cooler weather arrives.

I guess, aside from the trees, what I love best about the forest is the bird life. At the break of dawn, the forest comes alive with bird-song. I know some city folk, who think they can sleep through any kind of terrible noise, are alarmed at how noisy the bush can be of a morning, and so early in the morning! But I love identifying the birds' calls as they go to work looking for food. Lyrebirds work hard scratching under the trees and scrub for food. They are very shy birds, but they are clever. They can mimic any call in the bush.

When I used to go out in the morning to feed the horses, the parrots would swoop down and linger near the horses, waiting for them to drop any grain. They were pests, really. The grey bush thrushes seemed to be attracted to camp life and hopped around the forest nearby, watching with great curiosity any activity in the camp. They are fast fliers, would flit and zip from here to there all day, chirping away as if trying to give us instruction about how to conduct our lives. They are the best songsters to listen to. Kookaburras were also attracted to bush camps and used to perch up in the trees, watching everything that moved on the ground. With their laughter, they always let us know when rain was on the way.

The noisier birds were the bellbirds and the pigeons, who never stopped all day long in the mating season. The yellow-breasted robins would follow the post splitters for termites when the logs were split open, and the wrens and tree clingers followed the robins.

My favourite birds were the currawongs, who moved around in families and were knowing and unafraid. They used to watch me from the treetops, and when I would knock off work and boil the billy for tea, they would know I was about to have dinner. When I grabbed my tuckerbag and sat down for dinner, they would fly down and have lunch with me. I would test them by putting crumbs out on the log very close to me. They would stand on the log, tilting their heads, looking at me, then the bread, then back to me. They knew I wouldn't harm them, but it was a game. They always got their lunch. Butcherbirds were similar, knowing and friendly, but there was something noble about the currawongs that made me like them best.

Life was good, but now I was going to have to start thinking about the future. Euphie was going to have my child. I was surprised at how excited and proud I felt. There were lots of kids being born at the Track all the time: Roy and Gina Rose had Lionel and Raymond by now; there were five girls in the Marks family; Axel, Daphne and Eileen Harrison were all running around, and the Austin kids, the Kennedy kids, lots more. I always took notice of new babies on the place but had never been overly interested. I liked having the kids around and loved their chattering and laughing, but I was always at a distance from it. So when Euphie let me know a kid of my own was coming, my strong feelings took me by surprise. As Euphie got bigger, she let me put my hand on her stomach and feel the movement inside. We were happy.

I went out to work every day. Nothing actually changed, but my mind was on the future in a way it had never been before. I was looking forward to the birth of my own child. And Euphie was looking forward to it, too. That was something about Euphie. She anticipated each child as if it were the first child. This was her fourth baby, but it was clear it would get all the love the others had received.

Of course, we planned that Euphie would have the baby in the hospital at Warragul. We went to see Dr Power as the time drew near to make sure everything was all right and to make arrangements. Dr Power was a giant of a man, towering over me, but he was kind and gentle, a man you could trust. What surprised me was that he treated us like a normal couple, no hint that he was even aware of our mixed colour.

That first visit with Dr Power was the first time since I had been with Euphie that I had felt relaxed and confident in white company. Of course, I didn't mix with whitefellas very often, but once a week Euphie and I would go into town shopping. Sometimes we would go to the races or a rodeo or the market. We would get looked at. One thing I had learned since I had been with Euphie was that you could tell what you were by the way a person looked at you – at least you could tell what they thought you were. And there was no changing it. We walked proudly, but we would hear comments.

With Dr Power, there was nothing but acceptance. He said Euphie was strong and healthy and doing well. We went home and waited. The cart was ready to hitch up to the horse to take us the quarter-mile to the van, which was full of petrol, water and oil, the minute there was any sign the baby was coming. I had absolute trust in Euphie. She was calm and knowing. I learned later, with all of the children we were to have, that Euphie always seemed to know the right time to get to the hospital. She never left it too late, never had a false alarm, never panicked.

The people at the hospital were marvellous to us, just as Dr Power had been. Not a hint of disapproval. Again, I had been expecting bad treatment, but was pleasantly surprised. Immediately I could see Euphie was in good hands, that they would be good to her. So I left her to have the baby and went straight home to work. Back in 1950, men didn't have anything to do with babies being born, and there was no sense hanging around the hospital in idleness. No one was going to let me in to see what was happening, and, as a matter of fact, I was just as glad not to be there. I wanted to be home working. It seemed natural for me to get on with my business while Euphie got on with hers.

I made my way to the main house the next day when I was certain Mavis would be away and rang the hospital to find out I had a son. I felt fine about that and went off to tell Stewart and Dora. Then I went back to work. Of course, the news spread around the black-fellas' camp, and it was through the blackfellas that Harry found out about it. Harry didn't have much to say. There were no congratulations. It was all too late. Already I was beginning to realise that a mixed-race couple was bad, but a mixed-race couple with a child was worse. I didn't care.

I didn't go back to the hospital until it was time for Euphie to come home with my son. He was a very light-skinned little fellow. When he got older, people began to say he was me all over again. And he was tiny. His name was Philip. Philip Mullett. Like many of the Aboriginal women, Euphie gave all her children her own last name. Although we never discussed it, I know that she was protecting me from my own family by using the name Mullett rather than Tonkin. I was happy with her choice because I had no especial pride in my name. A name is a name, I say. I didn't believe in marriage in a church – didn't believe in anything in a church – and didn't believe a woman should have to alter her name in a church or name her children after anyone but herself. Even though Euphie's birth name was Hood, she had been forced to marry Crockett Mullett in a church on the mission station, and I guess she figured she was given the name Mullett for keeps. I was satisfied and so was she. So our new boy was named Philip Mullett. But the funny thing is, we never called him Philip. To us and to everybody else, he was Mac. I don't remember where that name came from, but it stuck. All the blackfellas seem to have two names: the one they're born with and the one they're called.

With Mac there, I found myself making up reasons to linger at home more than I used to. I helped Euphie bath him in the mornings. Bath time was a regular thing every day. I held him and I watched him being dressed. I wasn't like other men. I always helped and I liked family life. I liked my kid. I built him a little bush bunk: four forked posts in the ground covered with a bit of bark. There were no railings on it, but we packed blankets and clothes in around the sides to keep him from wriggling out. We would rock him to sleep in our arms before we put him on the bed. I was good at getting fractious babies to sleep. As often as not, he would sleep with us in our bed. Sometimes we just all slept on the floor. It was a family time.

Proposition

ONE DAY, about dinnertime, I set about boiling the billy after spending the morning splitting logs and stacking them for the carters at the landing when Harry walked up to me.

'Will you have some tea?' I asked.

Harry nodded. He squatted down near the fire, sitting on the backs of his heels. Even though it was a warm, summery day, he put his hands out over the fire as if he were cold.

'I've located a property near Toora that's up for sale,' he said, staring into the fire.

'Toora?'

Toora

'Down on the coast between Foster and Welshpool. It backs onto the Gunyah State Forest, sits at the bottom of Mount Fatigue.'

'Cleared?'

'Scrub. Some grass. Few fences. Good house, I'm told. Some sheds. Running water. Used to be a dairy farm.' He turned his head to look at me.

I nodded, turning over in my mind the possible reasons for his telling me this.

'How many acres?'

'About three hundred.'

'Steep country?'

'I'm going to look it over in a couple of days. Will you come?'

Two days later, I picked Harry up at the main house and we set off on the eighty-mile drive for the property near Toora. We went through Warragul, headed towards Thorpdale, hit the Grand Ridge Road that winds itself along the top of the Strzelecki Ranges, through Boolarra South and down to Gunyah south of the ranges. The property was north of Toora, along a winding track in the hills. It was steep country all right, and facing south.

It was a beautiful summer day, one of those quiet, windless days with a slight haziness when the grass looks lush and the smells are sweet and moist and the bird calls sound gentle and lazy. The farm had gone back to scrub somewhat, with plenty of ragwort, bracken and blackberry to keep a man busy, but there was a good cover of thick, sweet grass that would do horses very well. There was enough fence to keep them in and good yards. I ran my gaze along the line of the clearing to the forest and saw that it worked its way up Mount Fatigue and that it was difficult to tell where the property ended and the state forest began. Good timber there. But steep.

There was a good weatherboard house with glass windows, bedrooms, lounge room, kitchen, bathroom, brick fireplace. Solid enough. Good roof. And a tap with the water laid on.

There was a dairy in a good shed. There was a garage.

You could make a living here.

'Does this suit you, Daryl?' asked Harry after a while.

'Me?' Here it comes.

'We thought this place might suit you.'

I was expecting something. I knew Mavis and Harry would get their heads together to work out some way of getting rid of me, but this was a surprise.

'What have you got in mind, Harry?'

'You could buy this place, Daryl, if I bought you out of your share of Jackson's Track.'

'Why would you want to do that?'

He ignored my question.

'Mavis and I have made some inquiries and this seems like a good business proposition, Daryl. Think of it like that.'

'Good business for who?' Mavis is a hard woman with nothing generous about her nature and I knew she wouldn't have arranged things for someone other than herself to make the profit in a business proposition.

'It will profit all of us. You can have your own property to run as you please. You can run sheep or cattle. You can still work the timber.'

As I said, it was a fine day. In my head I knew the country was as rough as guts, steep and ferny and facing the wrong direction, but in my heart I thought, on that beautiful day, the place looked well enough. I felt I could make a living there.

And in my heart I knew I didn't want to fight Harry. I knew he was uncomfortable. I knew this proposition came out of Mavis's head more than his. I knew he was unhappy, that between Mavis and myself he felt backed into a corner, that this seemed like a solution and he would go along with it if I would.

We looked at each other, two stubborn men. No matter how much it hurt we wouldn't change.

'It seems like a fair idea,' I said.

We shook hands.

On the way back to Jackson's Track, we didn't say much. I was thinking about Harry. I didn't hate him. He was only trying to straighten me out. Maybe he thought that if I moved away from the Track and lived out amongst other whites instead of with all blacks, I would realise what a terrible choice I had made for myself and that I would change and that I would, in time, be back at the Track as his partner once again. Maybe he didn't think that at all. Maybe that's what Mavis thought, but I was sure Mavis didn't want me back. Mavis was a hard woman. She saw me as a hindrance to the property because, according to her, I was the talk of the district. She wanted me to fail. But Harry didn't feel the way she did. I could see he was unhappy.

Back at the Track, Euphie seemed pleased at the idea of shifting into a good house on our own farm. She said she was happy to go any-where with me. So I made arrangements to buy the farm at Toora, and Harry and I drew up a contract for him to buy my part of Jackson's Track property from me, a deposit now and the balance to be paid in twelve months.

I visited the place several times before final settlement and decided, when I saw the ragwort in bloom, to run sheep on the place to clean it up. There was enough fencing to keep them in and I didn't have to worry about them on the forest side since they wouldn't get far in the thick bush. But before the sheep were brought in I'd have to get my horses there so I could drive the flock from the railhead at Toora up the ten miles of track to the farm.

I had two hacks, three draughthorses and a stallion to get to Toora. I saddled up my red mare, borrowed Harry's hack for the return trip, strung the rest behind me and rode to Toora from Jackson's Track. I went the same route Harry and I had gone in the van. Once I was out of Warragul and heading up into the Strzeleckis I saw hardly a car the whole way. The trip only took me a day. I could do a hundred miles in a day, and this was only eighty. I could get on a horse and do it now if I had to and I wouldn't get sore.

Some people say it's impossible to go a hundred miles a day on a horse, but I say they're wrong. Of course, the horse has to be hardened so he's up to the journey, you can't just take him out of the paddock and expect him to do it. On a long journey, I just stand up in the irons and let the horse go at a fair clip, a jog or a trot. It's a balanced ride and easy on horse and man to keep going. If I were to sit down and let the horse canter, he'd soon be worn out, or if I let him walk, we'd never get anywhere since even a good walking horse will cover only six miles in the hour. So I stand up and off we go. You can cover miles like that.

After I put up the horses and had a good sleep in the new house, I saddled up Harry's hack and returned to Jackson's Track the next day. People don't do those kinds of trips nowadays, but it's nothing to me. When I get on a horse, it knows it's alive because it's got to work. Of course, you work a horse day after day like that, you have to get rid of him after five hundred miles.

My next task was to locate some sheep. I went up to the Euroa sales and bought three hundred merino ewes and some Corriedale rams and arranged to have them trucked to Toora. I met them at the railhead on my horse. No dog. Now, I have had plenty of experience mustering sheep and cattle in my time, but that experience was on the flat, wide country of the Queensland outback and it did not correlate one tiny bit to the steep hills and winding tracks of South Gippsland. I knew what it was to muster flocks of three and four thousand, but that couldn't hold a candle to the difficulty of trying to push three hundred confused and restless animals from Toora to Mount Fatigue.

Up north, a mob of station merinos will 'ring' or circle when you let them out of the yards and it takes a bit of work to get them to head out. But I soon found that in a small town closed in by streets, houses and tall trees, the lead merino will strike out blindly in any direction as soon as her feet hit the ground once she's bounded out of the yard gates, and all the rest will follow. I also found that in a town a stock-whip will frighten them out of their wits. I'm sure there were many townsfolk left shaking their heads and chuckling as I clattered out of town in a less than controlled manner that day. I would have been laughing myself if I weren't so mad.

Finally, the flock was gathered and heading in the right direction along the Mount Best Road. We had to go over Mount Best to get to Mount Fatigue. The sheep were all hemmed in by the scrub along the track, and I thought it wasn't going to be such a difficult run after all, when, from behind, a milk tanker came around a bend, its engines roaring and its hydraulics pumping as it came to an abrupt halt. The driver nodded to me and I to him and then, to my surprise, he put the tanker into gear and moved forward in an attempt to get round the flock.

These merinos from up north had obviously never experienced such a beast as this truck up their backsides in such a narrow space before. They wouldn't let the truck pass. The faster it went, the faster they went, leaving me behind. But, of course, the truck could outlast the ewes for stamina. As the weaker sheep fell back and let the truck come up close, they panicked and leapt off the road down the steep embankment. More and more of them ran off the road into the thick bush, scattering every which way, up hill and down dale. After the last one of them completely disappeared from view the driver, way up in the distance, put his foot down and roared off, giving me a final toot as he rounded a bend.

Where just a few minutes before had been a controlled flock of sheep was now an empty road. I couldn't see any animals, but I could hear plenty of bleating and crashing in the bush.

Three hours later, a trip that should have been calm and uneventful was completed and the flock was home – exhausted, confused and frightened, but home.

The next week, I went to fetch Euphie and Philip and all our gear and we were home as well, maybe the same as the sheep, a bit dazed and confused, but hopeful.

Toora

EUPHIE HAD BEEN ANXIOUS to get to see her new home. The winding Grand Ridge Road through the Strzeleckis made the going slow, but she was patient. The forest was thick and beautiful through the ranges. Once we passed Boolarra South, she began to show some signs of excitement, but when we turned off the Toora Road onto our track, the excitement turned to a kind of horror. The road in was very narrow and very steep and right on the edge of a sharp incline with a sheer cliff rising up on one side and a sheer drop off the other with a bluestone quarry at the bottom of the drop. Euphie was not one to keep quiet when she was frightened. She would soon let you know

Daryl and Mac on the jetty at Port Welshpool

just how frightened she was. By the time we negotiated the track, there was quite a bit of screaming and howling going on in our van.

But when she saw the house, she recovered her senses quickly. It was a well-made structure, built completely from split timber, not sawn, that had been harvested from the Mount Fatigue forest. The studs, beams and weatherboards were all split from local timber! The first thing Euphie did was go into the kitchen and try the tap. Water from a good spring above the house about a hundred yards away came gushing into the sink. What a delight for the cleanest woman that ever kept house.

I had stacked wood ready for the fire in the beautiful brick fireplace and the first thing I did was light it because it's no good without a fire going. I had brought in plenty of supplies ready for our arrival: a few bags of spuds, flour, rice, tea, sugar. We always had plenty to eat at Toora, with mutton in constant supply, apples from the old orchard, gooseberries in season, milk from the two cows I milked every day and vegetables from a garden Euphie kept.

I remember, the day we moved into the house, the wind was blowing and from that day on I don't think it stopped blowing for two years. The house was fairly sheltered from it by the hill behind it and a row of cypresses that acted as a windbreak on the western side. But it took the full brunt of any easterlies which, when they took hold, blew with ferocity for days on end. An east wind carries moisture with it and it would leave the boards on the east side of the house dripping wet, even when there was no rain in sight.

For a bushman used to the shelter of the forest, the wind was a shock. I couldn't work in it. It would set my teeth on edge and make me cross and irritable. Maybe that's another reason why I hate fences so much, because my first task on the new farm was to set the fences right, but fences are usually out in the open on cleared paddocks where there is no shelter. The wind made me blame the barbed wire for tangling round my leg or sticking into my hand. It made me misplace the fencing pliers or twist the strainer round the wrong way or bend the staples. If it wasn't blowing from the east it was coming from the west, right off Bass Strait. I was glad when I was able to retreat into the forest to cut fence posts for the repairs I was doing.

Despite the wind, Euphie and I were happy enough. She thought a house with water laid on and a bathtub in its own room was all she would ever need of luxury. The rest didn't matter. She and I both knew it doesn't matter where you are if you're with someone you like.

And we weren't lonely, for there was plenty of movement between Mount Fatigue and Jackson's Track. Of course, Stewart and Dora came down with Gary and Buddy to look at the place soon after we shifted. They were mainly concerned to know just how far Euphie was from them and Dora wanted to cuddle Mac. I guess they took note of the house and the wind and the steep country, but they made no comment one way or the other.

Euphie's brother, Collin Hood, and his wife, Mavis Kennedy, came from the Antwerp Reserve not far from the old Ebenezer Mission Station at Dimboola. Along with them came Sammy and Dickie Kennedy, Mavis's two brothers who had been such good company at the Track. They all camped on the floor in one of the bedrooms. We were happy with people around. It was always warm with plenty of firewood and plenty of food.

There was lots of laughter, yarn telling and singing, especially when Roy Rose and his family came to stay. Roy always carried his guitar with him. He wrote his own songs with all bush words. Back at the Track, he and Harry were a good team. Because Roy was self-taught and couldn't read music, Harry, who had learned to play the piano when he was a boy, wrote out the music for the songs so others could play them, and he copied out the words as well. Thing is, I don't know where all that wonderful music went to. If Roy wasn't entertaining us with his songs, we had the wireless on full volume tuned to the hillbilly music stations that came in across Bass Strait from Tasmania.

Another of Euphie's brothers, Clifford Pepper (Dora's son from before she married Stewart), came down from Lake Tyers with his wife, Mona, and their six kids. They came to live and stayed two or three months before they headed to the Track. We liked their company, especially the kids'. We were always glad to have the kids around. The oldest was Betty, aged about ten, and she led the pack of them all over the farm, dancing and playing, running and skipping in their bare feet, never worried about snakes or prickles or cow pats. Of course, whenever one of the little toddlers couldn't keep up, Betty would hoist him up to rest on her hip and away they'd go. She was a regular mother hen with all the littlies tagging along behind her.

While the Peppers were with us, Euphie had another child, a girl this time, that we named Cheryl, but straight away everyone called her Curly. She fitted right in to the large family surrounding her. It's easy bringing babies into the world when there are so many people waiting to love them and help out with them. Euphie never brought a baby home that wasn't happy, contented and secure from the start.

Mona and Euphie were great mates. They spent their days chattering away while they washed and cleaned and cooked. They would laugh long and loud, sometimes till they were weak with it, who knows about what. At bath time, they would sing out to the kids, who knew there was no way to avoid this daily ritual, and so they would line up with lots of giggling and wriggling. Their clothes would go in a heap for tomorrow's laundry and they would step in the bath to be scrubbed down by their mothers until they were white with lather. The little ones would twist and squirm, slither out of their mother's grasp with great splashing and laughing. Mac was in the middle of all this, slapping the water with his chubby little hands, grinning like a kitten until he got soap in his eyes. All together they would sing some song or other from the radio while they were dried off and bundled up ready for bed. Bath time was a jolly and noisy ritual. The only time Euphie missed supervising the bath, no matter where we lived, was when she was off having another baby.

Once a week Euphie would brave the track into town and go shopping with me in Toora. I'm sure it was a shock to the town people to see us, a man and a woman, sometimes a baby, white and black, obviously a family, going about our business, stopping at the greengrocer's, the grocery, the feed store, the newsagent, the chemist, as if we were just like everybody else. Brazen, they might have said, but not to our faces.

The thing is, Euphie was a tall and broad, imposing woman and very dark skinned. In spite of my bushman's tan, I seemed a pale white next to her. There was no missing us. The people eyed us as we walked down the street, some looking away as we got close, others nodding almost imperceptibly, never smiling. Euphie's bearing did not invite smiles or small talk, even if someone had been inclined to common courtesy where we were concerned. She was absolutely withdrawn in the company of whites so her expression was closed down and dark when we were in town.

Of course, everybody knew who we were, which farm we had bought, how we were doing. They knew where we had come from, how much we owed on the land, who was living with us. They probably thought they knew a whole lot more things about us, fantastical things that had nothing to do with our real selves, but that's how it goes in a one-street town. We must have been very worrying to them, exactly as Mavis knew we would be. The thing is, they weren't worrying to us. Had no effect on us. Poor Mavis, her plans for making me come around to her point of view were not working.

Clifford, whom we called Rats – I don't know why he had that name, but I know no one, including me, ever called him anything but Rats – never, in all the weeks he stayed with us, went off the property. He had lived a good part of his life at the mission station and probably felt shy about facing an all-white town like Toora, where the people would look at him and never smile at him.

I didn't ask him to work for me since I was working with horses and the Lake Tyers blackfellas had no experience handling horses, preferring to stay away from them if they could. He occupied himself exploring the property, which I suppose you could say was an interesting and varied place if you didn't have to work it. There were several creeks running through pretty rugged gullies that contained plenty of tucker if you could be bothered getting down to it. The trouble was getting back up again. There were also some very scrubby, almost wild, paddocks on steep hills which took some serious negotiating. The state forest that spread onto our place lured Rats into it often. He was a good, honest fellow and a few years later I would come to rely on him as a good worker.

Farming

PROGRESS ON THE FARM seemed slow but tolerable with the fences holding the sheep, the yards holding the horses, the grass holding, and the weather holding particularly well, but at the end of May it suddenly changed from summer to winter with no season in between.

I will never forget the change. I was out in the shed milking the house cows in the late afternoon when a wind storm suddenly whipped up out of nowhere. In the blink of an eye it became the worst wind I have ever been caught in. The cowshed was about a hundred yards from the house and I had a battle to make the distance. As I made my way, I actually had to hold my clothes on me.

Looking down on the farm from Mount Fatigue

I was amazed to see the milk I had just collected get blown right out of the buckets I was trying to carry. Sheets of iron began to fly off the sheds, the garage and the roof of the house. The verandah on the house just blew away. The thick cyprus hedge on the south-western side of the house where the wind was coming from saved the whole house from going with the verandah, and we only lost a few sheets of iron from the roof.

When it all died down, the place did look a sorry sight. We were all a bit shocked. It took us a while to get moving, but we had everything back in order again inside a fortnight. The whole time we were cleaning up we were wondering what else Mount Fatigue had in store for us.

After that blast it turned cold and began to rain. And then the fog moved in. No matter how windy it was there was always a chill fog hanging about. I don't know if it was fog or low cloud, but we were in it the whole of the winter.

My merino ewes didn't like the damp. They soon developed footrot, standing as they did in soggy grass day after day. Now, a sheep with footrot is no good to anybody. The rot is a kind of fungus which spreads from one sheep to the next. It must be painful, for when they've got it the poor animals can't stand or walk on their sore feet to feed. Nothing more pathetic than seeing a ewe crawling on its front knees, then lying down to get the weight off its back feet only to be driven back up on its feet by hunger. If you've got footrot, you've got to deal with it and quickly.

I had to reorganise the sheep yards and dig a bath to dip the ewes' feet. It was a hell of a job digging the pit, lining it with concrete, realigning the posts and rails in the yards, all in the damp cold wind. Then I had to get the ewes into the shed to trim their feet before I could dip them. The smell of rotten feet is what you'd expect: rotten.

What an awful dirty job it was bending over the ewes, trimming their feet! Merinos are quite placid sheep to handle in the shed, but no matter how placid they are, wet sheep are difficult. The wool holds a great deal of water and this makes them heavy and awkward. The smell of steaming wet wool on penned-up sheep can be overpowering. Quite a competition of smells in that shed between wet wool and rotten feet! To get started, you go into the small pen and grab the ewe under the chin to tip her up backwards and pull her out onto the boards on her rump. The wet wool combined with the sheep's natural lanolin makes the floor greasy and slippery. There is no way you can keep your hands dry handling wet sheep so the foot trimmers are slimy and shoot out of your hand before you can get a good grip.

Pushing the ewes through the dip was worse than trimming their feet, however, because the formalin you had to stand them in was treacherous stuff that you didn't want anywhere near you. Of course, the sheep baulk and panic, jump around, splash, fall down. It's awful work. All the while, the wind is blowing and the misty rain is soaking through your jumper and dripping off your nose and chin.

The season wore on and the weather closed in so we thought we would never see the sun again. The sheep were heavy with lamb and wool when the worst storms in history struck. Just my luck to try my hand at farming and strike the worst year ever known. We had thirteen inches of rain in one fall at one point, a record for the district. There were landslides all over that steep country, which should never have been cleared of its thick forest cover in the first place. Some farms even lost their houses. There were six landslides on my property alone. Roads all over the district went down with the slides along with uprooted trees and fences. It took the shire months to repair the roads, leaving people stranded.

The rain continued to bucket down, and the sheep burdened

with soggy wool just lay down, rolled over and drowned in it. Some of them overbalanced and toppled down into the gullies to be swept away in the flooded creeks. Others got stuck in the mud made by the slides. It was a disaster.

Immediately, the weather turned particularly cold and it began to snow, a rare occurrence in South Gippsland. Our place was covered in snow and it was three weeks before we could drive out. We were warm and well fed in our house, the horses were dry and standing with full bellies, even if they weren't warm, but the sheep that had survived the floods were out in it, wet, freezing and hungry. All that lush grass I had seen in the summer before I bought the place had gone to nothing as soon as the cold weather set in. The snow was covering what was left. Those poor creatures would soon be falling over with hunger if I didn't do something.

I began to scout around for paddocks to lease and found out that normal practice amongst the farmers in these ranges was to abandon the steep, high country and winter the stock down at Snake Island just a mile off the coast from Welshpool. In late autumn, the water was very shallow at low tide so they could force the stock to wade over to the island. By stock, they meant cattle, not sheep. But it was too late in the season to get any stock over there now, no matter what they were.

One morning, while I was making my mind up what to do about the poor ewes, I went out to check on them and saw that some of them were down over near the neighbour's boundary. As I got closer to them, I saw that they had been mauled. Their throats had been chewed out and there was some wool spread about, but whatever had done this was not after a feed. It had clearly gone on a rampage for sport. It had to have been a dog, most likely a well-fed working dog bored with inactivity that the winter brings. The next day, I went out early to see if I could catch this dog at play amongst my sheep, for if a dog has had fun once, it'll more than likely return for more sport. And there it was, a black kelpie from next door!

I went to the neighbour to tell him what I had seen. He didn't believe me. I understood that. A farmer relies on his dog and if he's a good worker is willing to trust him out of all proportion. I knew this was a good dog and it was tragic that it had got a taste for killing. I also knew my neighbour was an honest man, who would begin to watch to see if I wasn't a liar. Three days later, he came over to my place with his beloved kelpie on a chain.

'Well, Daryl, you were right.'

I nodded.

'I can't kill him myself,' he said, handing me the chain. 'Do with him whatever you think is necessary.'

I looked down at the dog sitting obediently at my heel.

'I know what to do with him,' I said.

He turned to go.

'I won't kill him. He'll be right,' I added.

'Thanks, mate.'

And I did know what to do with that dog. He was a bright, friendly animal and Stewart Hood would love him. At Jackson's Track there would be no sheep to kill and he'd get all the care and attention and activity he needed. He became a loved dog at the Track and lived to an old age.

What with floods, snow and a larrikin dog, those sheep needed a change, and quick. I found some paddocks to lease on deserted farms on the other side of the Grand Ridge just above the prison farm over there. I saddled my mare and drove this haggard bunch of exhausted ewes over Mount Fatigue, through the forest to a place where they could get some feed, find some shelter from the wind and stick their noses up out of the fog towards the sun once in a while. It certainly felt like a different country on the north side of the ranges.

Late in winter, the ewes lambed. They were doing fine where they were, but it was costing me money leaving them there. I waited anxiously for the feed in our paddocks to come away with the spring weather. I waited and waited. I discovered that this was 'late country' and that nothing begins to grow until late October or November. That made it a very short growing season.

'Blow it!' I said to myself, and in January I cut my losses and I sold the lot: rams, ewes and lambs.

'I'm better off sticking with timber. Timber is clean work.'

Horses

I HAD BEEN CUTTING fence posts all along for cash because I must have known from the start that the sheep were going to get me nowhere. There had never been enough sheep to keep me busy anyway. And I had to give my horses work to do. I would have been at a loss if I weren't working with my horses every day. And it wouldn't be right if I didn't swing an axe every day. How would I keep my hand in?

No, if the truth be known, I had never got out of the timber industry at all. I had just played with sheep for a while and found it too messy for my liking.

Just as I had at Jackson's Track, I advertised in the local paper that I was cutting and selling fence posts. I soon began getting orders by mail. We didn't have the phone on at Toora, but it made no difference since people were used to using the post in 1952.

Cutting fence posts at Mount Fatigue was very different from cutting them at Jackson's Track simply because the steep grade of the mountain made every task difficult and dangerous. The snig track up the mountain was so steep the horses would be on their knees going up, with me hanging onto their manes. Then the logs we were pulling out would chase them down the hill. Most often if a log tapped a horse on the heels, he would go faster and then smartly step to the side to steady it. But sometimes a freshly barked log would shoot out when it started to move and be going so fast that it would be impossible to steady or slow up. It would tip the whole lot of the horses over. Then there would be a tangle of harness, legs, chains, logs and hooves. The whole pile – log with grunting and struggling horses – would go sliding down the mountain with me chasing after.

The horses were often hurt, not only by renegade logs, but by almost anything. It's pretty easy to cripple a horse, especially in rugged country. They went lame by bruising their feet on the rocky ground that covered the mountain. There was no time for them to be careful about placing their feet when they were scrambling up the hills. They were draughthorses, built heavily for heavy work, and it took a lot of energy and speed just to get themselves up the mountain. They virtually galloped up and stood at the top, their sides heaving, while I set the chains on the logs ready for the dangerous haul down. It would take months for a horse to recover from lameness.

Sometimes they would get a fern stuck in the frog of their foot. The fern would fester and an abscess would form and the animal would go into shock with the pain. If you've ever had a toothache that seems to inflame your whole body with throbbing, you'll know how a horse feels with an abscess in his foot. Usually, when the abscess bursts the pain will subside, but with a fern, the pain doesn't seem to let up. I've known a horse to just lie down and die rather than put up with it.

A horse will do that, give up and die quickly. Once they give up, they're finished. They die of stubbornness. I had one horse I was spelling after he had bruised a foot who got himself down in a gully at the height of the bad weather that first winter. He couldn't get out. It was too steep and too slippery and he was too heavy. He decided to lie down and there was nothing we could do to get him to budge. He was determined to die and that's what he did.

I lost more than one horse at Mount Fatigue. One got staked by a small tree. That is something that often happens in the forest. In fact, I was staked myself by a stick I never saw which ran up my shin. It was that painful! And it never healed, possibly because I was always working in the damp. But I began to wear an aluminium shin guard and put up with it, just as I put up with lots of things on that mountain.

I didn't like losing my horses. You never like losing a good working animal, but you have to put up with some hard knocks in the bush. You look after your animals the best you can, you feel bad when you lose them, but you know they can be replaced. Nothing sentimental about the bush. A horse was only a horse in those days of hard physical work.

I went to the horse sales in South Melbourne regularly in search of good horses. South Melbourne was like a country town in the fifties, with wide cobbled streets and even a horse-drawn dray making its way to market now and again. Not like today where the traffic is thick and fast and the noise of it all makes a bushman like me nearly jump out of his skin.

Usually I would rise early in the morning and get down to the market with plenty of time to wander through the stalls and look over the animals before the auction began. The sellers would often be within range and try to convince me of the worth of their animal if I looked interested. I never took any notice of a word they said, but I would run my hands over the legs, feel the hooves for warmth, run a hand up the neck to the ears to see how flighty it might be, press my hand strongly along its back, looking for weakness. A horse will flinch or lift a back leg if a sore spot is found and that always raises suspicion. Sometimes the horses were too wild to get close to and then I'd have to run my eye over them. You work with horses the way I do, you soon develop an expert eye. No matter how I checked them over, the sellers would back off, realising I knew what I was looking for, and let me decide for myself.

I enjoyed the horse sales, being in amongst the beasts, breathing in the clean, grassy smells of healthy animals, listening to the stamping and snorting and nickering of the nervous horses. The swagger of the dealers was amusing to watch, and listening to the tall tales they told to green buyers about the marvels of their horses made me laugh.

I made a sport of following the sales, looking for a horse I fancied. I often came home with something. A few extra horses didn't make any difference. They always came in useful whenever there was an injury. And they didn't cost much in those days. Once I bought a beautiful black hack with saddle and bridle for three pounds ten shillings. It was a young, honest horse with no vices. Sometimes you might be lucky and strike a seller more green than the buyer. Lucky for me I was there that day.

I wasn't always lucky. We had been at Toora only three months when I went to the South Melbourne Market and bought two of the best draughthorses in the yard. They had come down from the north with a mob of sorry-looking creatures, but these animals were beautifully put together and I was looking forward to training them and working with them. I arranged to have them railed to Toora where I would meet them the next day and lead them home. But when I got to the yards in Toora, I found them both dead. The stationmaster, fool that he was, had unloaded them and let them out into a yard where there was a trough with water laid on. Now, these horses were stressed from the long trip down south from northern Victoria, the yarding at South Melbourne and then the trip down to Toora. Everyone knows you don't let a thirsty horse fill his belly with water after a long stretch without it. He'll drink more than he can stand and he'll die of gripe. That's just what happened. When I got to them, there they were, still warm but stiffening.

Another bloke was there collecting his own mob of horses when I found my two dead. He helped me cut those beautiful animals up and cart them away. Then he sold me two of his scrawny animals to make do until the next sale. That incident was a real blow and I've never forgotten it. I guess, looking back, I should have realised that was a sign, just like all the rest I was ignoring, telling me that Toora was not going to be the place for me. But, at that time, the weather was still good and the world still looked new and hopeful from our verandah, so I kept working and planning.

I built a special round yard to break horses in. I seemed to have good luck breaking horses. The main thing is to mouth them properly. First you handle them, touching them all over, running your hands along their backs, down their rumps, down their legs, lifting their feet. In the beginning they don't like it, but it doesn't take long before they will stand still, quivering and nervous, but no longer afraid. You keep handling them until they're standing almost asleep, then you put a girth around them and a bridle and bit on. This wakes them up considerably, but usually talking and rubbing will settle them. Then you attach the reins, running them from the bit to the girth, tight on one side and loose on the other, and leave them alone in the yard to argue with the bit on their own, walking around in circles, flexing their neck, chewing on the bit until they find out for themselves the purpose of it all. You leave them there for a couple of hours, then change sides.

This is called mouthing the horse. It takes a couple of days all up, and it makes all the difference between an easily handled animal and a hard-mouthed, stubborn one. We had a neighbour at Jackson's Track who believed the best way to mouth a horse was to tie back both reins tight and leave the horse to fight the bit until he was exhausted. Their horses always ended up mean and, to my way of thinking, it was because they were made hard-mouthed from the outset and you had to be rough with them to ride or work them. I guess they did it that way because they were in a hurry. I believe breaking a horse takes patience and you need to know just how tight to make the rein to keep a horse's mouth soft and pliable.

Not all horses worked out, of course. I was gentle and patient and tried my best to fully break a horse without provoking him to buck at all. Naturally, I didn't want them to buck, but I have to admit I got a bit of a thrill when they did. Some horses are just plain bad. A bad one will buck all day; it just can't help itself. You can't blame the horse for its natural traits. A bad horse will often be a cunning one. It will learn how to kick with purpose and with extreme accuracy. I've had my foot in the stirrup painfully cow-kicked many a time by a cunning horse.

With the working horses, after they've been mouthed and worked in the round yard with long reins from the ground in full harness, they get put in the shafts with chains next to an experienced horse and usually they don't look back. An experienced horse will soon put a young, flighty horse in its place. From then on they learn as they work.

I loved working with horses. Each morning, I would go out, bring the horses into the yard and give them a feed of chaff and grain before I cut the day's wood for Euphie. Then I would milk the cow and leave the bucket on the kitchen table for her to use. I'd stop for a breakfast of damper and jam and tea, then go out to harness up and be off. The horses in the main stood quiet and calm as I slipped the collars round their necks. If they stamped or shifted away from me, a deep 'Whoa' would come from my throat. I talked to them constantly in deep, soothing tones. My voice, the jingle of the chain on the harness, the creak of leather, the sound of horses' molars grinding the chaff, some snorting and stamping and the swish of flicking tails are the sounds of the morning mingled with bird calls and, of course, the whistle of the wind.

Just as I was ready to pull out, one of the kids, usually Betty, would run up with my dinner wrapped in a towel, which I took and stuffed in a saddlebag along with the billy. I headed out towards the back paddocks and Gunyah forest.

Mount Fatigue

I NEVER REALLY KNEW where my boundary was and what's more I wasn't interested in boundaries, only in finding straight trees that would be good splitting logs for fence posts. One day I was cutting a tree which had fallen across a road in the forest when two forest officers came along. It was a scorcher of a day in February. I was stopped for lunch, eating my pasty while I waited for the billy to boil, when they came upon me.

'Good day,' the driver said through the window of the four-wheel drive.

I nodded to him, aware that I was about to be caught red-handed

Daryl holding Mac on Jet

cutting wood in a state forest without a permit. He turned off the motor and he and his mate climbed out of the truck to have a yarn. They weren't looking at the tree. They were looking at my small fire.

'Hot enough for you?' asked the driver.

I nodded, still not saying anything, wondering what they were going to do to me. Everything was still, no wind amongst the tall trees and the heat had pretty much silenced the birds. The only sound was the fire quietly crackling and the billy just coming on to boil.

'You know it's a total fire ban day?' asked the other one.

I shook my head.

'That fire could earn you a hefty fine, mate.'

So they weren't worried about the tree, they were worried about the fire. I figured I'd better start talking.

'I'm just boiling a billy. That fire's not going anywhere. You boys stopping for a cup of tea?'

They scratched their heads and then nodded and squatted down, resting on their heels. I poured them some tea in tin cups and immediately put the fire out.

'Got to have tea with me dinner.'

They nodded.

'Where you from, cobber?'

I told them I had a farm on Mount Fatigue, running some sheep, that I was new in the district, had spent the last fifteen years in the forest near Jindivick, that I knew when there was no danger in lighting a fire to boil a billy, that I had lived through the '39 fire. It took about half an hour to get all this information to them as we swapped yarns. When I told them about the '39 fire, they looked at each other.

'The Forestry Commission is looking for a bloke like you, an experienced bushman, to do a job. You interested?'

'Depends on what it is.'

'We want a clearing made at the top of Mount Fatigue so we can set up a watch for fires in the fire season. What do you reckon?'

'Sounds good.'

'You live practically on the mountain. It means you could get home every night instead of having to camp up there.'

I didn't have to think very hard about this proposition for I could see straight away it would suit me down to the ground. If I were set to work clearing an acre of forest, I would have plenty of straight trees for fence posts and twisted trees for firewood at my disposal without having to worry about a permit whenever one of these officers came along. I would be working for myself but be doing a job for the forestry people at the same time and getting paid for it.

'Yes, that'd suit me well. I'll take it on,' I said, probably with a grin on my face.

'We'll tell our boss about you and he'll come by your place to give you the details of the job.'

They finished their tea, placed the cups alongside mine, stood up and we all shook hands before they got in their truck and drove off. Lucky thing I boiled that billy so these fellows would find me.

About a week later the boss, a Mr Ryan, turned up at the house. We went together in his four-wheel drive to inspect the site on the summit of the mountain. The acre was already marked out. It was thick with scrub and good, straight trees. Firstly, I was to cut the scrub and burn it to clear it away from the trees. Once I had done that, they would send an explosives man up and we would blow the trees out of the ground with gelignite. That seemed a pretty exciting prospect to me. Later, I was to cut the logs into lengths, heap them and burn them as well. I knew it wasn't economical to waste all that wood in a bonfire on the mountain. I quietly began working out that it would end up as fence posts round the district and firewood at home.

I told the boss I understood the task and that I would start the next day. It was the beginning of March.

It took me about three months to finish the clearing. Of course, I had the horses working with me the whole time, except for when it came time to blast the trees out of the ground. Then I left the horses at home and went up to the clearing in a four-wheel drive with a fellow sent up by the Forestry people, who showed me how to set the gelignite. This bloke had been an explosives expert during the war and he knew a thing or two. He taught me how to mould the gelignite, put the fuse in and set the detonator, but don't ask me how to do it today. I couldn't tell you. We had real sport setting off blasts and sparks, the likes of which that mountain hasn't felt since, I'm sure. We blew up whole trees, maybe fifty of them all up. We would set the explosive under the roots in a certain way, take cover and let her rip. It was amazing to see whole trees leaping into the air, spinning and humming like whirligigs before they toppled and crashed lengthwise to the earth, ploughing up great hunks of dirt and scrub, sending branches flying in all directions. What a noise! I remember we had to use a case and a half of gelignite under a huge mountain ash that was at least eight feet in diameter and more than two hundred feet tall. Upon explosion the trunk, with a great scream, split upwards fifty feet before it fell.

The site looked like a war zone when we were finished and it was my job to clean it up. The horses returned to the mountain with me and we pulled the logs I cut out of the fallen trees down that mountain through the forest to the property where I cut them up either into fence posts, which I would then cart to the roadside, or into firewood for Euphie. Up at the clearing, we piled up all the toppings, branches, roots and stumps into huge mounds ready for burning.

Of course, the Boss wouldn't let me light a bonfire when it was still dry since he judged it too dangerous. He made me wait until the weather broke, until it began to rain a light, soaking rain that didn't let up. Rain doesn't make burning off very easy. The Forestry Commission's solution to the wet was to give me drums and drums of kerosene to dowse the woodheaps with. Makes sense, doesn't it? Makes you remember the Forestry Commission is a government agency. I had some fantastic kerosene fires, but not a lot of wood burnt at the same time. It took me months to get those heaps turned into ashes.

In the meantime, I was asked to put a dugout in the middle of the clearing where a person assigned to be a fire lookout in the summer season could escape to in case the area went up in smoke. It had to be eight feet by ten feet by eight feet. It was hard yakka digging that out by hand but I've never complained about good honest work. I covered the hole over with slabs I split from some of the cut logs and put all the dirt I had dug out of the hole onto the slabs. I then dug a winding track out of the underground room through the side of the hill. I put a blanket over the entrance and a bucket of water just inside. A bushfire would pass by without even noticing.

The last thing I had to do, just before the fire season began the next summer, was to secure in the middle of the clearing a small hut which the Forestry Commission had sent up already built on the back of a truck. The hut could be locked up. It had a radio receiver in it so the person on lookout could communicate information about possible fires to Yarram. The hut also had a chair and a table for the radio in it. All it needed was a pole for an antenna to make the radio usable.

The Boss came up to have a look. He looked around for a tall thin sapling to serve as a pole. He didn't know what to do. All had been cleared away and burnt. I had done a thorough job.

'We'll have to go pinch one out of the Gunyah Reserve,' he said with a worried look on his face.

I started to laugh. To me it was a huge joke.

'You're the boss of the reserve! What are you worried about?' I hooted.

He looked sheepish. 'I'm not the boss; I'm supposed to be the protector. I suppose one pole won't hurt anything.'

'If you think about it, it might save the whole forest one day,' I laughed.

He laughed, too, and we put up the pole, ran up the antenna and the hut was ready. The Boss paid me off. We stood and had one last look at the place and then, just before we turned to go, the Boss looked at me.

'Would you like to keep working for us?' he asked.

'What have you got in mind?'

'How about if you be our lookout here this summer? All you'd have to do is watch for fires and report to Yarram on the wireless three times a day.'

I raised my eyebrows and looked at him, considering.

'You've made this place. It wouldn't be right offering it to some-one else if you want the job.'

'I'll take it.'

We shook hands, and so it was that I watched for fires on Mount Fatigue for the next two seasons.

Return

THE FIRE SEASON BEGAN the first of December and ended in the middle of March. I had to be up on the mountain every day so I could radio into Yarram on time three times a day. Some days, the cloud was so low visibility was zero, and it seemed a waste for me to be up there, but I had to radio in anyway. On those days, I would occupy myself pulling fallen trees out of the bush to drag home for firewood. But mostly the summer days were fine, and although I did see a fair bit of smoke and send in quite a few calls, only some of which actually turned out to be wildfires, to tell the truth I did little more than sit around reading books throughout my two seasons as a lookout on

The lookout at Mount Fatigue

Mount Fatigue. Each fine morning, I would settle myself in a position where I could see all around me. I would open my book on my knee, smooth back the pages and let myself enter another world. About every three or four pages, I would lift my head, check the horizons for smoke, then go back to my book.

I got the books from the Toora library and brought them up to the summit by the armload. I would read anything to do with land or pioneers, but I avoided mysteries, detective books, stories about murder in the city. I liked Ion Idriess, who wrote about the outback, and I enjoyed the stories of Lasseter's Reef and the writing about Australian history. But the things I liked reading most were the Zane Grey westerns. I liked reading about wild horses and life on the open plains in the American West. I liked reading about cattle rustling and all the trouble they had with fencing, how fencing changed the country, changed the way of life for most men, changed the wide land from a place where people were free and generous to a place where people killed each other to protect what they thought they owned.

Even though lots of these books were nothing more than yarns, there was still a lot of truth in them. They gave me much to think about. For instance, I knew for a fact that Zane Grey understood about fences. The same thing happened, was still happening, here. I was stumped about Lasseter's Reef. I couldn't decide whether I believed it or not. How could there be such a lot of gold in the ground without anybody ever finding it and all the sophisticated ways they have of locating the precious metal these days? But on the other hand, the man must have believed it was there or he wouldn't have died trying to relocate it.

I began to think of myself as a bit of a sceptic. I've only ever believed what I see. My world is the real world around me. I once saw a kangaroo that was eight feet tall and I believe in that. I once saw a white snake. Although I have never seen a dinosaur, I'm inclined to believe they existed, but it doesn't worry me one way or the other. I've thought about it hard and long and I don't know if anything in the Bible is true. Maybe the sense of some of it is true, but it's all yarns if you ask me. I've heard some funny yarns about the truth, but I need to see it to believe it.

Sometimes, when I looked up from my book to check that the country wasn't ablaze, I wouldn't go back to my book but I'd find myself gazing into the distance, thinking about my life and the way things were going. I had a lot of time to think up on Mount Fatigue.

I'd think about Stewart and Dora and their camp at Jackson's Track. Stewart didn't like money or the work you had to do to get it, but he had a good camp anyway, which Dora kept in good order. He loved to have his wife, his children and their families around him. He loved the noise and chatter of the grandchildren. He loved visitors, loved singing and loved telling yarns. The fire was always lit at Stewart's place and there was always good talk there. Here I was sitting alone on the summit of Mount Fatigue, I thought, while Euphie was alone with her babies at the bottom of the mountain. And I bet you we were both thinking the same thing about the movement and laughter around the campfire at Stewart's. And I thought about how we couldn't stay away. We drove over at night, maybe once a month, and spent a few hours with the mob that was our family, catching up on news and getting a good dose of warmth and laughter from everybody. I often thought that being over at the Track was a lot more natural for us than being here.

Sometimes, right in the middle of a description of a cattle drive or a gunfight, I would read something that reminded me of Harry and I'd stop reading and start thinking about him. When he was young he had been a bit of a cowboy, a bit of a larrikin, always ready with a yarn and a laugh, but he'd got serious once his personality rubbed up against Mavis's. I wondered how he was going on the Track. Stewart told us Harry had closed the saw mill driven by the gas engine and had erected one right next to it driven by a diesel engine. I chuckled at the thought. I wondered who he'd got the engine from and what kind of a deal he'd made. I wondered if he was able to send a lot more logs through the blades now. I thought about Harry buying a bulldozer to pull in the logs. I shook my head and probably said out loud, 'You'd never catch me using a machine!' Besides, a bulldozer would be useless on these mountain slopes. They said he was working weekends with the dozer clearing, as well. I wondered how the place was changed. I hadn't seen it in daylight in almost two years since we'd left.

I tried not to think about Mavis but, of course, I did. She was rarely mentioned at Stewart's camp. No one ever said anything bad about her, but since they couldn't think of anything good to say, they said nothing. When I thought about Mavis, I always thought about money. I remember one day thinking how I was sure I was at Toora because of her more than Harry. I was sure the 'business proposition' to buy this place was her proposition, but I had never received one shilling in payment for my part of Jackson's Track in two years. Was that because of her? Was she trying to cheat me? Had she never intended that I should be paid? Or – and I jumped up as the next thought entered my head – was it Harry? Had he made no attempt to pay me off because he knew if I still owned half of it I would find a way to return to the Track? Was that his way of saying he wanted us back?

'Yes,' I shouted to the treetops. 'He wants us back. I'm sure of it!'

I guess my startled horse looked up and snorted at that outburst. I walked around the clearing for a bit, thinking through this new idea. I realised Harry had left me an excuse to go back. But it was fairly crafty.

'He'd never ask me to my face to come back,' I said aloud.

I knew we couldn't go back onto the property straight out. We'd have to return to the forest and slowly ease our way back into things. Get back and establish our camp and settle the family quietly before Mavis realised what was happening so she'd have no chance to find a way to stop us.

I sat back down again. After all, it was only midday and I had my job as lookout to complete before I could go home. I wasn't sure I would tell Euphie about my new understanding just yet. I had lots to mull over, lots of considerations to deal with in a sticky situation. What better place to do it than up on this mountain with nothing to do but watch for smoke and think?

I thought about my neighbours here on the mountain. There wasn't one person we'd met up here who had been here very long. As I thought about it, I realised that, in my experience, no one ever stopped in this district for long. After the last winter, our Polish neighbours called it quits. They reckoned it was the worst climate they'd ever lived in, even worse than any winter Poland could dish up.

Once I understood that we could go back, I began to realise just how much I wanted to be away from this place. It's amazing how you won't let yourself think some thoughts when the consequences of them are impossible to face. I suppose if I hadn't seen Harry's signal, I could have gone on convincing myself forever that I could make a go of it at Toora.

When my thoughts went to the Track I could see that we had never properly left it, not in our minds and hearts anyway. We would go back. It was fated.

Euphie, patient Euphie, had been waiting for me to realise we couldn't stay at Toora. She was ready to move as soon as I gave the nod.

At the end of the fire season, I arranged to sell the farm to the

Forestry Commission. Then Euphie and I prepared our move back to the Track. I drove over to Stewart's camp one night and dropped off my gear: axes, saws, chains, harness. I returned to Toora to pick up the horses. I rode my mare and led the draughthorses in a line behind me through the Strzeleckis just as I had brought them here two years earlier, but my heart was much lighter going north than it had been coming south. I put the horses up in a temporary yard I quickly built near the spot I had chosen for a new camp in the forest.

I stayed in the forest for about a week, building the best camp I ever had. It was on Wattle Creek, still in the thick forest but within easy access to the creek along a path down the bank. We wouldn't have to fight our way through thickets of dense scrub at this camp, but we would have to think about snakes on the path. Snakes are scarce now, but there were lots of them then, just part of life. Tiger snakes mainly. We had learnt long ago to keep our eyes peeled. I loved that week in the forest back at the Track, building a large bark hut and yards. The work went well; all the things I built seemed to belong where I put them, seemed to fit snugly amongst the trees, seemed in the correct relationship to each other in the forest. Oh, it was good to be back in this forest. I will never lose a feeling for it. Nothing gives me more pleasure than building a camp.

When the camp was ready, I caught a lift back to Toora, loaded up Euphie, Dot, Mac and Curly along with all our belongings in the van and took off with hardly a backward glance. There are some of my kids, born after our return to the Track, who have only recently learned that Euphie and I ever spent any time away from here. I never talked about Toora and hardly even had thoughts of it enter my mind after we left. We had never belonged there and it was no use remembering why we went there.

Home

ALL I HAD TIME TO PREPARE in the week that I was away was a bare-bones camp: basic horse yards and a hut with no table, chairs or beds, no shelving, no proper hearth. Only walls and roof and, of course, a good fireplace. So the first few weeks of our return to the forest were spent building beds and tables and shelves, strengthening the yards, erecting a shed for harness and feed, clearing the path to the creek, establishing a woodpile for the fireplace, getting in stores from Longwarry, widening the snig track to enable the van to negotiate it to the camp. I took the time to make it the best camp I ever built.

I knew I was going to be cutting fence posts and firewood, just as

Cheryl, Dot and Linda Mullett

I had always done, but I wanted to have a look around and get a feel of the changes around the place before I started. I wasn't in any hurry. One day I was walking through the trees on the property, taking note of what had been fallen and dragged out and what was left, when I met Harry. He was coming along a snig track on the crawler tractor, pulling a log towards the mill on Gipsy Creek. He stopped and turned off the engine when he saw me. He waited for me to walk up to him.

'Well, here goes,' I said to myself.

I remember that walk of about twenty yards and all the things I was thinking before I actually greeted him. I wondered what he was thinking as he watched me approach. Was he shocked to see me here? Surely he'd heard rumours that I was back. Would he be wild and go crook at me? I thought he might, but I also knew that in the back of his mind was the fact that he hadn't held up his end of the deal and that he had an obligation to me. As I got closer and could read his expression, I got the sense that he had been waiting to come across me somewhere in this forest, that he was glad I was there in his path, that he wanted me there.

I came alongside the tractor and had to look up to see his face properly.

'You're back,' he said.

Pause. We studied each other. It was a bit like looking into a mirror, I've been told, although I've never been able to quite see my own features in Harry. We both had thick brown hair, although Harry's was covered by a felt beret which he always wore when he was working. Harry looked strong and fit, but I could see he had put on some age. Was this hard life catching up with me, too? Both our faces must have looked ruddy and weatherbeaten.

'I sold the place at Toora.'

He nodded.

'It was no good.'

'What will you do now?'

I knew I could tell him whatever I wanted to since he had no right not to agree. He knew how stubborn I was, as stubborn as he was, and he knew I had the same sense of fairness that he had.

'I'll be working on my own. Fence posts. Firewood,' I said, looking him fair and square in the eyes.

He nodded, not shifting his gaze from me for a moment.

'I'll fall the trees you have rejected for the mill.'

'You're entitled.'

'I'll keep to myself.'

'Fair enough.' He let out a breath and seemed to relax a bit. 'You can spell your second team of horses in the grass paddock.'

'Right then.'

We shook hands. He leaned over to start the motor and then continued on his way, giving me the slightest nod as he pulled out. I watched him go. He never asked about Euphie, never asked about my children. I knew he wouldn't. He didn't want to know. He knew if he spoke to me about my family, he would somehow be admitting how wrong he had been.

He'll never admit to that, I thought. I'll stay in the forest to protect my family and give no cause for interference. I'll work my own property, but I won't live on it.

I was sure he wouldn't put anything in my road from then on. And he never did. I'll never know what he told Mavis or how long it was before she was aware that I was back. I never heard from her and I never saw her.

Before I began the serious business of logging, word came through from some of Euphie's people who were camped along the Tambo

River at Mossiface near Bruthen that they wanted to see us. Euphie was keen to go so we bundled ourselves into the van and went driving. This wasn't the first time we had suddenly taken off to go visiting. We had been up to Dimboola to see Euphie's grandmother several times; of course, we had been making frequent night-time jaunts to the Track from Toora; and Euphie often came to the markets with me in the city. Euphie liked travelling around, especially to see her people, and I liked driving. I liked driving fast and I liked driving at night, which makes me think I must have been game in those days. It surprises me to remember that I was a bit of a night bird once.

The ground along the Tambo was rich, black soil on the river flats. Euphie's cousins were there working in the market gardens, picking spuds and peas. There was also wild fruit to be had by the bucketful, which brought a whole mob of people to the camp about the same time we arrived. It was a real summer picnic with lots of laughter and swarms of children swimming in the river.

We stayed for the weekend with Gene Mobourne and his wife, Effie. Effie was Euphie's aunty. She was nicknamed Mother Effie because she was always looking after somebody's child. In fact she had adopted her daughter, Gillian, who was living with them.

I had never met Gene before, but immediately he and I seemed to have much in common with lots to talk about. Effie was a lovely woman, who as a rule mistrusted whites, but sometime during the two days we were there she told me she thought of me as one of her own. Before the weekend was over I found myself agreeing to bring Gene and his family back to the Track with us and arranging to have him stay at our camp in our bark hut, which, as luck would have it, I had built big enough to accommodate many people.

I was happy to have Gene and Effie come and stay as long as they wanted. There's one trait I've always loved and admired about the blackfella and that's generosity. It's the most natural way to be. They always love to see people come and hate to see them go. I'm the same. The people who stayed with us over the years never stopped too long. An unwritten rule of any camp is to always show respect towards each other, and they all seemed to have an uncanny sense that allowed them to detect when that rule might be broken just before it happens. They seemed to know just when to go, so we were always sorry to say goodbye.

The only time I've seen trouble in a blackfellas' camp is when there is drink on hand. But we have never opened our house up to drink. I can't stand even the smell of alcohol myself, never could, and Euphie's temper will flare up if someone ever tries to bring a bottle over her threshold. Most of the women on Jackson's Track felt the same as Euphie about drink and, since they ruled the camps, it never became a problem for our mob. If a blackfella did turn up drunk, he would apologise for his state and go somewhere to sleep it off before he joined the group.

Gene drank wine, but never during the week and never on the Track. Effie used to get cross with him and scold him in a high, angry voice when he came home late, but she always looked after him well, no matter what state he might be in. Of course, I often hung out with Gene and, if I came in late with him, Euphie would have a go at me even though I wasn't drinking. No matter. The women managed to keep us in line pretty much.

We had a good camp with Gene and Effie there and the children. It was a busy and friendly place. Everybody liked Gene wherever he went. So after he stopped with us, many new people who had never had any connection with the Track before began to turn up. They were friends and relations of Gene's who wanted to work for me. Gene was particularly happy because two of his best friends, Jack Patton and Bob Nelson, had turned up and we were all working together.

They helped me get the fence post and firewood business re-established. I found a good buyer for split fencing posts and fencing materials who wanted three truckloads a week so there was plenty of work for all. I made landings near the road to work on. I used two draughthorses to pull the logs out of the bush onto them to be split and loaded onto the trucks. Things were going well. Even Harry seemed compliant and encouraging. Whenever my buyer rang the main house at the Track on the phone, Harry would get the message to me. However, he never came himself and I rarely saw him except from afar.

Another buyer rang to ask me to supply him with six-foot firewood for his wood yard where he had a firewood bench and one-foot blocks for sale. I had seven regular fellows working with me on the fence posts and four more regulars on the firewood as well as anyone else who wanted to swing an axe.

At last I was home with an established camp and an established business. It was the beginning of the best four years of my life.

Brothers

THE BLACKFELLAS AND I swung into a routine of work. I was always out and started by about eight o'clock but, in the main, working in the bush was fairly casual, with no strict starting time. I could count on two of them, Willie Marks and Jimmy Bond, to be on hand before I got out. Every morning about seven, they would arrive at our camp with their tuckerbags and billycans. They would stop for a cuppa, a chat with Euphie and a play with the kids, who loved them. Then we'd be on our way.

Of course, Jimmy had been a loyal friend and worker for years. He got along fine with Mavis and Harry and continued to stop there

Some of the mob at Jackson's Track

for a meal until I returned from Toora. Then he came to work with me and never went back.

Willie lived to work in the same way I did. Work made him happy. So he was always on hand from sun-up until sundown, putting in his hours every day of the week, and always in a good mood, laughing and singing. Willie was my main splitter. The logs would be brought to the siding where Jimmy, who loved cutting with the crosscut saw, would cut them into lengths and Willie would split them with wedges into six-inch posts and stack them ready to be loaded on the trucks. Both these men were reliable. They took pride in their skills and were interested in improving and becoming masters of their trades. At first, I would come in on the weekends and spend time trimming the posts properly after Willie and Jimmy had left them, but as time went on, the trimming became less and less a task since they were becoming better and better at their work.

I met the other fellows out in the bush to fall, trim and bark the trees before I hauled them back to the siding where Jimmy and Willie were. My main workers there were Gene Mobourne, Chook Mullett, Clifford Pepper, Ruben Wilson. They would work in pairs. I would always be on hand to choose the trees to fall. We worked on rejected trees that were no good for the mill, but they had to be solid and good straight splitters. The firewood trees could be hollow, but sometimes we would choose a hollow tree to fall for fence posts as long as it had outside wood that was at least six inches deep since that was the width of the posts we were selling.

There is a lot in it when you're falling a tree, and since most of these fellows were learners, they never fall any trees without me there. Once we picked a tree, it would have to be barked all around where we were going to make the cuts. Then I would decide on the direction the trees would fall and usually cut the scarf on each one to make sure it was in the right place for the safety of the falling. Then the boys would get going on the crosscut saws. It might take two hours to cut a tree with a saw. You have lots of spells while you're doing it. Once it fell with a slow creaking followed by a sharp crack and then a thunderous crash, the boys would set to trimming, barking and cutting the tree. We'd manage maybe four trees in a day. During the day, we'd be scattered about, working two or three landings sometimes, depending on how pressed we were to fill up the orders. I'd be working right alongside them. Chook Mullett was my partner whenever I worked on the saw. He was about six feet high, the same height as me, and we made a good team. He was a pleasure to work with because he knew how to pull a saw and then keep it free for me to pull back on the other end.

Other fellows were spread through the forest cutting firewood. They usually worked in pairs and stacked their wood together, which made it easier for me to tally the stacks of a Friday. Gene's mates, Bob Nelson and Jack Patton, worked together. Others were Sid Austin, Jackie Kennedy, Les Stewart, Roy Rose, Dave Moore. Jamby Wilson was one of my favourite firewood cutters. He was thickset, short, very heavy and slow-moving. He always left neat and tidy stacks of mostly small wood. He lived with his wife, Adelaide Rose, in a well-built, very tidy bark hut. The thing I remember about him was that he loved to eat wombat, a meat dish I stayed away from myself. By gee, Adelaide was a lovely woman. She was the mother of Roy Rose and was devoted to her grandchildren. I reckon she spoiled them.

Other workers came and went, but these men made up the main group.

These men were my mates. We were like a family. We always looked after each other at work, calling out warnings of danger, helping out with difficult tasks. In the bush you always become close friends with your workmates. Things you don't count on can go wrong and you need to rely on them. One day I was working and I thought I had something in my eye. I called Chook Mullett over to have a look, but he couldn't see anything. I went back to work but had to call for him to have another look. This time he said a leech was curled up on the pupil of the eye and that's why it was hard to see. Now, leeches were plentiful in the bush and if they manage to attach themselves to you and suck blood, they leave a fairly painful itch behind. Chook pulled the leech out of my eye, but the pain was so great I had to go to the doctor. My eye was inflamed and I couldn't see out of it for a few weeks. I was lucky to have workers who treated me as a friend. They saved my back more than once. If you don't become friends in the bush, if you don't work as partners and pull together, then it doesn't last and the enterprise fails. This is the way men were in the old working days: brothers.

Most of these men lived in camps they established on Wattle Creek, which is the same creek my camp was on, but they were about half a mile from us, on our property rather than in the forest, and down closer to the Track within cooee of Stewart's camp along the Labertouche. I knew all the people who came and went on the place because I was the main man they had to see to get work. Harry had a fixed crew on the mill, but my crew could expand and shrink as the blackfella chose. No man ever had to ask permission to stay at the Track. It wasn't a mission station. They could come and go as they pleased. Because the camp was some distance from me, I didn't always know straight away who was there. I never checked up on them, but I was always told about new people, just in conversation. Most people talked a lot in the old days.

A new man would come by my camp of an evening and squat down near the fire, stop there and talk awhile before he asked me for work. I suppose he wanted to know what kind of man I was before he made any requests.

'Where you from?' I'd ask.

That would be an opener. Some, like Bob Nelson and Jack Patton, had been soldiers in the Australian Army and had been restless and on the move ever since the end of the war. They had interesting stories to tell and kept us entertained, but I could see they were not so comfortable looking into an open fire and drinking tea. They had seen the world and had learned about possibilities in life. Maybe they thought a bark hut was a step backwards, but all doors were shut to them in the towns and so they resigned themselves to pick up an axe. At least they'd get the Welfare off their backs, but there was a lingering resentment in their bearing and it was hard to know if they would settle here. They would have been happier in a factory in town. No such luck.

Another man, named Jackie Green, had also been overseas in the army. He had come back shell-shocked and off his head. He never did find a way to ask me for work, but he lived on the Track for a while and was tolerated and cared for.

Some, like Jack Kennedy, had been brought up in homes in New South Wales. He had been orphaned or stolen and on his own all his life.

'I know how to take care of myself!' he bragged.

I could see straight away he was a terrible skite and blowhard, telling me how good an axeman he was and how his fighting ability was amazing. He was a big man with large staring red eyes that made him look mad. I was wary of him because he looked dangerous, but if he wanted to work he was welcome. He had a wife and two children with him. I wouldn't turn them away. I never turned anyone away.

Many people were from Lake Tyers. Some had been born and bred there, like Clifford 'Rats' Pepper. Of course, I knew Rats very well and regarded him as family since he had stayed with us in Toora, but I could see that he had the characteristics of a mission boy. A lot of people brought up on the missions lost their independence. They seemed always to be thinking about what the 'master' could do to them. It's my opinion that the mission managers didn't really like the blackfellas they were supposed to be looking after. They were kind-hearted religious people, but they had one-track minds and wanted to change the blackfellas to their way of thinking. For them it was one-way traffic. They never wanted to learn about the blackfellas' ways.

A mission black was not brought up to work. He sat down all day, played cards, gossiped, became soft. The house is not a place for a man. Blackfellas in mission houses lose ambition. They can hardly breathe. Rats was a depressed man. He was dull and found it hard to laugh. Although he was a reliable worker, he didn't enjoy his work. He appeared like an animal that's been mistreated. He'd been on the mission too long.

Many people came and went as they moved about from place to place. I was always pleased to see Dave Moore turn up. When I think back on old Dave, I believe he must have been the favourite amongst all of us. Euphie certainly liked to see him and the children would climb all over him when he appeared. He always stayed with us when he came to the Track. He would stay three to six months, then move on. He was a good axeman, but I never counted on his turning up to work regularly. No matter. He was a doer. He would do handiwork in the house, if he didn't go out with me, or he would go hunting and trapping to keep us fed with bush tucker while he was around. He was a clean and tidy man, which pleased Euphie. He would wash all his own clothes and do the dishes every night.

He was a fine, well-built man, about my height, but better built than I am. He was always clean-shaven and very concerned with his appearance. He wore good clothes. I remember the flashy brightly coloured shirts, completely different from Jimmy, who always wore dark work clothes and never dressed up. When he went to town, Dave wore a beautiful clean wide-brimmed felt hat. Stetson in those days. Didn't he think he looked fine?

He was a graceful man. He could throw an axe or a throwing stick as straight as a die. He was a great hunter, had a marvellous eye for tracking. To my mind he was the best blackfella on the Track.

His pleasure was telling stories, and real stretchers they were, too. He entertained the kids. I've got a picture in my head of Dave visiting us at the Wattle Creek camp with four of our kids around him. So it must have been around 1954 and Sandra, another girl, was about a year old with Russell on the way. He told amazing bush tales about what a great horseman he was up north on the stations. Of course, you couldn't get him near a horse here. He would tell us about his distant travels to the far north, but you wouldn't believe him. I do know that he went up to the Darling River near Brewarrina where the old blackfellas had fish traps in the rocks and he would tell us stories about these fellows and their ancient ways. I loved listening to him as much as the kids did.

He was part of our family. I would say Dave was my brother, and so were Jimmy and Willie and Gene.

Boomerang

SOMETIMES GENE would disappear for a day or two. When he returned he would be laden with crooked bits of wood which he had found deep in the forest – all sorts of hardwoods, but mostly blackwood. He would dump them in a pile out in the yard and then begin to sort through them until he found one that especially suited him. Then he would sit on a stump, lay his tommyaxe on his thigh and for a long while work at sharpening it to a gleaming razor-sharp edge. When he was satisfied, he would take up his piece of wood, looking it over, turning it this way and that, running his hands over it, before he set it on a block of wood just in front of his knees and got to work.

Freddie Bull, artist

Gene's father, Ernie, had been a master tool and weapons maker in his day. Not every blackfella knew how to make a good spear or boomerang or bundy. People would come to old Ernie and swap favours with him so he would make them a good boomerang to hunt with. He passed his knowledge on to Gene. I was very interested in watching Gene work his way through his pile of bent-up wood and turn it into a pile of beautifully crafted boomerangs. He worked at it night after night, listening to the talk around the fire, joining in, having a laugh, but never losing concentration. While he worked, I couldn't take my eyes off him. It was as mesmerising as watching a fire, the way those skilled hands would use the axe to chip away at the rough wood and slowly shape it into a smooth, perfectly tapered weapon.

'I wouldn't mind learning how to make one of these,' I said quietly one night after I'd picked one up and was holding it in my hands, getting a feel of the heft and shape and smoothness of it.

Gene smiled. Maybe he had been waiting for me to say that. He held up the one he was working on, eyeballed the edge of it to see how straight he was going.

'If it's going to be a thrower, it has to have a good bend in it,' he said as he continued to work. 'It has to be natural. You can't carve the bend into it. The best boomerangs are made from tree roots. You have to find 'em. You come with me tomorrow, hey?'

And so we went on the first of many treks through the forest looking for the right shapes for the best boomerangs. We would go for miles and miles and miles. We looked mainly for good tree roots because they were usually the right shape and size, but they could also be made from scrub trees if found with a suitable bend, or from limbs of trees if they had an interesting crook in them. We also looked for wood with an easy straight grain. Almost any hardwood is good to work with, but blackwood is the best because when you cut into it, it shines up instead of going furry like some wood. Wattle is not bad either.

We would wrap the wood in a large piece of hessian and cart it home, often well after dark with Euphie and Effie looking out for us.

I had to wait a whole day after our first search to find out the next step. Finally, in the evening I started on my first boomerang. I hung the Tilley lamp up outside for light and Gene and I settled down with two blocks of wood in front of us. I had a tommyaxe and a rasp, cleaned and sharpened, lined up next to me ready to use. Gene sifted through our collection to pick out the best shaped roots. He handed me a piece of blackwood.

The first step was to trim the root square along the sides into the shape of the boomerang with the ends cut the same length as each other. When the sides were straight and perfectly flat, I put it down flat on the block and had to work on the top side to shape it. The boomerang uses aerodynamics to fly and turn so the shape of the blade needs to be right. I trimmed a bevelled edge right around it with the axe, cutting with the grain from the sides to the middle until Gene reckoned I had got it to the right thickness and camber. I then used a rasp to level the wood off. I turned it over and did the same on the other side.

It was definitely looking like a boomerang. The sides were equal in thickness and camber, making the shape of the blades symmetrical on either side and equal shape on either end. But when I held it, it wouldn't balance perfectly on one finger placed in the middle. So I had to do some more trimming and rasping to get it right. Finally it balanced. It certainly felt good and looked beautiful with the blackwood grain running through it. But would it fly?

The old blackfellas who used boomerangs for hunting didn't really care if they returned. They wanted them to be accurate throwers more than anything. The returning boomerangs were for sport and show, but you had to be a master to make them so they would return. Gene's were so good because he had a good eye for shape, for the right curve in the wood and the camber of the blade. He also knew how to shape them with heat. If you want a boomerang to return, you have to heat it up over the fire and when it is hot enough, you have to apply pressure to the end of it with your knee to set a slight curve in the blade. If you don't do this – and there is a knack to it – you'll never get a good returning weapon.

Gene was pleased with the way I made the boomerang, it being my first, but he wasn't overly impressed with my attempt to heat it and set a bend into it. I never did learn to do that as well as Gene could. I guess that was his secret.

Once I made one boomerang, I couldn't stop. I had to keep going until I was good at it. Gene and I went out often looking for good wood to bring home and work on at night. It was a good pastime. I worked on the wood, shaping and fine-tuning my technique. Then Gene would take my boomerangs and bend them under heat. Lastly, he would decorate them. He was very good with a paintbrush and put wonderful designs on the blades and often an Australian coat of arms complete with the kangaroo and the emu in the middle. To my way of thinking he was a true artist and craftsman. I had picked myself a good teacher.

While Gene and I were making boomerangs, Effie would be working on her baskets. She knew how to make the tightly woven, deep baskets that her people had always used. Gene and I would be sent out to find basket grass for her to use. Now, I don't know the proper name for the grass that we called basket grass. You could find it anywhere, but the best was near the Koo Wee Rup swamp. It grew more than a yard high and its blade was thick and wide. She wanted to use more than one kind of grass in her baskets so she could weave in designs and patterns. We found a type of sedge grass in the bush near the Track. It wasn't so easy to collect because it was a cutting grass that could slice our hands if we weren't careful. She also liked a beautiful red grass we brought home whenever we came across it.

When we brought the grasses home, Effie would hang them upside down near the fire to dry them. They would dry to a yellow colour, deep or light, depending on the grass. The red grass stayed red and looked beautiful threaded in amongst the other grasses in a basket. While the grasses were drying, they would curl and kink. So Effie would have to strip each blade of grass with a pocketknife to straighten it and flatten it. She would sit there for hours pulling blade after blade through the knife edge and her thumb until she had enough to make a basket. She would separate each type of grass into piles stacked all around her as she stripped it. There would be a big stack of unstripped, tangled grass in front of her, a pile of scrapings at and on her feet, and smaller, tidy stacks all around her. She took up a lot of room when she got started on her baskets. I remember young Russell, our fourth child, was crawling then and very good at making a mess of her piles of grass.

I can't tell you exactly how Effie set about making a basket because for one thing I was busy working on the boomerangs while she was weaving baskets and for another I reckon basket weaving is a woman's job, although I have to admit that Russell became a master basket weaver. He learned from Alice Pepper, another woman on the Track, but he must have got a taste for it crawling around Effie's feet as she worked. You have to have a gift for making baskets, but you also have to have patience for it; if you ask me, it's tedious work. The result of Effie's effort, however, was a beautiful work of art.

There was another artist at the Track by the name of Freddie

Bull. He was a true bush black. He rarely wore boots of any kind, but went in bare feet summer and winter. He was a skilled bushman. I never saw a man throw a bundy as far or as straight as he could. And I never saw a better bush artist in all my days. He could carve things, he could paint and he could make incredibly detailed drawings by burning lines into bark. He came and went and never worked for me or Harry, never worked for wages ever, but I never saw him lying about doing nothing. The blackfella community supported him because they wanted an artist in their midst. They knew he had something to offer.

Gene and I used to take our finished boomerangs and some of Effie's baskets and travel here and there to sell them. We would pile everything in the van and take off, usually for a weekend. Sometimes we would cut across to Frankston on the Mornington Peninsula and work our way down all the tourist beaches from Mount Martha to Rosebud to Sorrento and Portsea. On Australia Day we would go up to Healesville, which was a real tourist haunt for Melbourne people. We used to set up in the local park and Gene would demonstrate how to throw the boomerang and we would sell the boomerangs for three pounds ten. Sometimes we would go to Dandenong. I remember one day we stopped for a feed at a fish and chip shop on the main street in Dandenong and Gene started talking to the Greek proprietor.

'Ya ever seen one a these, mate?' he asked, holding up one of our boomerangs.

'Sure I seen one, but I never seen one come back.'

'Then you've never seen a boomerang thrown properly, mate.'

'I don't believe you can make it come back.'

The boomerang Gene had in his hand was the finest weapon I've ever seen. It was his demonstration model and not for sale. It was made of blackwood and as long as a man's arm. It's very rare that you find a root exactly the right shape to make such a beautiful thrower. Gene could throw it so it just skimmed along about six feet off the ground and came arching back to him, making the most eerie humming sound as it spun around.

'Care to wager?' asked Gene with a wide grin on his face. He shot a glance at me and I was grinning, too.

The Greek began to grin, as well. 'Tell you what I'm gonna do. If you can make that thing come back, I'll buy it from ya and I won't charge ya for the meal.'

'Done.'

The Greek wiped his hands off on his apron, took it off, stepped from behind the counter and we all went outside. Now, Dandenong back in the mid-fifties was like a country town with wide cobbled streets which were mainly empty. Gene stood in the middle of the main street and threw that boomerang with all the strength and skill he had. It made a deep hum as it left his hand, flattened out, made a beautiful arch about thirty yards out and came spinning back to land right at Gene's feet.

The Greek was astonished. He gave out a holler, but instead of turning to Gene to congratulate him, he yelled at him.

'I never woulda believed it! That coulda bloody killed somebody! What you throw it out here for? Bloody dangerous! You bloody fool! Get outta here!'

'What about our wager?' asked Gene.

'Get outta here! Ya can't trust a boong. No way! Get out!'

It's not the first or the last time I've seen blackfellas treated like that in public, but I've never forgotten that incident. It made me angrier than usual. I truly admired Gene for having the skill to throw that boomerang like a champion, but the Greek took it all wrong and didn't notice anything but a black man threatening him. Or maybe not. Maybe that Greek was scared of a black man looking like he was better than anyone else. After all, what was a Greek in the 1950s but a fish and chip man? Who else did he have to yell at?

He didn't even notice me. Since I was with a blackfella I was invisible, not worth thinking about. But he turned on Gene. The cheek of him made me clench my hands into fists ready for anything. However, Gene was not about to pick a fight in the middle of Dandenong. We took off, and at least got away with a free meal. The Greek was still yelling at us as we rounded the corner to the van.

The place where we sold most of our boomerangs and baskets was back at Lake Tyers – well, Metung, actually, that beautiful little town in the middle of the Gippsland Lakes. Back in the fifties, people used to take excursions from the city to the Aboriginal missions to view the life of the blackfella. They would stay at Lake Tyers House and come on to the mission from there to visit the church, watch demonstrations of boomerang throwing, and buy baskets, spears and things. They would watch people going about their business at the mission, sometimes viewing schoolchildren at their lessons. They would entertain themselves by getting the children to dive into the lake for coins. The blackfellas tolerated being on show like that because a bit of pocket money from selling handicrafts was useful, but they told me themselves that they resented it.

A wonderful woman named Cora Gilsener, who was a champion of the blackfellas and helped them through many a bad time when they were faced with eviction or going to court or any such thing, had a property at Metung. She would get the blackfellas from the mission to come to her farm to entertain the boatloads of tourists from Lakes Entrance who went there for a sing-song and a barbecue each weekend. She, and the blackfellas who worked with her, thought it was more dignified for tourists to see them in a spot of their choosing rather than stickybeaking around their houses at the mission station.

We used to sell our boomerangs at Gilseners' farm rather than going to the mission. The Lake Tyers Gum Leaf Band would be there to play. There were about ten fellows in the band, each with a pocket full of gumleaves which they would hold up to their lips and manage to somehow make a high-pitched singing note with. They could play anything on the gumleaves, with all sorts of harmonies, while one of them pounded a big bass drum to keep the beat. It was a marvellous thing. One fellow named Jamesie Scott was the star of the show. He had a beautiful singing voice and led everybody in the singing of hymns. The blackfellas loved to sing hymns. Jamesie was a mission fellow but he had knowledge of the old ways and was deeply respected as an elder. He used to demonstrate how to light a fire with sticks while Gene demonstrated boomerang throwing and others showed off their handicrafts. I usually kept out of the way since it wasn't a whitefella any of these tourists came to see.

There would be singing, dancing, storytelling and demonstrations to keep the tourists happy while they ate their barbecue. When they finally left, each carrying one of our boomerangs or Effie's baskets, if we had our way, more wood would be thrown on the fire and the blackfellas would settle in for a night of more singing, dancing and storytelling. Finally, in the small hours of the morning, we would roll up in our blankets and sleep all together near the fire.

I used to love those nights on the lake. I was the only whitefella amongst them, but it never bothered anyone. Now, blackfellas can be as racist as whitefellas when they are talking amongst themselves, but their racism was never directed at me, or Harry for that matter. It was well known by the blackfellas throughout Gippsland that the Tonkin brothers were fair, but, in my particular case, they also knew that

I was a faithful partner and good provider for Euphie and my family. I guess the main reason I was accepted, however, was that I could mix with people without ever trying to tell them what to do. I never growled at these boys and I never tried to change them into white-fellas. I was no missionary.

I had no sense of class. I took each man at face value and assumed he was a good man until he proved to be otherwise. I listened respectfully to their stories and showed real interest in knowing these fellows. I suppose they weren't used to that from a whitefella and property owner. They were pleased to know that I had made some of the boomerangs, that I had taken the time to learn one of their skills and that I didn't do too badly at it. They called me a white blackfella. I was proud of that title.

A Notorious Place

JACKSON'S TRACK was a community of different types of people from many backgrounds. Some were orphans, some had been forcibly taken from their mothers, some had lived nowhere but on missions, some had been brought up camped on rivers outside of towns, some had been in jail and some ought to have been in jail. Some were real barefoot bushmen, some were workers, some were hunters and trappers, some were craftsmen and some were lazy. Some were drunks, some were teetotallers, some were gamblers and some were religious. Some were kind, some were responsible, some were selfish, some were larrikins, some were proud, some were cunning, some were

Some Mullett, Rose, Moffat, Coombes and Pepper kids

gentle and innocent as lambs and some were mean as snakes.

All of them had respect for the law, the blackfella law of tolerance and respect. So the community at Jackson's Track was generally a peaceful community where there was a sense of caring and a sense of order, where the elders, like Jackie Coombes and Wagga Cooper, but especially Stewart Hood, kept the law and were respected.

The way the blackfellas arranged their lives did not always fit with the white man's values. Their idea of work was not always in terms of paid work. There were about a dozen men living on the Track who never worked for money at all. They spent their time hunting through the bush. They were experts at snaring and trapping game and thus meat was plentiful and free to any of the woodcutters. The dogs were well fed, too. These men were an important part of the community. They were respected and welcomed anywhere.

In terms of whitefellas' idea of right and wrong, and if she had wanted to, Mavis could have found plenty to gossip about in town, but she never ventured near the blackfellas' camps, lucky for them. I remember two good mates who worked together on the firewood and lived in the same bark hut. The unusual part about this was that they both loved the same woman and all three of them slept in the same bed together. The two men looked after that woman and she cooked and kept camp for them. They seemed to be as happy as Larry with no sign of jealousy between them.

If there was going to be trouble on the Track, it often had to do with jealousy. Chook Mullett was my best working partner. He and I often found ourselves alone in some part of the forest working on a tree. We entertained each other with stories and gossip and jokes while we worked. Chook would confide in me about his wife and we would discuss the problems of understanding women in general. One day he told me that his wife, Nora, had left him for Bob Cockrane.

'I want her back. I want her back so bad.'

'Why do you reckon she left with Bob?'

'She's lonely. She doesn't have enough to do in the day.'

'She needs company.'

'I'm gonna go find her, Daryl. I'm gonna bring her back.'

'How are you going to keep her here?'

'How 'bout if I stop with you for a while so she can be with Euphie and Effie and have company?'

Now, a man asks for help in that way, it's not my nature to turn him down. If he wants to stop with me, I'm glad to have him, especially if it's an honest bloke like Chook.

'That'll be all right, Chook.'

He disappeared for two days, then arrived at our camp with Nora and settled in. We thought the world of Nora and we thought the two of them looked pretty happy together, but about a week later, I was driving along the road with Chook when he suddenly shouted at me.

'Pull up! Pull up!'

'What's the matter?'

'There's that mongrel!'

He jumped out of the van and took off across the paddocks for Bob Cockrane. Bob saw him and ran for his life. He was too fast for Chook and got away. I saw Chook stop and stamp his foot and raise his fist in anger, probably calling out something awful, but I couldn't hear him.

He came back to the van looking pretty upset because he knew as long as Bob was around, he had plenty to worry about. Sure enough, about a week after that, Nora disappeared. Chook moped around our camp for about a month and then one day he went walkabout. I never worked with him again.

We only had a few woodcutters who were bad and dangerous, but they had wives and children so we put up with them. Connie Coombes was down from Cumeroogunja in New South Wales. He must have been related to old Jackie somehow, but neither of them acknowledged the relationship. You couldn't find two more different men. Connie was a surly fellow who was touched by drink. Since no one liked him, he and his family lived off on their own. Everyone looked down on Connie because they knew he ill-treated his wife, Rita, but as long as she stayed with him, he was protected. Since he was an evil man, dangerous and unpredictable, they bided their time and waited for him to make a mistake.

One night he went too far and laid into Rita so badly she had to be taken to hospital where the police wanted her to charge him. This became a complicated issue for the poor battered woman. She knew the police were always on the lookout for any excuse to go into the community at the Track and throw the weight of their authority around. After all, a colony of blackfellas living independently made it a notorious place. She knew that if the people at the Track were united on one issue it was their hatred of the police. She wisely refused to lay charges against Connie.

When she returned to the Track, Rita moved to her relatives' camp with her three children, leaving Connie alone with his bad thoughts. Once he was alone, the others in the camp knew how to take care of him. Blackfellas will tolerate just about anybody in their midst. They put bad behaviour down to nature and don't take a set against wrongdoers, but they don't let incidents go unpunished either. It wasn't long before Connie Coombes took off and never came back.

Jackie Kennedy was another who was trouble the whole time he was here, but he had a wonderful wife named Anabelle who we all had lots of time for, so we kept him on. He could tell a good yarn and he laughed a hearty laugh, but he could suddenly turn mean and then you got out of his way. He was not right in the head.

Jackie was not a good provider for his family. He would wander around the different camps bragging about how powerful and dangerous he was; he would skite about his skill with an axe and challenge anybody to try to chop better than he could, but he rarely worked for a whole day and his stack of cut wood at the end of the week was always too small to give him a living wage. Anabelle and the kids were half starved.

It was after I saw his infant drinking weak black tea out of a tittie bottle to stave off hunger that I began dropping into Jackie's camp to pass the time with Anabelle. I had a lot of respect for her. She had a little girl about four years old, a small baby and she was pregnant again. So I wanted to quietly keep an eye on her. I wasn't a stickybeak and I didn't go around reporting what I saw in that camp. I knew the others were aware of Anabelle's plight and were looking after her somewhat, but I just wanted her to feel comfortable enough to come to us for help if she ever needed it. We've always helped the blackfellas out if they've run short of things. In the old days, Dora used to send the kids up to the main house for flour or sugar if she needed it. It was always paid back eventually in all sorts of ways.

Jackie made everybody mad, always attempting to find out other people's business, trying to steal wood from others' stacks, always huffing and puffing and yelling at people, bullying them if he could. He was a big bloke and when he got worked up his big staring eyes would go red and he'd look as mad as a mallee bull. People stayed away from him.

One day, when she was heavily pregnant, Anabelle had had enough and she was forced to come to our camp for some food. She came in and sat down at the table near the fire and Euphie was handing over a cup of tea to comfort her when in walked Jackie as bold as could be. He went straight for Anabelle and threw her off the chair and began to kick her, going crook at her in his bellowing voice.

'Ya stupid black bitch. Walk out on me, will ya?'

For Jackie, coming into my camp was a huge mistake. He wouldn't have dared come in if he had known I was there, which he didn't, but there I was, standing in the corner, astonished beyond belief to see him in my hut. There is nothing more despicable in my mind than a man who will attack a woman. I pushed my way between him and Anabelle and breasted him out of the way. He was shocked. I stood up to him real close.

'Get out.'

He took two steps back. Surprised. Then came in again.

'That's my woman.'

I stepped into him.

'Get out,' I said right into his face.

He backed out, but when he got outside he stood his ground and started bellowing like a wounded bull.

'Come out here, ya coward. Come out here and fight me if you dare. I'll fix you!'

I stood in the doorway looking at him. I've never ever had a row with any of my blackfellas before and I certainly never fought one.

'Come out and fight like a man!' he shouted, almost like a curse. Then he put his two hands to the front of this silk shirt I remember he had on and ripped it off his body. He thumped his chest. 'Come and fight me!'

Now, I'm nowhere near as big as Jackie Kennedy, but I could hear his wife wailing behind me, the kids crying, Euphie trying to hush them and I saw red. My hands formed into fists and I stepped outside and took a fighter's stance directly in front of that big oaf.

'Yer on,' is all I said.

As soon as Jackie saw that I was ready to do battle, his bulging red eyes suddenly glazed over, his dripping face went slack and he began to back away. Suddenly he turned and ran. I stood there, my body tense, my hands up, and watched all this with amazement. My mouth dropped open, my hands fell to my sides and, although my heart was still racing, I relaxed and began to laugh. I could still hear him crashing wildly through the bush in flight as I turned back into the hut to comfort the women and children.

About a week later, Jackie found himself cornered by some of the fellows and he couldn't turn and run away. He had to face his assailants, who'd had enough of his bullying. After his conflict with me, I guess he thought he had to save face, so he spent a great deal of his time attacking anyone who was harmless, trying to frighten them about how much damage he would do to them.

'Just try me!' he'd skite.

Finally this tactic backfired on him. He made the mistake of cheeking three woodcutters as they walked past his camp, and this played into their hands. They attacked him no more than a hundred yards from his camp. They did him some damage, too. I remember seeing him in a bad way at his camp later on. They had rubbed his face in the dirt and this left him blinded for two weeks, but they hadn't done him any permanent harm. They were just trying to mete out justice as they saw it. They seemed to know the difference between real justice and unfair justice.

Jackie had the sting taken out of him for a while, but he knew people at Jackson's Track would get him if he acted up again and that he had to watch out for himself. His relationship with Anabelle changed, too, so he was never able to bluff her the way he had. Finally she found strength to leave him and he knew his time was up.

He packed his swag and pleased everybody by leaving. About twelve months later, we heard that he was up on a murder charge, having killed a man with an axe.

There were other people, white people, who lived and worked around Jackson's Track who could outdo Jackie Kennedy for villainy. Two other mills operated near our property and employed some of our blackfellas. One was the Wentworths'; they put in a saw mill and about twelve months later a mean drinking man named Ivan O'Shanessy put in a paling mill at one end of our property. He would drink on weekends with the other mill workers, and always end up in some kind of brawl.

You never see a true-blue fight these days; a few punches and it's all over. Back in the old days blokes like Ivan O'Shanessy used to go hammer and tongs all day long. His fights used to begin as proper fist fights but end up as nothing more than a couple of men rolling around in the mud, stopping now and then for a drink. Finally one man would give up, or they'd both be out cold, and only then would they call it a day.

One weekend, O'Shanessy got so drunk and so mad that he hauled out his gun on a dare and shot Bill Regnier dead. Now, nothing like that ever happened among my mob of blackfellas. Of course, O'Shanessy was arrested for murder. He was out on bail awaiting a trial when he went and drowned himself in a dam out on his brother's property.

It was a notorious place all right.

Police

I'M NOT SURE if people in the white community knew about Jackie Kennedy, but of course word about Connie Coombes and Rita spread like wildfire. There was one other bad bloke that I can remember, by the name of Foxy McGee. He was so gone on alcohol that he was drinking metho in the end. He was a worthless, surly bloke who didn't last long at the Track. We never fired him, but he was too mean-spirited to be part of any community. That was only three bad apples out of the whole bunch of hundreds who came and went over the years.

Nevertheless, it was assumed that drunkenness and violence was the order of the day out on the Track. To be honest, drinking was not a general thing in our community. The women hated it and the men were too busy to waste their time getting drunk. Once in a blue moon tempers would flare and it often was when somebody had had too much to drink. My trusted friend Willie Marks used to drink on a weekend, but he was never violent. He was a crying drunk and needed a bit of pacifying. One day he did stumble into our camp with a huge cut across his forehead near his temple after someone whacked him with a lantern, probably to stop him from being a nuisance. We couldn't get boo out of him to find out what really happened. Incidents at the Track were rare, which is probably why I remember them so clearly. It was a peaceful, industrious and honest community.

But the police accused us of harbouring criminals just the same. On weekends some of the woodcutters would go into Drouin for entertainment and a bit of a drink, just like any worker would do. Gene often went in with Bob Nelson and Jack Patton. Since these two blokes had been soldiers in the war, they weren't shy about mixing with white folks in the Drouin pub, but the police thought they had a kind of swagger about them that they didn't like one bit. They put a curfew on all blackfellas, saying they had to be out of town by six o'clock or they'd land in jail. What a terrible thing to do. Now, that's a case of unfair justice. Instead of putting them in jail, however, more often than not they would drag any lingerers down a back lane and let them have it before they put them on the road home. One man in particular who seemed to enjoy doing over the blackfellas was called Up-the-Lane Jack by the people at the Track.

'Keep clear of Up-the-Lane Jack!' Effie would call out as Gene and the boys headed towards town.

If ever anything of a criminal nature happened in Drouin, before you could blink the police would be out at the Track questioning anybody and everybody. They came out here first, no question. Blacks were all criminals to the police. As soon as they saw a black face, that was it. The police in Drouin gave our community a bad name. They would have liked to get rid of the lot of them. The black-fellas were scared of them because the laws kept changing with each situation. There seemed to be no fixed or equal law for everybody. In the blackfella's mind, the only thing unchanging since white man came in contact with blacks was that the police were out to get them. They had a terror of being sent to French Island out in the middle of Westernport Bay and being left to rot regardless of the nature of the wrongdoing or regardless of the truth of their guilt. I only know one fellow who was ever sent there, but it was a terror that loomed large in the minds of the people.

We did have one thief in our midst, a known thief who was in and out of jail. Edgar Green was well liked for his brightness and was always good for a laugh, but he was a born thief. It was his game, like a sport. There was never a hint of violence about him; he was fright-ened of his own shadow and everything that moved in the bush. It never would have occurred to him to try armed robbery. No, he was just light-fingered; an honest thief I called him since he never meant any harm. He couldn't help himself and he took his punishment in good faith, never hid behind the law like a lot of legal thieves.

He used to play with the police, seemed to love having them chase him. One evening, I was passing the time at Stewart's camp when Edgar came in carrying a wireless which he had playing at full volume. He was laughing and proceeded to dance around all of us to the beat of the music.

'Where'd ya get that thing?' asked Stewart.

'Found it,' was Edgar's cheeky answer.

'Fell off the back of a truck, more like.'

'Nice, isn't it?' he said as he turned it back and forth, pretending to admire it.

'You take care, boy,' said Dora. 'The police'll be after you.'

'They're on their way now,' said Stewart, looking across at Jackson's Track where a cloud of dust was moving through the trees towards us along the roadway.

'Yahoo!' shouted Edgar and he took off.

Now, there was one detective who was always the first one out at the Track. He seemed to like hunting blackfellas, liked to stir them up. He pulled up to Stewart's camp and got out of the car.

'Any of you seen Edgar Green?'

No one answered him, but we were having a hard time keeping straight faces because Edgar hadn't turned the wireless off and you could hear it plain as day. Every once in a while, Edgar would let out a yelp as if he were teasing the detective to come and get him. The detective stood there, with two uniformed police behind him, look-ing at us one at a time, looking as mean as he could, not quite understanding the queer expressions on our faces. Suddenly the detective cocked his head and we could tell he was beginning to lis-ten, that he had heard the wireless and was beginning to realise what it was. He looked back at us. We were all grinning by then.

'Come on, boys!' he yelled and he took off after the sound.

But Edgar was hard to catch in the scrub. We sat there listening and laughing for about half an hour as the sound of the pop music coming out of the wireless moved back and forth through the scrub, with shouts of the police coming from every place except where Edgar was. Finally everything went quiet and we thought Edgar must have been caught, but the police came straggling out of the scrub with no Edgar in sight.

The detective came and stood himself in front of us as if he were getting ready to threaten us or lecture us. He took one look and must have thought better of saying anything. He let out a big sigh and left in disgust. Pretty soon Edgar returned with a grin on his face. It was quite a joke Edgar played, but in the end it probably did him and all the blackfellas on the Track more harm than good since the police had gone away angry, knowing they'd been made to look like fools. Edgar ended up being picked up eventually.

Most of the fellows didn't like spending too much time in town because they were shy of the whitefellas. To my mind whites cannot tolerate difference and blacks were considered different. So the men spent the weekends at the Track. One of the men never worked but was a good talker and organiser and well liked by everyone. Every Friday night he held card games at his camp. He made the players chip in for costs: he took money for supplying drinks, his wife was paid for cooking up meals for the gamblers, and he hired one of the fellows to keep the fire stoked all night. The boys who played were mostly woodcutters because they had some money. They played all night. They were mostly quiet, but at the end of each hand you could hear them through the bush discussing the play and then it would get quiet again. There was a rhythm to it. There were never any fights that I knew of.

Jackson's Track was a community, just like other communities. It was the police who made people think it was a notorious place.

School

THE COMMUNITY OF BLACKFELLAS at the Track grew to well over a hundred people at times, but usually stayed around one hundred and fifty. Euphie and I were adding to the population. We had Sandra in 1953 and Russell, who we always called Snag, in 1955. Even though we lived out off the property, our children always had plenty of company and were spoiled like all the other children at the Track. They hung out at Dora's camp whenever they could since she was so fond of children. Or along with all the children they would wander over to Jamby Wilson's camp where Adelaide would spoil them with too much love.

There were about fifty children all up, but it's hard to remember

Some of the children from the Mullett and Rose families

all their names. Roy and Gina Rose had three kids by the mid-1950s; we had four of our own as well as Dot, who always lived with us, and the two boys, Gary and Buddy, at Dora's; there were a fair few Austins: Willie, Murray, Lena, Ricky. Stewart's son Collin had two kids. At Stewart's camp, Dora was always looking after a mob: there was Ruben and Jewel, getting pretty old by then, as well as the Harrison children: Eileen, Daphne and Axel. The five Marks girls who had come down from Dimboola where Willie was originally from stopped with Dora since they had no mother. All the children were well looked after and never excluded from the activities around the camps.

Sometimes the older kids would wander out with their laughter and antics to our work, staying just out of our reach, romping like puppy dogs, until we told them to scat because a tree was coming down; then they'd scurry to stand behind one of us where it was safe. They always did what they were told. Once the tree was down, they'd swarm all over it as if it were a jungle gym in a playground. If there was a nest in some of the branches they'd pounce on it and lift it from its mooring as if it were a lost treasure, all surrounding the one who got to it first, reaching out to feel for eggs, touching the downy lining in the heart of the nest. Laughing and chattering. They loved to be involved in the barking process and often someone would allow the bigger boys to have a go at tearing bark away. Of course, they all waited eagerly to get at the sticky resin on the freshly barked wood.

I liked having the kids around. They were good, lively company. I didn't mind walking along with them. That's how they learned, and they always did what they were told.

When they weren't hunting, the men of the camp played with the children, teaching them how to make snares and traps, making up games which gave the kids hunting skills. Les Monta was an excellent teacher for the kids. He knew how to make a wombat snare out of a long bent stick which was somehow designed to snap up when the wombat came too close and hang the poor animal upside down. He showed the kids what to do and where to set the traps, since he had a sort of sixth sense where to put them. It is not hard to imagine the kids' delight when the snares Les helped them set actually caught a wombat. He and the others taught the kids how to make fish traps out of wire and mesh. The kids loved helping the men with their hunting and would play at it all day.

Dave Moore used to take them for long walks in the bush, pointing things out to them, telling them tall stories. I can see them now, Dave tall amongst the kids, with them swarming here and there as he pointed towards one thing and another. They had an idea how to make boomerangs from watching their parents, especially Gene and me, but Dave helped them find roots and let them have a go at making their own. He spent time teaching them how to throw the weapons. Dave was a true teacher. The kids loved his stories, and he loved the kids.

The kids were getting plenty of education, but they weren't going to school. In the mid-1950s, whitefella preachers used to come to the camps – looking for converts, I suppose. They made friends with Siddy and Margaret Austin and convinced them that the kids on the Track should go to school. The Austins had no schooling, but they wanted their kids to learn to read and write. Recently, Dot said she remembers an official-looking man coming into Stewart's camp one day when Euphie was there visiting. The man told the women, Dora, Euphie and Gina, to get the kids to school. If that's true, then I reckon the preachers dobbed the blackfellas in. Nevertheless, this was one idea from the whitefellas that many of us took notice of.

Although I had never been much of a student myself, always wanting to be out with the animals and nature rather than sitting cramped up in a schoolroom, I thought it was time Mac and Curly began school so they could get along in a whitefella world later if they needed to. Euphie agreed, but she was not ready to send Dot, who didn't end up starting until she was ten years old, although she did want Dot to learn to read and write and add up. Maybe she wanted to see how the other kids got along first. The Roses wanted to send their kids. For all the parents who wanted their children to go to school, there were many who would have nothing to do with it. Stewart and Dora didn't think much of the idea and never sent any of the mob of kids stopping with them. So, Euphie's boys, Gary and Buddy, never learned to read and write. The blackfellas who had come down from Dimboola had no room in their souls to trust whitefellas and wouldn't send their kids to whitefella school. Never.

Some kids went anyway just to be part of the excitement. Euphie and Gina Rose took it upon themselves to walk the three miles over to the school to enrol the kids. That was a brave effort from those two women because, as I recall, none of the adults ever wanted to have anything to do with the school, never wanted to speak to teachers at all. They were shy of them. They kept away from people outside the Track in general. Once the kids were enrolled and had started the daily trek to school, Jimmy Bond began walking with them every day, but he always left them in the morning and met them at night some distance from the school.

No one took them to school that first day; they just went. I believe they knew the neighbours' kids went off to school each morning and wanted to follow them. And that is what they did, followed them right into the little one-room building called the Labertouche school. It was a fairly easy three-mile walk in those days because there were no fences to speak of to get in the way, but I remember Jimmy would end up carrying the littlest ones home after school on his back the last mile or so since they were just about asleep on their feet. My daughter Curly remembers the kids often rode one of my old Clydesdales, the one we called Fat Horse, to school. He was so big and so gentle four or five of them could get up on his back at a time. The prospect of riding Fat Horse made it an exciting adventure for some of the kids to go to school.

Now, I was the only one on the Track who really had any idea what it would be like at a proper whitefella's school and I thought the kids were in for a shock, but I knew they had to survive it and learn to read and write for their own wellbeing in the future. I knew that aside from the three R's, what students really learn at a white man's school is to be a silly fool because they are taught to be greedy, to try to be better than others and to be dishonest by cheating. I knew that our kids would learn by having whitefella values drummed into them with the strap and with humiliation. I knew our kids had never been faced with such discipline before. I knew they didn't understand about the whitefellas' sense of rules and punishment.

The blackfella way of teaching is by warning and experience rather than discipline. The kids in our camps were indulged absolutely, and never, never given a hiding, although sometimes experience was allowed to be a cruel teacher. I remember one day I raised a hand at Mac, and Euphie went mad. She turned from the fire where she had been scratching at the coals getting ready to cook some damper and screeched.

'What are you doing?'

'This boy needs a hiding,' I said.

'What? A hiding! I'll give you a hiding before I see you hit one of my kids!'

'He's my boy and he needs to be taught a lesson he'll never forget, woman.'

'Don't you woman me, Daryl Tonkin,' she yelled in full voice.

She looked around for something to threaten me with, a lump of wood, perhaps, but nearest to hand was the small axe we keep next to the fire for kindling. She grabbed that, raised it over her head and came at me with the expression of a demon on her face. Mac twisted away from me and raced off. Euphie came around the table and I took off, too. She chased me out the door, curses coming thick and fast out of her mouth. I couldn't repeat anything she said, it was that harsh. She had a powerful temper, all right, but it was usually for a reason.

I never again tried punishing any of the kids with a hiding.

Kids were taught by example to respect their elders and their relations and to care for one another. They were rewarded for good deeds rather than punished for bad ones. They learned above all to be honest, that it's low to be a liar and to be someone who is untrustworthy.

I thought that our kids would have teachers who would yell at them. I couldn't imagine our lively, squirming mob being able to tolerate being told to 'Sit down at the desk and wait for the bell!' My own experience at school told me that teachers loved to give you a crack over the knuckles if you didn't mind out.

But these kids were lucky. When they began at Labertouche school, there was a wonderful teacher there named Ryan, whom they all loved. He must have had a knack with kids and a generosity of spirit because our kids kept wanting to go back to him day after day. My belief is they liked him because he liked them. Generally, I think, our kids got on well with the teachers.

Of course, our laughing, energetic, dancing kids soon met with name calling from the other kids out in the playground and that would take the light out of their eyes. I knew this would happen, but I also knew that every kid is good at name calling, that it's natural. At home when my kids would ask questions, I wasn't upset and knew how to back them up.

'Dad, what's an Abo? They're calling us Abo.'

'It's nothing. Being called Abo is nothing.'

'What's an Abo?'

'That's what you are. You're an Aborigine, another word for blackfella.'

'But they laugh at us.'

'It's nothing. Be proud of what you are. But if they laugh at you, stand up for yourself.'

'Fight?'

'It's better to have a fight and get over it than call each other names.'

And so I taught my kids to stand up for themselves. I taught them to be patient and decent and tolerant, but that if anyone ever called them 'nigger', they could do as they liked.

My kids were lucky, I guess because I was there to set them straight about all the shocking things they were coming up against at school. So they kept returning day after day. Others weren't so lucky because their parents were as confused about it as they were. I remember Lionel Rose went to school for one day at Labertouche and played the wag from then on. In fact for several of the kids, going to school and being there were two different things, but even though truant inspectors were lurking about in those days, our kids were never caught.

My kids continued at school and they got good marks, too, better than their old man. Euphie finally sent Dot to school and she did very well. She had the neatest handwriting out of all of us! At night she would sit at the table in the room lit by the big Tilley lamp and do the most beautiful work to take to school the next day. Before we were finished, Euphie and I had nine children, and each one of them went to school and high school. I was proud of all our kids.

The Mill

ABOUT THE TIME our fifth child, Linda, was born, which would have been 1957, I met Harry in the forest and he told me Mavis had left. Well, didn't that surprise me! I thought she'd be the one to outstay us all just for spite so she could take over the place, but when Harry said she had gone to live with our mother in Melbourne, I wondered what she was up to. Our mother had recently been widowed and wasn't faring too well on her own. I thought Mavis had her mind set on the estate and wanted to be close by to keep her eyes on things so she could grab the lot. I have to admit, where Mavis was concerned, I had learned to have little generosity in my heart.

I suppose I should have felt free to go up to the main house now,

Euphie and Russell

whenever I wanted to, that I should be able go in and talk things over with Harry in front of the fire in the main room, but I couldn't bring myself to go there. It still seemed more comfortable meeting Harry on common ground in the bush where we were equal and the past did not hang over us. Harry had never been to my camp, never acknowledged my family, although I am sure he knew all about the kids and could identify them when he saw them. If he still couldn't bring himself to go to my camp, I couldn't bring myself to go to his, even though the spectre of Mavis was gone.

But a kind of quiet tension did lift from the whole property. I had an impression that Harry had had some sort of final row with her, and she had left for that reason. I never found out, but I began to come across Harry in the bush more often, and there was a lightness in our greetings that hadn't been there for years. We discussed our businesses with each other, made suggestions for improvement, told stories about incidents which might have happened. We never met for long, but I felt a kind of satisfaction in it.

One day, Harry came and found me while I was in the middle of putting a scarf in a tree. Ruben Wilson was there leaning on the saw, waiting for me to finish. When he saw Harry, he greeted him, then laid the saw across a fallen log and moved away to leave us alone. It was not usual for Harry to seek me out, so I stopped my work, dropped the head of the axe next to my foot and leaned on the handle.

'G'day, Harry.'

He put his hand on the tree I was about to cut, looked over the line of the intended fall, looked up at the lean of the tree and nodded to himself. I took all that in and thought he will always be my older brother, checking up just for good measure. Then he looked at me.

'Daryl, I've got a proposition for you.'

Immediately my guard went up.

'This have anything to do with Mavis?' I asked.

'Well, yes, but I think it'll suit you.'

'Go on,' I said warily.

'Mavis has come across a place in Seaford–Carrum that would be perfect for a timber yard. She and I talked it over and it makes sense that we start our own timber and firewood business. She can handle the books. I will control the business of the timber in the yard. And, well, we've had a row over this, but I want you to take over the mill and supply the timber for us.'

I looked at him. He was asking me to go into business with him. After all these years! I was immediately excited about the idea, but I slowed down my responses and remained guarded.

'Why would you want to leave here?'

'I don't really want to leave here, but I can see this is a good opportunity.'

I knew Harry could never pass up what he saw was an opportunity and that he loved setting up new works. I was satisfied with that answer.

'How did you manage to get the timber yard?'

'Mavis has borrowed some money from Mother.'

I didn't like that idea, but I kept quiet. Harry kept speaking. I could see he loved the whole thing.

'She and Mother have sold the house in Essendon and they've found one to buy in Seaford, with money to put down on the timber yard.'

Like Harry, I could see that the whole thing was a good idea, but I felt uncomfortable because I knew Mavis was too shrewd for the both of us, that as far as money was concerned she would manage to get the lion's share. I wasn't really interested in money myself, but the idea that Mavis thought I didn't deserve any used to goad me and make me want to foil her although I had none of her shrewdness. But in the eyes of our family, now that Father was gone, I thought she was probably right about my not deserving anything. That thought always stopped me in my tracks. Since I had let the family down so badly, especially since I had been a disappointment to Harry, I had no right to question their decisions. If Harry was asking me to go into business with him, then I should accept and help him out.

Next, Harry said something which made my heart soar.

'You and your family should move into the main house.'

Now, that may sound like just an ordinary, practical thing to say, but to me it was like a song of rejoicing or a hymn or a prayer or an announcement of triumph. By saying 'you and your family' Harry was making peace, letting me know that the future could only get better, declaring that we were brothers again. I put out my hand to Harry and we shook hard, looking each other in the eye.

'I'll accept your offer to work the mill, but I would rather move Euphie and the kids into the big mill house. You keep the main house. You might be back one day.'

'It's your choice, Daryl.'

'That way I'll be on hand at the mill regularly,' I continued.

'Done. As soon as you're organised, I'll make my move down to the yard.'

We shook hands again and he was off. I turned back to my work and Ruben quietly slid into view, picked up the saw and resumed his position. It was as if nothing had changed, but it had. Something had taken a great leap forward and my mind and heart were full to brimming. I wondered if Harry had any idea what a change his few words had made.

The real reason I wanted to live in the mill house was that it was in the bush, while the main house was now standing in about three hundred acres of cleared land. Once I began living with Euphie, I had lost all interest in Harry's vision of clearing the land and eventually becoming a farmer. To be sure, I had helped him with the clearing at first, but after our row, I left off clearing forever. I became a bushman, a man of the forest. I loved the beauty of it. Even though my work was taking down trees, the forest was not being thinned out for I was taking one tree at a time, working along the contours of the land, letting the creeks and big trees determine where I went and how I logged.

All of our cut trees were being replaced by thousands of saplings whose seeds had been germinated by the '39 fire. A fire is good for a forest; the seeds cannot germinate without hot ashes to cover them. In the old days, the blackfellas who lived in the bush looked after the animals and birds by burning the bush for them. If the bush is not burnt, native grass and scrub grows too hard for the animals and makes them sickly. After the bush is burnt all the insects, grubs and everything that crawls thrive. Plants that have been dormant for years will grow after the fire. The bush then has good feed for five years, when it should be burnt again. Those young trees from the '39 fire were getting on to twenty years old by now. They were tall and beautiful. The forest seemed no less fresh and wild than it had a generation ago.

Living and working in the forest was more important to me than making money. From the time I met Euphie, all I wanted was a living, not a fortune. I was never a hungry man who charged more than I needed for my work. I trusted people to pay and never chased a bad debt. The only debt I ever ran up myself was at the Jindivick store where we bought all of our supplies, including horse feed and kerosene, and where the blackfellas could put anything they might need on my tab. At one point I remember the tab crept up to two thousand pounds, but I always paid it off. Yes, the Jindivick store kept us poor, but we never worried about that. It was life we loved, life in the forest.

Euphie was pleased to be moving into the big mill house. Our camp on Wattle Creek, although it was the best camp I ever made, was getting too small with all our children. The new house was made of weatherboard, had a tin roof, three bedrooms off the main room and a six-foot fireplace you could practically sit in. It was surrounded by a picket fence to protect a vegetable garden right outside the front of the house, with a little concrete path running through it to the door. To Euphie's delight, it had a washhouse and a toilet. There was also a water tank which gathered water off the tin roof, something you have to do without when you've got a bark roof. The water in the tank supplemented the running water in Gipsy Creek, which ran right by us.

Our new house was part of a compound of houses built near the mill for Harry's workers. There was another house right next to ours, with the washhouse in between. These each had outhouses or sleep-outs where a single man could sleep and keep his belongings. Close by were two more huts made of palings with paling roofs that were very steep. Four more houses were down the other end of the mill about a hundred yards away. We had never lived so close to other houses before, but the forest was thick so we could only see bits of the houses and yards peeking out from the trees.

When we first shifted there, Dave Moore came with us and moved into one of the outhouses. Jimmy Bond was already living in one of the mill houses, always had, but all the rest of my workers remained in their own camps on Wattle Creek. The other houses were occupied by a new team of men from Powelltown I'd hired to work the mill with me. They were all whitefellas and, except for Carl, my main sawyer, they only lasted about three months with me before I decided I liked working with my own men better.

Carl was an excellent worker but he was a heavy drinker – drank wine all day long every day. He never seemed to be drunk, which was odd to me, and he never made a mistake at the mill; just kept working and drinking. He was a character. I remember he had a new ute that he was proud of and he used to drive it all over the countryside, running here and there. The repossessors would regularly come to the property looking for Carl because he hadn't made his payments for the ute, which was getting pretty battered by then. I paid a cheque to them every month since he was such a good worker and I wanted to keep him on. Finally they saw him one day on the road, chased him and caught him. They threw him out of the ute onto the road and drove off in his car, leaving him to find his own way home.

Carl stayed on for a while. After the whitefellas departed, I put Jimmy and Willie Marks on the mill with me. The others had learned enough about falling trees by now to do it unsupervised. I would go out and mark the trees they were to fall that week and leave it to them. They would fall them, top and bark them, then leave them where they lay. On the weekends I would pull them into the mill yard ready for the week's milling. Because I was short for time, I realised I had to give up using my beloved horses for snigging and begin pulling the logs in with a Ford Blitz, an army four-wheel drive with a winch on the back. It was very quick, quicker than the horses, but I felt bad about it. I knew that by turning my back on the horses I had let something change which could never be recovered. I guess what changed was a set of values. Somehow I was working too hard, altering my life to keep up with the orders coming in from the timber yard at Carrum. Why were the orders so big? Because Mavis was finding new clients. New clients meant more money.

We worked the mill Monday to Thursday, then on Thursday night I'd load up the truck and drive down to the timber yard to help Harry on Friday morning, sorting out the lengths, stacking the firewood and bagging up briquettes which came by rail from Yallourn. It wouldn't have been a typical timber yard without a sideline of brown coal for the customers. We'd then make up orders and I'd spend Friday afternoon and Saturday morning delivering before I'd drive back again to the Track to spend all Sunday snigging. Harry would drive to the Track on the weekdays and take loads of wood back to the yard with him. We had to keep up with him. Work? I never stopped.

At night, after the day's cutting was finished, Carl and I stayed back to sharpen the huge circular blades. You have to go around the blade twice to sharpen it: first to gullet it, which is what they call deepening the grooves between the teeth, one at a time; second to sharpen the point of each tooth. We had a machine the blades sat in which made the process easy, but it was tedious and took a long time. We had several blades to sharpen each evening. We also had to be vigilant about maintaining the machinery so there would be no accidents. I never loved any of this machinery the way I did my horses, axes and saws, but I became a jack-of-all-trades and nothing went wrong.

Eventually Carl left the Track and I had to do the sawing and maintenance myself. It was a long week I put in, but I was fit and strong and I kept going.

I was working with my brother.

My wife and family were living on the property where they belonged.

We were making money.

The kids were going to school.

Everyone was well fed.

Health and Welfare

ONE BY ONE, my workers began shifting to the mill houses and setting up camp. There was Gene Mobourne and his family, Les Monta, Jackie Green, Willie Marks, Jack Patton and Bob Nelson, and the Kennedy boys. The others all stayed in their camps along the creeks. You'd never get Stewart and Dora to shift.

At the mill on Gipsy Creek, we were all closer to each other than we had ever been. Usually, you won't find blackfellas setting up camp anywhere near anyone else when they're in the bush. You'll never see a tight little compound or a large group of huts in a circle or a row. They are found willy-nilly through the bush, usually along creek beds

Euphie doing the laundry

which meander here and there. They are always within cooee of each other, but never on top of each other and never in the order a whitefella likes to make.

The mill houses were close to each other, but they were also placed according to the terrain and the path of the creek rather than in a row. And they were all back in amongst the trees. Nevertheless, we all saw a lot more of each other, once we all lived together, than we ever had before. It was so easy to pop over to the neighbours' to see what was going on. Since anybody who came to the Track came to my place first, everybody else would drop in to see who it was. So our place became a social centre. Most nights you'd find us sitting outside under the trees around a roaring fire, telling yarns about the day's mishaps, catching up with visitors, scaring the youngsters with ghost stories. There was no television in those days so everybody was a good talker.

I loved it. I never felt so secure or happy. As I listened to the yarns, many of them sorry tales of woe that I found hard to believe could be true, I learned more about the blackfella, and I began to realise that I was more secure in my wellbeing than any of the people around me.

Because I've always been a free man, I have taken my freedom for granted, assuming it is my right as a living, breathing man. All my life I have been able to come and go as I please, to work where I please, to own land if I can find a way to pay for it and hold onto it, to vote as I see fit. The blackfellas in the 1950s had rarely experienced freedom in the way I had. They had no right to vote; they owned no land according to whitefella law; they had the Aboriginal Protection Board breathing down their necks wherever they went, whatever they did. But because it was a thriving community, full of busy people who were proud of their independence, people from the

'Welfare' never came to Jackson's Track. The people at the Track had a kind of freedom and they knew it and they cherished it.

Whenever an unknown whitefella showed his face at the Track, he was met with a defiant, cold courtesy that soon had him retracing his steps back off the place as quick as he could. Euphie, whose closest family, apart from Stewart and Dora, were from Dimboola, knew what whitefellas, especially if they were from the Welfare, could do. As did every other blackfella on the Track. They could steal children from you. They had tried to steal the five Marks girls up at Dimboola and put them in a Home, and they had stolen a niece of Euphie's right from her mother's arms before anyone could stop them. Not that anyone could stop them. Many children had disappeared into the Homes, but that would never happen at Jackson's Track.

Euphie had our children schooled well. If ever they saw a whitefella coming they sang out 'Gubbah! Gubbah!' and ran into the house and slammed the door shut. Other children all along the Labertouche and Wattle Creek camps did the same. They'd screech out a warning, 'Gubbah! Gubbah!', and scramble behind any adult, hold onto their legs and peer out to look at the stranger with wide, frightened eyes. Whenever a whitefella stranger came, the place closed up behind a steel wall impossible to penetrate.

The people at the Track were a proud mob. They were workers, living busy lives. They were independent and confident and did for themselves. Their camps were tidy, well cared for and full of activity. Nobody had a right to step into this community and lecture people about their way of living, and no one did for almost twenty years. The people here were free, but I was aware they were not as free as I was. The only protection they had was the fact that they lived deep in the forest on private property and the only hope they had was that the Welfare might not see them and might forget about them.

I have been to Dimboola many times with Euphie. Compared to the Jackson's Track mob, the Dimboola blackfellas had a hard time keeping the Welfare from interfering with their lives.

The people lived on crown land along the Wimmera River. Out in the open. I found at their camps that the sun was too bright, with a real sting in it, but that's because I am a man of the forest. Since there was no forest, their houses were not bark huts like those at the Track, but they were well made and comfortable. The Dimboola mob lived more on bush tucker than we did at the Track, for across the river from their camp was the Little Desert where there was some excellent hunting with more game in it than the scrub around the Track even. It was great sport going out early in the cold desert mornings with a group of men to bring home some tucker for the camps, especially roos and possum. Possums love red gum and were plentiful. The river was full of fish and the women knew how to dig for roots and grubs in the old way.

The people kept themselves busy maintaining a healthy lifestyle, but things were harder for them than they were for our mob. There was plenty of work for a blackfella in the Wimmera, but not much work at home close to the camps. Some of the men were shearers or rouseabouts in the big wool sheds, others worked on the railway or on the salt mines, but these jobs took them far from home, which was against their grain. There were market gardens on the river that employed the people for seasonal work, and, for some, that's all they cared to do. They weren't interested in a lonely life separated by miles and miles from their families for weeks and months at a time. Blackfellas live for their families and children. Part of the reason so many Dimboola people ended up at the Track was because the work was constant and close to home.

The Dimboola mob lived in the camps on the river instead of at

Ebenezer mission station, where they wanted to be, because the station was closed. Some resisters had managed to set up their camps there and elude the authorities. Those old fellows were looking for freedom to live as they wished, just like our mob, away from the prying eyes of whitefellas. It was harder for them to be free on the river because they lived closer to town, in plain view with nothing to protect their privacy. The Welfare was on the prowl every day for no reason at all. They would come with the police to find out who was in the camp, where they came from and how long they were going to stay. They were especially suspicious of me because I was a whitefella in amongst blacks. It's true that the police north of the divide were much tougher on the blackfellas, and anyone who associated with them, than they were in the south. Dimboola felt more like a prison camp than anything else to me, the way the people at the camps were harassed as if they were inmates.

The Welfare people had the right to search homes of people who they thought were starving or ill-treating their kids. Now, I think it's probably fair that children should be protected above all else in the community, but the welfare people who searched the blackfellas' homes seemed to have no understanding of blackfella values. They couldn't recognise a happy, healthy blackfella as long as he was living on a dirt floor. I have been in lots of camps with large families and have found them cleaner than a lot of whitefella houses I have visited in the past. But the Welfare thought it wasn't right that children lived in the camps and felt it their duty to find a way to take them away and put them in mission homes. No wonder the blackfellas hated and feared these people who would give no notice when the camps would be invaded.

I've seen the Welfare myself walk into a person's house and go through the cupboards looking for food, then making note of what they did or did not find. It was these notes which gave them the right to walk in another day and take the children away. This made the people keep whitefella food always in the cupboards, even if they never ate it. In fact, they only had cupboards to keep the whitefella food in. Since they lived on bush tucker, and since they had no electricity for refrigeration, their food was either hung up in a cool place or in containers cooling in the river, not in hot cupboards inside the huts. The welfare people never even noticed any of this healthy bush tucker in their searches.

I never saw any of the children actually being taken. I don't suppose they would do such a thing in full view of a whitefella who wasn't one of them. But I heard plenty about it in the sad tales told around the campfire at night. And I saw the result of stolen children. I saw a woman a few days after her daughter had been taken. She was standing outside her shack across the river from where I was. She was leaning against the door, a high-pitched, keening cry coming from her wide-open mouth letting all of us in the camp know her heart was broken.

The Dimboola people who were related to our people became so concerned and so frightened that they sent down to Dora and Stewart to ask them to take some of the children in at the Track where they would be safe for a while from the assimilation policy that the whitefellas kept going on about. Stewart came to me.

'Daryl, we need your help.'

I was part of the family. I didn't need to be asked twice. I put all other business aside and early the next morning put my tuckerbag and billy in the one-ton truck. I told Euphie I'd be back in a day as I pulled away towards Stewart's camp to pick up Dora, who was coming with me to Dimboola to look after the children on the trip back. Dora was mother to everyone who needed mothering. What a lovely, wise woman she was. She had a kind face, but if you looked closely you could see more than kindness. There was sadness there, too, and determination and pride, but most of all you could see love in her expression. She loved her home, she loved her family, she loved Stewart and she loved her people.

We picked up two families of children to bring back with us: the Marks girls and the Harrisons. They were sad to be leaving their parents and their home, but they weren't scared because they knew many of the people at the Track and knew there would be lots of other kids to play with. They thought they were going on a holiday. They liked travelling. Back in those days every blackfella liked getting into a car or riding on the back of a truck. The big kids tumbled onto the back, Dora in the front cradling one of the little ones on her lap with another littlie between us, and we took off before any Welfare people might take notice of us. The kids' parents were satisfied that the children were going to be safe, so they showed no sadness no matter what they felt.

It was a fact that the people in the Dimboola camps schooled themselves to show no sadness, if they could help it. They faced their trouble with a blank expression in order to protect the other children from what was going on whenever one of them was taken. My niece Carol remembers that when she and her sister were taken, their mother told them not to cry, not to let the others see them cry and, most importantly, not to let the Welfare see them cry. And so they were taken away acting like little wooden dolls and stayed wooden until they reached the Home where they were to grow up. It was only then, in their new, strange beds, Carol says, that she began to cry, 'and I didn't stop crying for two months'.

All of the children Dora and I picked up that day were taken in by Dora and Stewart, who gave them their love and care. Some of them stayed for years at the Track while others went to stay with relatives at

Lake Tyers and were back and forth as long as their beloved Dora and Stewart were here.

The blackfellas at Jackson's Track knew how lucky they were and they took care of themselves. They were a healthy lot. There was very little sickness. I do remember Tootie Hayes had consumption, which finally killed him, but that was only one serious ailment out of the lot. Of course, the kids got the usual measles and chicken pox and every once in a while you'd catch a chill. But the women knew what to do about it so it didn't stop us from carrying on with our work. Effie used hot ashes in a flour bag as a cure for a sore joint or stiff muscles or even a toothache or a boil. It worked. If we had a cold, Euphie used to collect armfuls of gumleaves and burn them down to ash on the ground. Then she'd have us lie on the hot earth to draw the fever out of us. That worked, too.

It wasn't hygiene or illness that gave us problems at the Track, it was fleas. We had plagues of fleas in the black, sandy soil and since there were a fair number of dogs about in the community, it was hard to conquer them. They would get into the blankets and ride around on the rims of our hats. The fleas drove us crazy. We all tried at some time to burn the very ground where they were worst, but that only gave temporary relief. We also used to spread phenol around, but to no avail. Euphie used to go mad with the washing. She was a clean person anyway, but the washing became a serious ritual at our house in an attempt to control the fleas.

I'd say Euphie's life was made up of washing. To my mind, she loved washing like I loved working in the bush. She always did the washing outside. She had me cut a forty-four-gallon drum in half and rest it on two logs outside the washhouse. She would fill that with water and build a huge fire under it to get the water boiling hard and she would keep it boiling all day long.

She would transfer some of the boiling water into a big iron tub and dump the clothes in. She would grab the Velvet soap and rub the clothes with it. I don't really know what she was rubbing at since most of the clothes were already clean before she even started, in my opinion. She'd never let us wear anything more than a day.

'Get your clothes off,' she would command, 'so I can wash them.' And we always did what she said.

Once she was satisfied the spots were rubbed out, she would put the clothes into the rest of the water boiling in the drum, cut some shavings of soap into the water and let it boil and boil until it got thick with soap. She had a strong stick, washed clean with use, she used to pick the clothes out of the boiling water and dump them into a tub of cold water to rinse. Then she would take the clothes out one at a time to wring them out with her hands. She had real strength in her hands and could wring out those clothes better than I could. She would hang the clothes out on the line, or, if it was wet, she would hang the line up inside and you'd have to walk through a forest of clothing to get to the fireplace.

Once the clothes were hanging out to dry, she would take a big steel bucket, dip it in the still boiling water, take it inside and tip it on the wooden floor. Then she'd get down and scrub the floor with a brush and sand soap.

Euphie would work all day in a cloud of steam to keep me and the kids and the house clean. Euphie's clothes on the line were always cleaner than anyone else's. The clothes were faded with all that washing, but absolutely clean.

We still had fleas.

Spiritual Matters

MOST SUNDAYS, while I was out pulling the logs into the mill yard, Euphie would take the kids over to Stewart's camp and attend a church service if one was being conducted that day. Doug Nicholls used to come out from the city at least once a month if it was fine weather and spend the day at the Track, starting with a revival meeting in the morning. He was Pastor Nicholls to all of us. His wife, Gladys, and his family and any friends he could fit in his car would come from town with him. They would set up their little travelling pump organ and singing would begin. I'm sure there was a lot more singing than preaching. I know my kids politely listened to Doug

Families singing hymns at one of Doug Nicholls' church meetings on the Track

preach, but to their minds Doug's arrival meant a good rollicking singalong more than anything else. After church there would be cups of tea and lunch, lots of talk, lollies for the kids. Roy would get out his guitar and play along with the organ while the rest sang. This would go on all afternoon until Doug and his mob would depart in the evening.

Pastor Nicholls was a friend to everybody, no matter if they attended his services or not. I used to see him and have a yarn sometimes early in the morning before he started the service. I had first met him in my travels with Gene Mobourne. We would often have dinner with Doug at his place near the Fitzroy footy grounds where he was caretaker during the week. Doug was a man who could cross the colour line, who felt comfortable with blacks and whites. He used to encourage the people to have faith and to take courage in their independence. He was ever hopeful and believed a day would come when there was no longer a need to be afraid of the white law. Pastor Nicholls was an exceptional man, quiet, kind and gentle.

One thing Pastor Nicholls' mob did was throw a big Christmas party for the kids at the Track each year. A whole group of city black-fellas would come in three or four cars to Stewart's camp with their hampers full of food, tables and chairs, and pillowcases bulging with presents for the kids. The first thing they would do was go out and cut a tree, a cherry tree, I remember, that we used to call a Christmas tree. It had beautiful white flowers all over which looked like bells. They would decorate it and put all the presents under it. One of the city fellows who came with Pastor Doug would dress as Father Christmas and pass out gifts to everyone before there was a great feast of Christmas food. The women of the Track would prepare for Doug's visit with their own contributions to the feast. My son Russell, who would have taken more note of the exciting preparations for

Christmas than I would have, remembers them making Christmas jellies and setting them in enamel bowls in the cold water of Wattle Creek.

Stewart especially liked Doug because he did not harangue the people about changing their ways. He loved it at Jackson's Track and let the people know they were doing a good job bringing up their children. It was not so with white 'bible-bashers', I call them, who came to the Track some Sundays, not to hold services but to speak individually to anyone they thought would listen. They called themselves Christians. That is supposed to mean they are from a kind and loving religion, but to my way of thinking these people were self-righteous, which made them blind. They thought they knew what was best for the blackfella, and came out here to stir the pot if they could.

At first these whitefellas came here only once in a while, but that was enough to make them experts on what went on here. What they saw through their narrow, do-gooder eyes did not especially please them. They could not see the bark huts for what they were, nor could they see the abundance of food in the creeks and the bush. They could not see that a scattering of logs around the ashes of an open fire indicated the centre of a social life that was rich with stories and comradeship. They could not see the blackened camp oven or the billy hanging on a wire over the open fire as anything but deprivation. They could not see that here was a preferred way of life, not a life of poverty and hardship on the fringe. They ignored the happy chattering and laughter of the kids and were blind to the polite confidence and pride of the adults. They misread the place entirely. I didn't like having them here, but Stewart told me he thought they were kind-hearted people doing what they thought was best. He said he wouldn't tell them to leave since they seemed to want to be here, although he had to admit he didn't pay much attention to what they said.

Those whitefellas would roll over in their graves if they knew that alongside their preaching about Jesus and salvation the black-fellas had another deeper and much more ancient sense of the spirit world that was alive and bubbling just under the surface. I have known ever since I was a lad working with the blackfellas in Queensland that they have a gift that allows them to sense the world and the things in it on many more levels than any whitefella can fathom. Blackfellas have an instinct – they feel things, they are intu-itive – and they are pretty right about things, in my experience.

The two elders, Jackie Coombes and Wagga Cooper, who lived in the mia-mia on Labertouche Creek, knew more than anyone. Jackie, especially, was connected to the old ways. He could speak in the old language. He was smart, but at the same time a bit queer. I thought he might be a bugeen, which is a spirit person, or what whitefellas might call a witchdoctor. Or, at least, he might have known the secrets of a bugeen. A bugeen is said to be a solitary spirit who wants to be left alone, who can turn into anything – bird, fish, reptile – and can travel swiftly like a flash. Bugeens are said to like sitting around fires, but if anyone walks over their shadow, it is an offence. The people treated Jackie with respect, but left him alone with his own powers.

I have seen the work of a bugeen, who can point the bone to kill someone or cure them. One day word got about that Dave Moore had been boned. After two weeks this healthy, happy-go-lucky man looked sick and skinny and on the verge of death. One night, while he was lying on his bed in a hut near Stewart's camp on the verge of death, a bugeen visited him and took the curse away. Within three weeks Dave Moore was the picture of health and back to his old ways. I can't say I understand it, but I saw it.

Around the camp fire I have heard many stories of mrartches, which are ghosts. There can be good or bad, white or black mrartches. Jackie Coombes claimed to be able to see them even in the daytime. Stewart reckoned there was a black mrartch living under the bridge where the old Jackson's Track Hotel had been many years ago. He refused to go anywhere near that bridge. Blackfellas reckoned that they had encounters with mrartches all the time, that there was no use being frightened of them, although you wouldn't want to provoke them. Their philosophy was that the living can do worse to you than the dead.

I must admit, I believe I've been visited by a mrartch. One night I awoke and sat straight up in bed. There before me was an old woman whose long grey hair was streaming down over her shoulders and back. She looked at me and shook her fist, then disappeared. I was shocked. I put my hand on Euphie's shoulder.

'Euphie, Euphie. Wake up!'

'What is it?'

'I don't know. I've just seen something. There was an old woman in here.'

'What did she look like?' asked Euphie, who was suddenly interested.

'Old. She looked at me and shook her fist at me. Then vanished.'

'A mrartch!' exclaimed Euphie. 'She was angry. You've done something wrong.'

'What could I have done wrong?'

'Something to offend her. You'd better look to your own heart and make amends.'

I shook my head.

Euphie laughed. 'Don't worry, she'll probably come back, but she won't hurt you.'

I don't know how Euphie knew I was safe because I had heard around the camp fire of violent mrartches who try to smother anyone

they don't like. I lay awake all night thinking about it. To my knowledge, that mrartch, if that's what it was, never returned, except my
son Cat, who was born at the mill house in 1958, reckons there's one
in the house with me now. I'm not aware of it, but I keep my senses
open. Maybe it's her. If it is, she doesn't worry me, now.

Around the camp fire there were stories told about dooligahs,
which frightened the children, and this made them stay close to the
camp. These are hairy creatures, half-man, half-ape. They hunt for
food only at night and are especially dangerous to boys and men. If a
boy approaches, the dooligah will rip him apart. A dooligah will not
kill a woman, but it will kidnap her. Dooligahs smell strong and
awful, like a tip full of rotten and dead things, and you can smell
them from a long way off. They live in holes in the ground, especially
in thick bush. Dooligahs are everywhere, but they are afraid of fire.
That's why it's safe around a fire, and that's why I reckon so many stories are told about them around the fire. I can't say I've ever seen one,
or even smelt one, but Stewart swore he saw them and I believe him.

Blackfellas seem to know wherever there is trouble. They can
sense when someone dies. If a bird comes to them, they read that as
a message that someone has died or is sick. The blackfella tracks
throughout this region are full of significant spiritual places where
signs have been left or spirits have shown themselves or things have
happened. The elders have a map in their heads of this area that is
unlike any map a white man has ever seen. I respect their knowledge
and take their stories seriously although I'm only a whitefella.

Harry

THE TIMBER YARD in Carrum was doing well. Harry came to the Track twice a week to pick up loads of cut timber and firewood. He never stopped, never came to the mill house, never saw the family, but I had a feeling things were going to change. I saw a lot of him every week and we would talk – about business mostly, but sometimes while we were talking about the happenings on the Track, it would spill into family, just a touch, and move off again.

'Roy Rose's cousin, Punchy Rose, has turned up. I've got him working on the firewood.'

'Where'd he come from?'

Harry Tonkin

'He's been travelling with boxing troupes around the country shows.'

'Hasn't had his brains knocked out, has he?'

'He's teaching the boys how to box. They've built a ring and all. Lionel's turning out to be a champion, and Euphie's son Gary is good. Tootie Hayes's boys, Harry and Brian, have also taken it up.'

'These boys won't go travelling with the troupes, will they?'

'Who knows? One thing is certain. The kids have more respect for them at school these days.'

Harry chuckled appreciatively. He was always interested in the blackfellas. He had remained great friends with Stewart and Dora in spite of the stand he took with Euphie and me. He was especially fond of Roy and Gina.

The more we worked together, the more relaxed we were, the closer we were to a true partnership, the way it had been in the beginning. We both worked as hard as each other and one didn't let the other down. I was sure that one day he would get sick of living away from the bush and return to the main house, that he would eventually get to know his nephews and nieces and feel relaxed and comfortable in my house with my family. In fact, I realised later, I was looking forward to that day with more hope than I knew.

But it wasn't to be.

One day, Harry didn't show up at the Track to pick up his load. He had complained of a headache to me two days before, which was unusual because as a rule he never said a thing about his health, but I paid little attention. When he didn't show up two days later I rang my mother's house. I hoped Harry would answer the phone and not Mavis or my mother, who was more like Mavis than she was Harry or me. But Mother answered. I was blunt.

'I'm looking for Harry.'

'He can't come to the phone, Daryl.'

'Why not?'

'He's sick.'

'Sick?'

I'd never known him to stop in bed because he was sick. He'd never really been sick, nor had he ever been laid up with an accident. Harry was like a cat, agile and smart. Even though he spent most of his working life benching on the mill – which is a dangerous job – he was never caught. If he were thrown from a horse, something that happened now and again to the best of horsemen, he was never hurt. No, I couldn't quite imagine Harry being sick.

Mother said that by the time he got near the timber yard with his last load, he felt too tired, so he pulled in at the Seaford house, thinking he would stop there and unload the truck in the morning. While he was parking the truck he miscalculated and took the rail off the fence with the back corner of the trailer, something he had never done in his life. He just left the truck where it was, up against the fence, tumbled out of the cabin, somehow got himself into the house where he collapsed on a chair exhausted and complaining of a raging headache.

'We've had the doctor out,' continued Mother. 'He said it's just a nervous condition from overwork and Harry'll be fine. He's given him some medicine and told him to rest for a few days.'

'Right, then. I'll see him on Friday when I come down.'

I hung up and went to work as usual, but I was uneasy. I'd never known Harry to complain of overwork. Was Mavis driving him too hard? That didn't make sense. Harry would drive himself, but he was a sensible man. Overwork? No, it couldn't be that.

I drove my usual load of wood down on the truck that Thursday and was surprised to find Harry still in bed. He looked pale, but he was talking normally enough, telling me he would be up the following week, giving me the orders for delivery and telling me to keep up with the mill work – all the usual big-brother commands. In the morning, I went over to the yard and filled hundredweight bags with briquettes, loaded the firewood and went off for my first round of deliveries. My work was fast paced that day because I had to do twice my usual work, Harry not being there. That's all I thought about. I knew he'd be on the job next week.

But the doctor wouldn't let him out of bed.

I had to take a load down myself mid-week. I dropped off the timber at the yard, unloading it all alone. Mavis was in the office, but she never came out. I had to go in there to give her the invoices. Usually I found a way to avoid the office so I wouldn't have to speak to or look at Mavis. I told myself it was to protect her from my own foolish villainy, but I know it was to protect myself from her sharp opinion and angry tongue. This day I had to go in.

'How is he?' I asked.

'Doctor's coming tonight.'

'I'll go see him now.'

'Clean yourself up first,' was all she said.

I banged the invoices down on the counter and left. There is no brotherly and sisterly love lost there, I thought to myself as I walked to the truck.

Harry looked crook. But he insisted that he was sick of staying in bed and that he'd be at the Track on Monday. I thought he was right. I thought he'd get over whatever it was that was ailing him. Why wouldn't he? Neither of us ever considered sickness in the scheme of things.

The next week he managed to drive the truck up for a load, but I noticed as we were piling wood on the tray that he had lost a lot of weight and his face was looking drawn. He seemed tired and didn't have a lot to say. After a cup of tea straight out of the billy, he climbed slowly into the truck. He started her up, nodded at me.

'See ya next week.'

And he was gone. He never returned.

Mother rang me one evening at the mill house just as we sat down to eat our meal. I remember the line was usually a bit crackly because it was connected to our place via the Jindivick store where there was a small exchange. Wind, rain, leaves falling, birds landing, anything made the line crackle. But on this night Mother's voice came through loud and clear. In fact, as I remember it, it seemed to me to boom across with a great cavernous sound.

'Daryl, your brother is dead.'

The line seemed to respond with a splutter, but I didn't say anything.

'Daryl? You there?'

'Yeah,' I muttered.

'Yesterday he took a turn for the worse. He got so bad he couldn't even walk. We called another doctor. He took one look at him and put him straight into an ambulance. They operated on him this morning.'

'Operated? What did they operate on?'

'On his head, Daryl. He had a brain tumour.'

I couldn't take that in. What's a brain tumour? How do you get a brain tumour? How long had it been there?

'He didn't have the strength to pull through, son. He died on the operating table. Mavis and I were there waiting for him. Your brother is dead, son. It's a terrible blow. We depended on him so . . .'

I didn't want to hear any more.

'Goodbye, Mother,' I said and quietly hung up the phone.

All the while I had been talking, my back had been on Euphie and the kids. When I turned around, I must have looked terrifying, for all noise stopped and the kids faded away. I didn't have to speak. Euphie knew. She came up to me and guided me to a seat at the table. She patted me on the shoulder and then left me alone.

Mother was right. This was a terrible blow. Couldn't get a worse kind of blow than this.

The next morning I awoke earlier than usual, saddled my horse and rode out to where we were falling some trees. I needed to work. I eyeballed a fine, straight silver-top, estimated how tall she was, lined up a fall-line, checked to see how free the scrub was behind it. I took my axe from its scabbard on the saddle and began to cut a scarf. I stood side on to the tree, planted my feet about shoulder-width apart on the ground and I swung the axe straight and true. It bit deep into the hard wood and the lovely smell of sap rose from the cut. I swung again and again until a perfect wedge was cut which would guide the fall of the tree.

I went around to the other side of the tree and began to swing the axe on a line a little higher than the wedge around the front. Usually, I would cut this side of the tree with a crosscut saw, but I had a need to swing an axe this day. Blow after blow of the axe sounded through the early morning forest as I cleanly and accurately used all my strength to work through that tree. By the time I was halfway through, I was down to my singlet and the sweat was flowing freely. The forest rang with the sound of my axe.

One more blow and the tree began to lean forward. I stood back. The great tree moaned and creaked as it broke its mooring and with great dignity fell straight and true to the fall-line in amongst the other great trees around it. There is something majestic and final about the falling of a tree.

I decided to leave the topping and barking to the men, and I turned to the next tree marked for falling. I spent the whole day swinging my axe until I was exhausted. I just kept working. I had to. Working keeps your mind off things, but no matter how hard I worked that day or successive days, I couldn't keep thoughts of Harry at bay.

I kept thinking about that tumour. Where does a tumour come from and how can it kill that quick? It could have been my fault. One day – early in the piece, could have been even before Stewart was here – I caused an accident which left Harry with a cut over his eye. Harry was helping one of our workers fix a broken spring on his car. I was standing next to the car watching the proceedings. They jacked up the vehicle and Harry prepared to get in underneath to have a look. As he bent down, I gave the car a kick – just a little kick, you know, the way you do when you're making out you have an opinion about the workings of something. This innocent kick made the car fall off the jack and whack Harry on the head. He gave out a yell and scrambled out from under the car with a deep two-inch cut over his eyebrow, blood running everywhere.

We managed to stop the bleeding and have a good look at the cut. Harry refused to go in to the doctor. There was too much work to be done, no time for that. Just like the time I lost the tips of my two fingers when I was young and silly. I was going too fast pulling out flitches at the mill and managed to get my fingers in the wrong place. The flesh was pulled off and the bones were sticking out, but there was no time for a special trip to the doctor. I had to wait until the next day when the truck was fully loaded. No one stopped work for me – it was only fingers – and we didn't stop work for Harry either. He sported a mean-looking scar over his eyebrow after that. He was as tough as nails. We all were. It had to be something really serious to stop us. That was bush life.

But maybe we should have taken it more seriously. Maybe that was the beginning of the end for Harry. Who would have thought it? I couldn't believe my brother was dead. I had never, in my whole life, thought of myself without him. When I was a lad, I couldn't wait to be old enough to follow him up to Queensland, and then couldn't wait to be allowed to ride on the boundaries with him, and finally nearly burst my buttons when we went into partnership on this property. Even though we worked independently of each other after I went with Euphie, I always knew we were still partners in the ownership of this land. And when it looked like we were coming back together in a true partnership, I felt the world was climbing back up on its axis where it should be. But now he was dead and I was alone.

Finally, no matter how hard I swung my axe, or how far out into the forest I rode my horse to get away from it, I couldn't keep my mind clear of thoughts about my brother.

The blackfellas felt the blow of Harry's death just as I did. They were quiet and respectful around me and at night Euphie told me they told stories of the man and made sure he had a place in their memories. But, of course, I went to the funeral alone. My family and Harry's best friends, Stewart and Roy, were all left at the Track. I wished I had stayed at the Track with them because a funeral is a hard thing, too hard on a man to face such terrible sadness. Harry's is the last funeral I have ever been to. Everyone knows, now, I don't go to funerals.

At the end of that terrible day, Mother came up to me.

'You know, Daryl, Mavis believes she put a lot of time and work into the property at Jackson's Track.'

'You mean time and trouble – she caused trouble.'

'Is that fair, Daryl?'

'It was her idea to live there. We – I didn't need her there.'

'Be that as it may, I know she intends to make a claim, which she sees as her right.'

'It has nothing to do with "right".'

'Well . . . I love both of you. Be warned and see to your affairs.'

Of course, Mavis would agitate for ownership of as much as she could grab. The way I was feeling, I would have been happy to retreat to the forest and let her have all of it, except that I remembered Mavis's words as I walked out of the main house and into the forest long ago: 'You'll finish up with absolutely nothing! I'll see to that!'

I remembered back then that I didn't care, that I thought she was wrong anyway, that no matter what she owned, she would be the one to have nothing compared to what I had out in the forest. But now I felt differently. I couldn't let her take away the livelihood of all the people who depended on this property. I had a family. I had a wife and children and cousins and uncles and sisters and aunties. I had workers – all my blackfellas – depending on me. I knew Mavis would send them all packing if she gained the upper hand, so I had to fight her, even though I felt the fight had been knocked out of me. Harry left no will, which was a mistake, but then he had no idea of dying when he was only forty-four years old. Mavis thought she could take advantage. I thought if I let her have the timber yard – even though, legally, I could have forced her to buy me out – she might not try so hard for the Track property, but I was wrong. She wanted as much as she could get.

Harry and I were honest bushmen who worked on agreement and handshake; we never thought about one brother trying to undermine the other. So we never bothered to organise the three titles that made up our eight hundred acres into joint ownership. I owned the eighty acres we bought from George Rogers; Harry owned the 186 acres that had been Kelly's; and we both had signed our names on the title to the 550 acres of Eliza Peters'. Mavis knew she couldn't touch George Rogers' eighty, but she put a claim on the 186 and the 550. I wasn't too worried about her having the cleared 186 acres if she was determined to have it because I wasn't interested in working cleared land. I had had my fill of potato growing when we had the thirty-acre hill planted out during the war and I didn't want to be bothered with dairying or any such thing after my experience at Toora. No black-fellas lived on the cleared area. So I thought if I let her have it, she might give up her claim on the rest.

She wouldn't talk to me. She could not recognise the responsi-bility I carried because she would not recognise the worth of the blackfellas that made up my family. She must have known I had a stronger claim, but as far as she was concerned I was the black sheep of the family who deserved nothing. In fact, she thought nothing was too good for me. There certainly was no warmth between Mavis and me. She lodged a claim with her lawyer. I was disgusted, but I knew what was mine and I knew there would have to be a terrific row if she was going to get it away from me. I didn't put in a claim because I knew what was mine, and I turned my back on her.

Now, everyone knows lawyers will take their own sweet time to get things settled. So in the meantime I set my mind to finding a way to keep my family. My problem now was to find a market for the milled timber since I was no longer connected with Mavis and her timber yard. I didn't have to look far. A timber merchant from East Doncaster named Herb Nelson made himself known to me and we came to an agreement. He sold all the timber we could cut anywhere he could find a market. So we were still in the forest, still working, still living busy, prosperous lives in spite of the threat hanging over our heads.

As I think back on this time, I always mix it up with Lionel Rose's success, for it was about then that he began boxing at the Railway Hall in Warragul and people started taking notice of him. Even though he was still young and he was working with us as part of the mill team, we weren't going to have him for long. Right then Lionel was the future and Harry was the past. For me that past almost overwhelmed any future. From then on, there was always an empty space where Harry was. I often found myself remembering with regret the hope I treasured of our getting back together, but now, when I think of him, my memory speeds past the times of anger and disappointment to the beginning when we were strong and healthy, when we were laughing and full of dreams, when we were the Tonkin brothers.

The Track

WHEN THE BLACKFELLAS first began to settle on our property, we were
surrounded by two thousand acres of scrub on the one side, going
almost as far as Drouin, and thousands of acres of forest on the other
side. There was not a fence in sight. The blackfellas were free to walk
over this country just as they had always done, relying on landmarks
and stories and songs to tell them the way. When they gave each
other directions, they would talk about a certain tree or where
Stewart shot the old man roo or the dippy bridge where the mrartch
was waiting. They didn't talk about this road or that road the way we
did. My version of how they got to Drouin is probably not the same

Jimmy Bond

as theirs. They went from Labertouche Creek and headed for a crossing at Wattle Creek about a quarter of a mile off Jackson's Track, cutting through Jimmy Robbo's place and coming out near the Robin Hood Hotel.

They avoided walking along Jackson's Track, which was back then a narrow, sandy track that wound around trees in a difficult meandering pattern with potholes so big and deep you had to go off the road and cut another route around another tree to keep going. In the boggy spots it was lined with logs in a corduroy fashion to make it passable for trucks but difficult to walk on. The blackfellas had no cars and did not know how to drive. They had no inclination for driving, not like they have today. They travelled on foot wherever they went. They liked the pace of walking their country, observing the great trees, spotting game, paying respect to caves or rock formations. They went wherever the spirit took them until about 1950 when the shire brought the bulldozers out and slowly began straightening and sealing the Track to make the area more accessible to cars and trucks.

With the making of the road came new settlers into the area, people who bought the overgrown farms and set about clearing them and stocking them. Jimmy Robbo was the first to come. He built a dairy and slowly cleared his land. He was happy to let the blackfellas continue hunting. The Track was straightened section by section and work was slow, the clearing gradual, but in a few years the two thousand acres of scrub country around us which supported so much game was gone: the deserted farms were bulldozed and fenced and sown down to grass. Dairy cattle were put on, houses and dairies built. Where once a man could walk freely, there was now a maze of fences and barriers with 'no trespassing' signs threatening passers-by. The blackfellas had to walk along the roads now to get anywhere. Their quiet progress was interrupted by cars, vans, trucks rumbling past and splashing mud or throwing up dust and rocks. By the late 1950s, the country beyond our forest was changed. The pace had quickened and there was a tension in the air.

Not long before Harry died in 1958, the Track on the edge of our property was at last being straightened. The Track originally went right around our property, crossing the two creeks at shallow sections where logs could make do for bridges. The shire engineers decided that the new road would go through our property instead of around it, cutting off about a fifteen-acre corner from Eliza Peters' 550. Harry and I were not pleased with this development. We tried to fight it, complaining to the shire council, finding lawyers and making claims, but the road went through anyway. It was like an act of God; nothing could stop it.

The trouble was, the new road cut right through the blackfellas' camps. Once it went through, Siddy Austin and his family were like sitting ducks, camped just twenty yards from where the road crossed Wattle Creek. To my mind the Austins had a beautiful and tidy camp, but my values were bushman's values, and beautiful and tidy to me was one thing, but to a whitefella, who could now look straight into their camp every time he travelled the road, it was another. A white-fella doesn't like to see life spilling out of the house into the yard where laundry was done, dishes were washed and stacked, cooking was done over an open fire; where sometimes bedding could be seen and people were lounging about with children swarming everywhere. Stewart's camp was the same. Suddenly his bark hut, which had for twenty years nestled privately on the Labertouche, found itself only about thirty yards away from the road. Several other families found their camps were no longer even on our property, but cut off by the new road. It was a disaster. Suddenly these quiet bush folk seemed like fringe dwellers, on display to any stickybeak who happened by.

Almost twenty years earlier, in 1940, if Stewart's camp had been that close to the road, it still would have been secluded, because the tea-tree had been so dense and the silver-tops so plentiful that no one would have seen him. Back then the bush near their camps was a second-growth forest of trees which had never been cut into. But that made it a dangerous spot for fire, so Stewart and the others who made their camps nearby started cutting firewood close to their camps, clearing and burning the heads and scrub to make it safe. As they cut into the bush, tracks had to be made to get the wood out. They had to cut the stumps off at the ground to allow the horses and carts hauling the wood to go over them since the trees were only about two feet apart in that area. Over the years the area became opened out, with snig tracks making their way between the camps and log bridges placed over the creeks. While the road was in its original spot, the camps remained entirely secure and private in spite of the clearing, but by the late 1950s the people found themselves on show.

The Track continued on through to Jindivick and became the main route between Jindivick, Drouin and Longwarry. Soon cars and trucks were speeding along the Track in numbers that altered the feel of the whole place. The blackfellas, who had always been going back and forth between their camps and the Jindivick store through the forest, now found it quicker to go along the road, which had no fences to get through. New settlers and travellers, people who had never had anything to do with this country before, began to complain about groups of blacks along the road.

'They just meander along looking for trouble.'

'Most of them are barefooted, even in winter!'

'They're a scruffy lot.'

'Up to no good.'

'It's getting so you don't want to go past their hovels.'

'The way they live is disgusting.'

'If you should break down anywhere near there, they would bail you up for sure.'

'It's frightening and dangerous.'

The blackfellas seemed to go into town more often now than they used to. The fences made it difficult to walk, and going along the Track was too long, but the new sealed road meant that it was easy for the Drouin taxis to get out to the camps and take the people into town. There were three Drouin taxi services which were happy to come out because it was the beginning of a booming business for them. A lot of money started being wasted on taxis. At first the blackfellas just went into Drouin for something to do, and more and more often a drink, but they began getting caught by Up-the-Lane Jack and being sent for a fortnight's holiday at Pentridge.

So they started to go past Drouin, where the police were proving to be too dangerous, and go on into Warragul. They would often meet their relatives in the Railway Park for a get together. Their relatives were usually making their way from Lake Tyers into Melbourne or beyond to Warrnambool and would get off the train in Warragul for a day in the park with the Jackson's Track mob. Blackfellas will always do that, meet up with each other to catch up and keep in touch. They are a deeply bonded group of people and will go out of their way to get news of each other. It's their business.

The police and people of Warragul seemed to tolerate these gatherings as long as the blackfellas were polite and kept to themselves. Of course, no white mixed with the blackfellas and, in fact, every white child, especially every young boy, was warned to stay clear of Railway Park: 'Just walk fast and don't look back.'

One person who would never waste his money on a taxi was Jimmy Bond. He didn't like the way things had changed. He didn't like the new fences everywhere. He didn't like the new road. He liked the old ways and he tried to stick to his old habits. Every once in a while he was in the habit of going into Drouin, risking an encounter with Up-the-Lane Jack, and buying himself a bottle of wine, which is all he needed to get himself through a weekend. He didn't like to, but now he had to walk along the road, which took him longer than it used to when he could go through the forest and not be caught up by fences. He never drank in town, but would walk back to the Track at night with the bottle tucked deep in the pocket of his dark-blue greatcoat that he used to wear everywhere.

One night he was later than usual returning because of the new distance along the road. It was cold and raining. He was walking with his head down, barefooted, hands deep in his pockets, when a car came from behind him, hit him and killed him. Then kept going.

As I remember it, we got a phone call from the Drouin police telling us about Jimmy. I don't remember how the message was worded, whether there was sympathy or coldness in the voice relaying the message, whether the voice used his proper name or not, but I do remember the voice said it was Jimmy's fault.

'He shouldn't have been walking out that time of night. No driver would have been able to see him in that black coat and with that black face.'

I was too struck with the sadness of Jimmy's death to get angry. It was obvious there and then that no one would ever be charged for the killing of Jimmy Bond, that his death was a meaningless occurrence, but I was too stunned to react.

Jimmy Bond dead. What a blow.

I turned to Euphie, who was sitting by the fire having a smoke since all our kids were at last in bed. She looked at my stricken face with alarm.

'It's Jimmy,' I said. 'They've killed him.'

Euphie began to weep, quietly at first, then louder. Dot came out of the other room rubbing her sleepy eyes. She went up to Euphie and put her hand on her shoulder.

'Ma?'

Then she began to cry with her mother. One by one all the little children arose from their beds and gathered around their mother and began to cry, whether or not they understood exactly what was the matter.

I went out, started up the old van and drove into Drouin to take care of the business of identifying the body and arranging for an undertaker. I knew the blackfellas would want a decent funeral for him, that they would bury him in the Drouin cemetery with a mob of people as witnesses. But, if I had my way, I would have taken Jimmy with me and buried him with no ceremony deep in his beloved forest. Unfortunately, they have laws so you can't do that.

I had promised myself never to go to another funeral after the awful experience of Harry's funeral. To me a funeral should be a private thing, but for the blackfellas it's the opposite, with a large gathering of all the relatives. It is a kind of celebration because for a blackfella the dead never leave the earth, but become a part of the very air they breathe and the ground they walk on. So Jimmy had a large funeral with people coming from all up and down the line: from Lake Tyers, Warrnambool, Dimboola, New South Wales. People came and stayed on the Track for days, hunting, eating, yarning, remembering.

Me? I stayed away. I have no respect for the dead. If a person is dead he is dead. He might have been my best friend, as Jimmy was, but the memory is more important than the dead.

Jimmy was family. He was a friend to this property. He belonged to it. He worked it. He seemed to take an interest in or take responsibility for everyone and everything on it. He knew every tree, every track, every creek and billabong. He was one of the old breed of blackfella. It's hard to explain just what the qualities were that these old fellas had, but there's no match for them today. You never saw such workers as the old ones. Gee, they were skilful people and they had the heart to tackle any job. The old fellas like Jimmy could fell a tree six foot thick without blinking.

And they looked like quality. I don't know what it was that let you identify the quality in them, maybe the way they walked in a graceful, silent, powerful sort of way with their heads up noticing everything around them. It wasn't their clothes, although the clothes of the old ones were different from those of today. Work clothes were dark blue in colour, not khaki or green, and made of rough, durable cotton and wool. Not Tasmanian blueys, like the whitefellas wore, but the same colour. They – we – always wore hessian bags draped over our shoulders and hooked the corners together with a piece of twisted fencing wire at the front when we were working. And they hardly ever wore hats, or, if they did, they wore a kind of ex-military beret because as timber workers you get caught by a branch quicker when you wear a hat with a brim. Jimmy wore no hat, nor did he wear boots. He taught me that if you want to stay dry in a rainstorm, you take off all your clothes, put them under a dry log and work naked until the weather clears.

I don't know. There was something about Jimmy that it isn't possible to explain – a kind of spirit. I have strong feelings about the old blackfellas like Jimmy. They were brought up hard, they lived hard. They were very independent, strong of heart, mind and body. You couldn't get another Jimmy Bond ever again. He was a man brought up the right way – an honest man, a gentle man.

And he was run over in the road like a dog!

One thing the blackfellas believed – something which made their celebration at a funeral a sober affair – was that when one dies, there will be a series of deaths. Deep in my heart, I had a feeling that Jimmy's death was the beginning of the end of the blackfellas on Jackson's Track.

Change of Policy

ONE DAY, about twelve months after Jimmy was buried, people came home from a day at the Railway Park talking about a new policy the Aborigines Protection Board was threatening.

'They reckon they're gonna shift people off the missions and force 'em to live in government houses in the towns!'

'Why can't they leave people alone?'

'Some people like livin' at Lake Tyers.'

'They reckon they want people separated from each other.'

'More assimilation rubbish, hey?'

'Tell them blackfellas to stop here. No one can touch 'em here.

Stewart's camp on Labertouche Creek

This is Daryl's land. The whitefellas can't tell him what to do with his own land.'

'Maybe.'

The talk continued around the camp fire night after night as stories came through about people actually being put into houses in white neighbourhoods.

'What do they want to live there for? They don't know anybody.'

'They got their own telephone, and a refrigerator!'

'The government give 'em that much.'

'They have to pay rent, but.'

'How do they do that?'

'Government gives 'em money.'

'Do they work?'

'No work.'

'Crikey, bloody stupid if you ask me.'

Once the policy was under way on the missions, they then started rounding up families who lived on crown land along the river banks. The Dimboola families were being shifted. Talk around the camp fire became angry but also fearful.

'Why can't they leave people alone?'

'You know what whitefellas are like.'

'Hang on, Daryl's a whitefella.'

'Daryl's a white blackfella, you mean. Daryl's got law. The whitefella has no law.'

'What can you expect from the kind of man who has no law?'

'A man with no law shoots the people on their own land.'

'Then rounds the rest up and puts them on mission stations with whitefella food that makes people sick.'

'A lot of people die.'

'And the whitefellas with no law are glad of it as there are less people to look after.'

'They shoulda left us alone if they didn't want to look after us. We never needed to be looked after.'

'Now they're shifting us into towns, expecting us to live like whitefellas and blaming us for being ungrateful when it's against our nature to live all shut up and quiet and unhappy.'

'They know nothing about nature.'

'They have no law.'

The blackfellas felt they were safe on Jackson's Track. I was not so sure, but I was hopeful. I couldn't believe that anyone would make such a stupid decision as to put blackfellas on their own in a town. It was a cruel, thoughtless policy, to my mind. A cruel policy designed by cruel, stupid men. In my experience, wherever white men go, they damage things. Look at nature. Blackfellas are satisfied with nature and do nothing to damage it whereas the whites pollute all the streams, making them unfit to drink from. They starve the native animals and spread poisons all over the land. In the dry areas they cause man-made droughts by over-stocking, killing native animals, grasses, scrub and native plants, which allows noxious weeds to come in. The whites make laws which the rich break. They also look after their own, keeping thieves and murderers in luxury yet not allowing the blackfellas to live together in peace wherever they want in the land they were born in.

For a long time, nobody bothered the blackfellas at the Track. We continued to work and live in peace. Taxi rides to and from Drouin and Warragul, or maybe Bunyip or Longwarry, became more and more frequent. There were two drivers who became well known to us. Mae Plew was wonderful. Everyone called her Ma Plew. She looked after the blackfellas if she saw they were headed for trouble, bundling them in her taxi and carting them home. She would pick up the kids walking along the road to school and deliver them for free. She brought me home from hospital once after an operation on my leg and delivered me to my door, unlike other drivers who refused to negotiate the tracks into the place. She visited people who were sick and never hesitated to give away a free ride if she thought you needed it. She said she appreciated the blackfellas because they weren't greedy.

'They're never out to beat you,' she said. 'They're wonderful people who haven't had much luck since the white man arrived on this continent.'

The other driver who began finding his way out to the Track was a young fellow, and he came out our way in his taxi more often than we appreciated. He was a sly grogger, always carried a bootful of booze to sell specifically to the blackfellas any time of day or night – early openers, late openers, whatever. Ma Plew knew he was selling grog and it disgusted her. She would hit the roof before she would bring out grog, but she wouldn't dob on a bloke. Many people at the Track were against him, but he brought his overpriced liquor where it was wanted, never to my place and never did he go near Stewart's camp. His presence created ill-will, especially among the women, and especially with Margaret Austin, who was watching Siddy being pulled by the lure of alcohol. She would curse the unscrupulous villain and tell him to move off away from her camp, but he would just laugh. And there wasn't much she could do, being so close to the road.

Another visitor who began preying on the Austins more and more frequently was a bible-basher from Neerim South. Our family used to get together with the Austin family quite a lot since the kids were all going to school together and had become fast friends. By 1960, Euphie and I had eight kids with another on the way. Trevor (Cat), Pauline (Haggie), and Howard (Ben) were all born at the mill house, and Valda (Lilian) was about to be born. Russell (Snag), Linda

(Bic) and Sandra had all been born at the Wattle Creek camp; Cheryl (Curly) had been born at Toora; Mac had been born at the Gipsy Creek camp and, of course, Dot had always been with us. The Austins had Willie, Murray, Lena and Ricky, maybe more, but it's hard to remember such a swarm of kids. After work, we used to get together, usually at our mill house, visit each other, spread the food around, see what was going on. There was no television, of course, but everyone had yarns to tell. Siddy and Margaret began telling stories about Jesus and reporting things the do-gooder and his wife were telling them.

'They say if we love Jesus our bad luck will turn to good luck,' Margaret would start.

'What bad luck have you had since you stopped here?' I would say.

Another time she would say that the wife had brought them over some blankets and some food and recipes which would make them healthy.

'Whitefella food is not healthy!' I would say. 'Look how all the blackfellas started getting sick when they ate whitefella food.'

She'd say something like, 'The Bible says cleanliness is next to godliness.'

What was the use of responding to that rubbish? But those two bible-bashers came more and more often. Stewart still didn't see that they were doing any harm. He thought they were good, honest people who believed they were doing the right thing. Well, they were good people, but not as good as they should have been. I began to realise that if the Welfare hadn't the courage to come onto private property to gather up the people, they would let these churchgoers do their dirty work for them. I began to see a pattern in their preaching. They were onto the people about the conditions of their living. They were trying to make them think that for some reason Jesus

wouldn't approve of their bark huts and bush lifestyle. Stewart didn't
notice that Dora was taking a shine to them and beginning to swal-
low all their guff. Euphie noticed and didn't like it, but she felt she
had no right to tell her mother what to think or who to believe.

The church people didn't have much luck getting others besides
the Austins and maybe Dora to listen to their message so they enlisted
the help of an old-timer named Buchanan who had been coming to
the Track for many years even before we came here. He used to come
along the old sand track in his Model T Ford cleaning up bottles
along the roadside. He had a job for many years on the water pipeline
from Baw Baw, keeping it clean and sluiced out. He was a frugal man,
in fact so tight he was the only man I have ever seen with two tyres
on one wheel. He was a good bloke, but somehow, through his wife,
I think, he became connected with the church and came out here
with the others. He never actually preached, but became friendly
with the blackfellas, sold them cheap clothes from his house in
Drouin, letting his wife work her way into their lives that way.

Slowly more bible-bashers began to find their way out here,
going from camp to camp talking about Jesus and Christian values.
They were always on the backs of the blackfellas trying to get them
to improve their ways. What did they mean, 'improve their ways'?
Didn't they have eyes to see how good, peaceful and godlike the way
of the blackfella already was? Just like the Welfare or the mission
managers or the government, these church people were blinded to
any vision but their own. In their minds they saw every family on
earth living in a little brick house with a tidy garden, a fridge, a
washing machine and a car. They weren't fussed about a fireplace
anywhere in the house, but were happy for the kitchen to have a gas
oven. They saw a fine little family where father works and mother
cooks and cleans and children happily go to school and on Sunday

mother and father take the children to church. They were convinced this was everybody's dream, or, if it wasn't, as soon as they experienced it, it would be.

The silly mongrels were also convinced that if the blackfellas moved into town, they would immediately become the perfectly happy family of their vision. If they had taken any notice of the way blackfellas conducted their lives centred around the fire, with extended families filling up rooms and beds, with food being shared by everyone and care for the children and the sick shared around, they would have known they were setting up a disaster for the blackfella. If they had taken any notice of how difficult it was for a blackfella to be treated fairly, let alone find work in a town, they would have seen the trouble they were brewing.

I could see it and it made me angry, all the talk about Jesus and the good life going on in the camps. Others laughed at the rubbish these blind people preached, but were happy to take any handouts. No matter if they made you angry or they made you laugh or they convinced you of their ideas, they were becoming a powerful influence on the fate of the people of Jackson's Track.

One day late 1961, news came to the Track that the church people and the shire authorities had had a meeting about what to do to clean up 'the black problem' out on Jackson's Track. I can imagine what they must have said to each other at that meeting:

'The best thing to do is to clear them off the Track altogether.'

'The best thing to do is to split them up so they won't be such a frightening mob.'

'The best thing to do is to move the poor wretches into government houses situated in different spots around Drouin and Warragul.'

'After all, it is being done everywhere. It makes the control of these poor people easier.'

'It'll make it easier for us to look after them and help them.'

'Do we have any available houses?'

'We'll get to that later. First we must decide how to move them.'

It wasn't long before the people at the Track found out what the authorities had decided to do. The church people came around to all the camps one by one and explained how they had the welfare of the blackfellas in mind and that they truly felt this was the best thing for them. They said the good people of the church had worked together to build some housing for the blackfellas and that in one week a truck would be out to fetch them.

'One week? I'm not going!' was the response from every family. The do-gooders realised they would have to be more forceful in their explanation.

'You have a choice. Either you move into a fine house in Drouin or you will be shifted back to Lake Tyers.'

'This is private property. You have no right.'

'Yes, we have.'

'I've lived here more than twenty years!'

'Be that as it may, we have plans that will only benefit you.'

'I don't want to leave here.'

'You cannot stay here. Children cannot be brought up in these conditions. We will be forced to take your children from you.'

There it was, they would break up the camps and the families and steal the children for the 'good' of the people. These do-gooders called themselves Christians! The way people's lives get bent all out of shape in the name of God leaves me astonished. Look what Mavis and Harry had done to Euphie and me in the name of God; look what these people were about to do in the name of God. It was disgraceful. I had no belief in this God.

Forced Out

I HEARD ABOUT this final solution for cleaning up the Jackson's Track blackfellas around the camp fire. There was talk of little else all that week. I was sitting with everyone else just like always, but my position was uneasy. No one looked at me much or spoke directly to me. After all, a whitefella was under no threat. I was a whitefella, now, in this predicament, and I knew it. No one asked for my help and I remained quiet.

The thing was, I was feeling the frustration and anger as much as they were. For the first time in my life, I felt there was nothing I could do. This was my land, but I couldn't protect anybody from the

Families on the Track

Aborigines Protection Board, and to me and to the blackfellas it was absolutely clear they were the ones behind all this. When it came to blackfellas the Board had the final say. It was as if the blackfellas were their property, and the Board could do with them as they saw fit. The blackfellas were their wards, and they seemed to believe their wards were wretched people who weren't capable of making their own decisions, weren't good for much, couldn't be trusted. They were a responsibility, a duty, a burden. There was no way to stop the Board from telling the blackfellas what to do. They were like the police, with power to do just about anything they wanted to. This is what the blackfellas believed and I believed it, too.

As I sat amongst my family, my relatives, my friends, saying little, I thought to myself what I'd be doing to save myself. I would gather my horses, my tools, my family and sink back into the forest, deep in the forest where I couldn't be found. I would disappear. I knew it was possible. I also knew I was thinking that way because I had never had to face a Board that had authority over me. I had been treated like I was a fool at times; I had thought myself a villain for throwing in my lot with the blackfellas, but I had always behaved and acted of my own free will. The blackfellas, on the other hand, had had more than a hundred and fifty years of being bossed around, and they found it easier to give in than to take the law into their own hands.

But as I looked around the fire, I could tell there were a number of people who just might be planning to become outlaws themselves to stay out of the hands of the Board. They were the ones not saying too much, but listening hard and thinking. I respected them. After all, I was a kind of outlaw myself, a white man among blacks. But I was miserable all the same to think of the future for these proud outlaws, to think they would have to leave the Track for good.

There were several others sitting at the fire who were separate like me. These were the people who lived near the mill on Gipsy Creek and worked with me: Gene Mobourne, Jack Patton and Bob Nelson, Les Monta, Willie Marks, Jackie Green and the Kennedy boys. The church people and the shire and the Board had ignored them. The bible-bashers had never been anywhere near them – never anywhere near me, more to the point – and so there was no recommendation to move them. Besides, from the road no one could see people who lived at Gipsy Creek, so they didn't bother with them. Out of sight, out of mind. Shows you how hypocritical they were. They weren't concerned about anyone's welfare at all, just wiping out all trace of blackfella culture from whitefella view. These fellas were sitting tight and sitting quiet. They knew it was just the luck of the draw they'd been passed over and they were worried about the break-up of the folks on the Track.

The blackfellas argued through the nights about the best way to go: with them or away from them or against them. It was Stewart, Siddy and Roy who seemed the most lost. The do-gooders had got to them. Their wives, Dora, Margaret and Gina, were talking like it might be a good idea to go along with the shift and find out what it was like to live in town. I could see these men becoming more resigned to the move, becoming more and more quiet about it, and then even beginning to argue for it.

'The church people say they've got together and started building good houses for us. They've got one already finished.'

'It's better for the kids to live in a proper built place with water laid on.'

'The church people will take the kids to school every day. They say they'll get the kids uniforms and books and paper . . .'

'We'll get free clothes and boots. They're putting in a garden and we won't want for food. They say they'll see to that.'

'It might be a good thing to go along with them.'

After listening to those kinds of things coming out of Stewart and Roy, the conversations usually went quiet momentarily. A few people had been nodding while they talked, but many had eyed them with suspicion. Euphie just shook her head at things she heard her parents say, and kept her mouth shut, which must have been hard for her. I was dismayed, but I didn't know what to say. I wasn't really aware myself of what a lifestyle change it would be for them in town, never having lived anywhere near town since I was twelve years old. I shrugged my shoulders and knew there was nothing to do but let them go their own way. I could see everybody in the camp was resigned to what was about to happen, whether they were going to allow themselves to be shifted or not, whether they were under threat or not. In my experience, I have often seen blackfellas resign themselves. They never want any trouble with the authorities. They are always thinking of the children.

Two days before the deadline, Siddy announced that he was going to shift with his family to an empty railway house in Neerim South so they all, especially Margaret, could be nearer to the church.

'We hear the calling of the Lord,' announced Siddy, not too steady on his feet.

I moaned. How was Siddy going to survive alone in Neerim South?

'Siddy, you shouldn't be leaving here,' I couldn't help saying to him.

'It'll be all right, Daryl. Jesus loves us.' And he patted me on the shoulder.

The next day, Siddy and the whole family were gone. Their cleaned-out camp sat next to the road silent and cold. Abandoned. It was a shock to see it. It was as if the whole Austin family had been stolen.

This spurred some others into action. By the morning of the day before the deadline several more camps were empty, but these people hadn't been stolen; they had spirited themselves away. Siddy's brothers, Chris and Walter, were gone, followed by the Lovetts, the Somervilles and Freddy Bloomfield. All these empty camps made those of us left feel uneasy. There was bad spirit coming down on the place. I could feel my own sense of doom like a steel rod in my neck.

There was not much of a gathering the night before the trucks were to come. People were keeping to themselves, not talking much.

In the morning, about ten o'clock, I saddled my horse and rode over to see for myself the breaking up of Stewart's and Roy's camps. As I emerged from the bush, I stopped my horse at the edge of the clearing and looked around. More people had disappeared. Markie Harrap, Les and Joyce Dow with their sons, the Coopers and the Stevens had decided not to wait for the whitefellas to come and get them. I nodded my head with satisfaction, but there was no joy in seeing Roy and Gina Rose with all their children still at their camp as if nothing was about to happen. Stewart and Dora and several other families were the same, doing nothing about readying themselves or taking control of their futures. They were just waiting.

And so was I. I sat on the back of my patient horse, shifting in the saddle once in a while as he grazed at the edge of the clearing. Waiting. After a while I realised that some of my mill workers were lingering in the shadows of the bush behind me so as not to be seen, but close enough so they could witness the events.

And two trucks came. One a flat-tray vehicle and the other a low-loader carrying a bulldozer. They pulled to a halt on the road near Siddy's camp. The fellows in the cabins of both trucks got out and gathered in a sort of conference, deciding what to do first. They looked around, pointed here and there and then broke away from each other. Two went immediately to unload the bulldozer. The other two walked towards the camps, stopping at each one to tell the people they had half an hour to gather up their belongings and get on the back of the truck before the bulldozer would come along and clean up their camps. They looked over at me, but did not approach me. I felt a strong urge to spur my horse into a gallop and run those fellows over, but it was a dream. I sat and watched, letting them know they had a witness. I hoped it was clear to these whitefellas that this witness was sickened by them.

The members of the families left at the six camps began moving around, quickly gathering their things. While they were doing that, the bulldozer started up, moved off the road towards the Austins' camp. Everyone everywhere stopped to watch. My horse lifted his head. The whitefellas turned to look, too. The dozer moved without hesitation right over the bark hut that had been home to Siddy for almost twenty years. We could hear the cracking of the wooden posts that held up the table and beds inside, the tearing apart of the bark, the splintering of the beams and the ripping of corrugated iron that had formed the fireplace. The dozer backed off, lowered its blade and began to push all the debris together in one heap. The driver's offsider approached with kerosene which he splashed over the dry bark. Then he stood back and threw a match and the whole place went up. The dozer had already moved on to the next camp.

The people at the six camps began hurrying about their tasks as if they had been frightened out of their wits. No doubt they had been. No one would ever think they would burn the houses down right before the blackfellas' eyes. It was more than Dora could stand. I could see she was crying while she was moving about, hurrying up the children, deciding what to take and what to leave.

Finally, all the blackfellas, adults and children, and all of their belongings were piled on the back of the truck. Anabelle Tregoning, who had been married to Jackie Kennedy, and her kids were first onto the back of that truck. Anabelle had been living with her sister ever since Jackie had abused her, but her sister had left with her husband, Norman Lovett, the day before so it was the Lovetts' camp Anabelle left from, probably feeling frightened and alone. Others who followed her onto that truck were: Les and Nellie Stewart and their two kids; Norma Rose, who was married to Tootie Hayes, along with all their children, a stack of them, as I remember; Jamby Wilson and his wife, Adelaide, who was Roy's mother so, naturally, she had to go where Roy went so she could continue to spoil the grandchildren; the Roses, Roy and Gina and all their wonderful kids; and, of course, Dora and Stewart.

It was hard to sit there and watch that truck drive off with all those good people on it. It reminded me of the day long ago when Dora and her family climbed with their belongings onto the back of Harry's and my truck to leave the mission station forever. The feeling then was of hope and adventure. The feeling here was . . . I don't know, too many mixed feelings to say.

I sensed the blackfellas slip away in the bush behind me, but I continued my vigil while camp after camp was bulldozed and burnt. I couldn't bear to see Stewart's crushed. So when they approached his camp, I pulled on the reins, turned my horse and galloped off in disgust. At home I felt a great heaviness about my tongue and lips as I told Euphie what had happened.

'They came in with the bulldozers and they burned all the camps.'

Euphie, who had been listening to me quietly, slowly shaking her head with a sad disgust while she was making me some dinner, suddenly whirled around and looked straight at me with an aston- ished expression.

'What did they burn?' she asked.

'Every hut. To the ground. Nothing left,' I said.

Then Euphie began to yell. She stomped and screamed. She wailed and moaned. She threw herself into a chair, leapt up and hurled a cup across the room. The kids were standing staring at her goggle-eyed. I shooed them away. She cursed a steady stream of oaths until she was out of breath. She cursed the shire, cursed the Board, cursed the do-gooders, cursed all lawless whitefellas, every one of them. It took me a while, but I finally got hold of her and held her tight until she settled down.

'They didn't have to burn the camps,' she moaned in my arms. 'They didn't have to do that.'

We stood there together in silence for a long while. I knew she had always assumed her parents would return to their old ways at their camp as soon as they found out what it was like in town. I guess I thought the same thing. Now, with the camps destroyed, neither of us could contemplate what would happen. The future was black.

When she was calmed down she turned with a great sigh to continue cooking my dinner. I sat and waited and then I ate it for her, but it stuck in my throat. Finally, I left her and went out to work, the only way I know to settle a grieving heart.

Dispersal

IT TURNED OUT that no real plans had been made to move the people into houses in the town immediately. The shire had set aside a bush paddock of about four acres with some saplings on it along the Princes Highway near the Drouin golf course, and the volunteers from the church had managed to build a two-room house on it before the bulldozers came and demolished the bark huts. One house where they thought two rooms could accommodate two families! They crowded the Roses and the Hoods into the house, and for the rest of the families, the shire provided tents. Tents!

The water was laid on because the pipeline from the mountains

Claud Mobourne, Keith Hayes and Ivan Mobourne, in Wood Street, Drouin town

ran right past the paddock, but all it was was a tap sticking out of the ground. There were no toilets and certainly there was no electricity; not that these blackfellas were concerned about that, but how were they to keep themselves and their children clean and washed when they had left their washing drums and coppers behind? Hadn't they been told they would have washing machines? They wondered how they were going to cook on open fires when they had left all their camp ovens and billies behind to be crushed by the bulldozer. They had been told they no longer had need of those things. The women, Dora, Adelaide, Gina, Anabelle, Nellie and Norma, would have been badly disappointed. They were clean and house-proud women, wonderful women. Now they would have to start from scratch, somehow set up a home so they could keep their families together. How had they been so foolish as to believe a whitefella?

The six families were told they would be looked after until houses could be found in the towns, not to worry.

Well, they were all pretty disgusted. They had been told that their life at Jackson's Track wasn't good enough to bring up children, that living in bark huts and eating bush tucker was unhealthy, that living on dirt floors and cooking over fires was unhygienic. They were told that the only right way to live was in houses, with fridges and bathrooms. They were frightened into believing that if they didn't improve their lives, the whitefellas would be forced to take the children away to protect them from such rough living. And where had they ended up? Didn't the whitefellas think that living in a tent was rougher than living in a bark hut?

What were they thinking?

It was pretty plain to me that they weren't thinking of any blackfellas. They were all thinking of how much better the roadside out at Jackson's Track looked now that it had been cleaned up. The shire was thinking it wouldn't have to put up with complaints coming in from the good citizens who were developing the land out that way. The church people were thinking that now all the blackfellas were theirs to do with as they pleased. In my opinion, these particular church people were not genuine people. They would never send themselves broke helping people like a bushman would. They thought they were clean and a cut above. They were not working people. They had a sour look on their faces and all they thought about was their own prestige. It was plain to me they thought themselves pretty good, but they certainly weren't thinking of the blackfellas.

I guess the Board was the only body that was unhappy, because it was their responsibility to see that the Aborigines were properly housed and they would have to keep pushing at the shire to find houses. It became clear that the shire was going to take its time about being pushed. It took them at least eighteen months, maybe more, to move all those people off that few acres of bush. I know it was a long time because I remember they had to survive two Gippsland winters in those tents.

I went to see them regularly, stopping in to drop off supplies to supplement what the whitefellas weren't giving them. Sometimes a few would come back home with me to stop at the mill house with us for a few days. We could afford to have them all back to stay, but in reality we all knew that we could never turn the clock back. They had been shifted away from the Track and their destiny had been shifted as well. They weren't happy; they were living more or less out in the open and it was plain to me they were just scratching along, living hand to mouth, but they felt they had to put up with it.

Now, blackfellas, especially the old fellas like Stewart and Jamby, had lived rough all their lives, so they weren't overly concerned with their comforts. The main trouble for these fellas with being away from the Track was that they had nothing to do. There was no work for them; there wasn't enough land for them to be out hunting every day; there wasn't enough wood for them to be cutting much fire-wood; there were no creeks for them to spend time fishing and setting traps; there were no bark huts to build. They had to sit around and wait for handouts to arrive from the do-gooders who said they would take care of them. Sitting around waiting for handouts is no kind of life.

They were bored. The only thing that eased their boredom was when visitors from down the line stopped over for a few days. You can't keep blackfellas away from each other and as soon as word got out where the shire had dumped their wards, relatives began coming around. The Wandens from Lake Tyers showed up with a caravan, set up camp and stayed the duration. When visitors showed up, it was an excuse for a celebration. Now that they were living so close to town, it was easy to go in and get some grog. Grog made them forget how bored they were.

And so, for the first time since I had known them, alcohol became an influence in the lives of the people. Stewart and Dora still kept away from it, but Roy Rose took to it in a big way. And it was the grog that killed Roy. For a long time now, it had been known that Roy had a bad heart, or 'a weak ticker', as he called it. Out at the Track he had lived a healthy life, working and looking after his family, and never drinking any alcohol. He was too busy to bother with it. The work as a woodcutter kept him active and kept his heart strong. As soon as he was shifted, I imagine the heart went out of him. He used to love Jackson's Track and love the bush. He didn't love this old bush paddock on the edge of town. He did nothing but sit down day after day with a bottle of wine and his guitar for company. One day, he sat down and never got up again. His heart decided it had had enough. It was as if it had soaked up all the grog Roy was consuming, become swollen with it, and then stopped. At least that's what they said happened, but I wouldn't have been surprised to find that it had broken in two.

Roy was only the first to go. Poor old Siddy Austin was next. He and Margaret and the kids found themselves alone and desperate in Neerim South. They were in a house, sure enough, and the church people, in their righteous way, probably tried to support them best they could, but a bored and lonely man soon stops taking care of himself. Siddy had already been lured by grog before he left the Track, but once off the Track, he was into it day and night to drown his sorrows. I can imagine the do-gooders not knowing what to do with him, getting angry with him and even being tempted to wash their hands of him. Siddy was soon dead and the shocking thing was that Margaret was soon to follow in exactly the same way. Who would have thought it? A woman who never touched a drop and fought the demon drink with a vengeance, in her despair turned to it and killed herself with it. The orphaned children were taken in by relatives at Lake Tyers. We would have had them if they had come to us and asked to stay. We would never turn anyone away. But we didn't go look for them because we always thought it was better for kids to be with their true relatives. At least they didn't end up in the Homes. We were very downhearted about what happened to the Austins. They were a wonderful family whose luck ran out. They never should have shifted from the Track.

Finally, six months after Roy died, the shire saw fit to begin moving the people out of the tents and into good homes in Drouin and Warragul. I know many people in these towns were worried about the living conditions of the blackfellas once they realised it was not their choice to live in tents, and some council members campaigned hard to find houses for them. There were many more people who never even knew the blackfellas were there, and still others who thought they should be forgotten out on the edge of town and left to die.

Without considering how the blackfellas felt, the policy of the Board was to separate the people from each other, put them singly in white neighbourhoods, hope they would somehow turn white themselves and disappear altogether. And so it was that the Hoods found themselves separated from the Roses for the first time in twenty-five years, that Anabelle Tregoning Kennedy found herself on her own, that Adelaide Rose Wilson found it difficult to see her grandchildren. In my mind, separating the people like that was a needless cruelty, just one more betrayal piled on all the rest.

All the families were put on Aboriginal pensions. They were given furniture and some food to get themselves started and told to look after themselves with their pensions. Another cruelty. These people had never lived in a situation where everything they had – food, drink, electricity, telephone, water, housing, clothing – had to be paid for. Before they lived at the Track, most of them had come from mission stations where they weren't allowed to lift a finger to take care of themselves without being told what to do. At the Track, they had taken care of themselves in a traditional way: they hunted for much of their food, they built their own houses, fetched their own water, collected their own fuel. They worked for their own money to pay for clothes and staples, taxis and entertainment if they wanted it.

Even though they did not live on top of each other at the Track, they never acted as individuals, but always as a community, sharing the food and fuel and water, helping each other with their huts, swapping tools and utensils as well as kids, since every adult was an uncle or an aunty to every kid. I can remember, if somebody heard there was good entertainment on – a country and western concert, a rodeo, an Elvis Presley movie at the drive-in – they'd all tumble into my truck along with Euphie and me and the kids and go along. We all loved the Bunyip drive-in movies. We must have looked a sight, and people must have thought I was brazen, a whitefella driving a bunch of blacks around town, but we were all in it together.

Now in the towns, they were expected to live apart and act apart, taking care of themselves and no one else. Of course, things began to go wrong. Surprising things would happen, like the electricity being cut off – surprising to no one except people who had never had to pay bills before. The rent would get into arrears and then the people found themselves facing angry landlords. The phone bills would be unpayable, they were so huge. Even I was surprised myself at what a lifestyle change it was turning out to be. It wouldn't have occurred to me either that I would have had to buy a lawn-mower to keep the lawn tidy, or that people would object if I turned the front yard into a vegetable garden, my usual practice wherever I lived. It seemed out-rageous to me that Stewart and Dora had to pay for their water and it would have been difficult to get used to the idea of paying for meat.

The worst thing was that whenever the blackfellas had visitors land at their doorstep, the neighbours would go dotty. Stewart couldn't understand it. He was used to having his camp the centre of the community social life and now he was suffering under the watchful gaze of his neighbours, who resented it if anyone stopped by. He used to come out to the Track now and again just to get away from it. He would camp out, not stopping in the house, but have meals with us and entertain us with tales of woe and complaint. He was especially upset about blackfellas getting into trouble with the police because they had too many visitors and neighbours were complaining about noise.

'Whitefellas don't get it. Nobody's gonna turn away a relative, but I've seen them shut the door on their own folks,' he'd say. 'And they're so quiet and unfriendly. They never look ya in the eye. And they never smile.'

People around the camp fire would listen to him and shake their heads in wonder. 'It must be awful being the only blackfella in a street of whites,' somebody would venture.

'Bloody awful livin' in the town, no matter who's your neighbour!' Stewart would mutter. You could tell he was despondent about it. A year ago he would have shouted that like a curse. So someone else shouted it for him.

'Bloody awful!'

I know when Euphie and I visited Stewart and Dora in town it was like visiting people in jail. Stewart would start complaining the minute we walked in the door.

'Whites say stuff about you, but not to you,' he used to say as if he'd only just realised it.

I would nod, knowing full well what kind of things they said. 'You only have to look at their faces to know what they're thinking, Stewart,' I'd answer.

'They are watching every move we make. It's a terrible place.'

When we left, Euphie would often comment that she was worried about her mother's health. I knew what she meant. I was worried about all of them. In my opinion their living in town was even worse than having to put up with the conditions in the bush paddock. At least there they were together and had no neighbours worrying them.

None of them should have been moved off the Track.

Losing Heart

BACK WHEN Jimmy Bond died, the land settlement between Mavis and me finally came through. Just like I had offered her in the first place, she took the cleared 186 acres and I kept the rest. I never hired a lawyer or made a claim against the 186 acres, but I knew she had spent good money on lawyers trying to get more than she deserved. I felt a certain satisfaction about that. I was glad it hadn't come to a row, but I might have had satisfaction in beating her in a fight, as well. She, of course, sold her acres as soon as she could and it was many, many years before I saw her again.

It made no difference to us. We continued our logging and mill

The forest in springtime

work as usual, having known all along that Mavis would get away with nothing. It was Jimmy's death that made me feel that things had altered. There was a changed atmosphere, a feeling of emptiness, where Jimmy's hard-working honesty had been. Nevertheless, we had to work all the harder because cut timber was beginning to lose its market value. By the time the blackfellas were told they were to be shifted, the timber industry had dropped to its lowest ebb and many mills in the district were closing down, some even sent bankrupt.

Doing business was becoming increasingly difficult, especially for a man who didn't like doing business. I had been supplying timber to one company who suddenly went broke and failed to pay me thousands of pounds for loads of timber I had delivered to them. Money got tighter and tighter, and at the same time we were beginning to run out of trees big enough to use as saw logs. Well, there were still lots of large old trees, but they were gnarled and crooked, no good for timber and too good for firewood. They kept the forest ancient. In fact, the forest was thick with trees, but most of them were too young. They needed another twenty-five years' growth on them.

Spurred on by the responsibility I felt for all my workers and my large extended family, I kept the mill going by buying in logs from elsewhere and venturing out to the state forest. I stopped cutting palings and sold the radial saw bench I had for cutting them to the mill at Bunyip. Since I knew the people there well, I let them take it on trust, but the mill went into receivers' hands and I didn't get one shilling for it. We kept going. The timber and logging business had always been up and down. A man had to chase his money, something I wasn't very interested in doing, and you expected bounced cheques now and again. We had been through these times before and we would have weathered this economic drought, if the blackfellas hadn't been shifted and we hadn't had to deal with a sense of disintegration on top of everything.

The blackfellas who were left at the Track after so many had gone felt uneasy, as if they were living on borrowed time. When would the next change of Board policy capture them? At first they stuck around like a tightly knit group. We all did things together: ate together, worked together, told yarns to each other around the fire. We were like a large family, but everything had become quieter, darker, duller. Pretty soon, the blackfellas began to drift away. They went walkabout. Some came back, but most didn't.

Gene Mobourne left soon after everyone was moved into houses in the towns. A while back, his son, Angus, or Sam, as we all called him, had gone to Lake Tyers where he knew Janie Marks, one of the girls Dora and I had brought down from Dimboola. Janie had two children, and was shifted from Lake Tyers into a house in Drouin. Sam decided to move to Drouin to look after Janie. Effie decided she wanted to be with them to look after their two small children. Gene soon followed, was given the pension, and never returned. It was a blow to lose Gene. We were great friends and worked well together, but, in my experience, once they moved to Drouin, they never came back. Gene eventually died at Lake Tyers.

Soon after Gene left, Jack Patton and Bob Nelson followed. I didn't keep up with them and never knew what happened to them, but they never returned. Old Les Monta was suffering from arthritis. He decided to take some time off to visit relatives at Eden. He never returned.

Willie Marks was never the same after Jimmy died. He often went back and forth to Dimboola. One day he went up there and never returned, even though we expected him back. He had found himself a camp along the river, but then he was shifted into town.

He was a stubborn bloke and kept going back to the river bank. I heard he frustrated the tidy plans of the townspeople and the Protection Board. We missed old Willie and kept hoping for his return, but finally we got word that he had died. So many people were dying. No one ever died here at the Track.

My own oldest boys began working on the mill to replace those who had left. Lionel Rose worked with us as well until he left to go into training full-time for the lightweight boxing championship. Jackie Green was the last to leave. He went to Tarago and built himself a hut, where he stayed until he died. He was a mad old fella, never got over his shell shock from the war. I hated to see him go, but he needed to be nearer other blackfellas and there weren't many left here.

The only person who stayed was Dave Moore. Others came and went, but Dave was the only one to stay. It's true that one night of decision making at the Drouin Council meeting had broken up an entire community. People don't know what they do.

It got so that the only logs we were cutting were ones I carted home on my truck. I was down to a small crew of four working on the mill: Dave and my son Mac, who was about fourteen years old, Lionel, a few years older, and Smoky Mobourne, one of Gene's sons. I had to hire another man to help me keep the logs up to the mill-hands. Euphie's two boys, Gary and Buddy, were living with us now that their grandparents were in town. Gary worked at the mill, too, when Mac was at school. It was hard yakka, and the thing was the heart had gone out of it. You can work all day as long as you've got hope in your heart, but it was like a plague had been through a place and all the people in the whole community had been wiped out. What were we working so hard for, if no one was left? I had never felt this way before. Everything had gone quiet.

One weekend I was working in the log yard so as to get a good start for the next week when a well-dressed man approached me. I was startled to see someone with such shiny shoes walking in my yard. Behind him I caught a glimpse of a shined-up, flash car.

Must be a city slicker, I thought to myself. Must be lost.

'What can I do for ya?' I asked, wiping my hands along the seat of my pants.

He continued to come towards me, then confidently stuck out his hand and shook mine vigorously while he introduced himself.

'I'm out here looking over the countryside,' he said, turning his head this way and that. 'Lovely country.'

I nodded, trying to follow his gaze. What's he up to? I wondered. I looked back at him and caught his eye. 'You lost?'

'No, no! I'm thinking about investing in some bush blocks out this way.'

'What for?'

'I think it would be a sound idea to clear them and turn them into cattle farms or even dairying properties.'

'Hmmmph,' I snorted. No chance he will be able to clear this place, I thought. Too much ancient timber still standing to make it worthwhile, but I kept the conversation going out of politeness. 'What would you think of paying?'

'I'm willing to pay up to twenty-five pounds an acre.'

I raised my eyebrows. I was surprised. That didn't seem too bad to me. I looked around me again. This land, full of saplings and useless growth, seemed a burden to me just then. It was doing me no good and nobody was living on it any more. What was the sense of keeping it when I had a buyer standing right in front of me? Right then, I couldn't see any good in the place. I didn't care what happened to it, although I was sure nothing would happen. If Harry had been alive, he would have worked until he dropped trying to clear it. So why not let someone else break their back trying? This man had appeared before me at one of the lowest times in my life. Lucky for him.

This man and I sat down for a long talk. He offered me a deposit of four hundred pounds there and then with the balance payable in twelve months. We agreed I would keep five acres with the mill on it and have an easement through the property along the old track which was on the crown of the hill so I could have access to the state forest, my old home. I would have the mill, the houses, the Gipsy Creek and the main forest. It seemed a good deal to a broken man, who didn't know he was as down as he was. Nothing would really change and the burden of the property would no longer be mine. In fact, when I shook on the deal and pocketed his cheque, I was feeling clever, like a good businessman.

Now, I can't believe I did it. If the blackfellas had still been there, I'd never have done it.

For a year, nothing seemed to change. We kept hearing bad news about the blackfellas in town. Alcohol was now part of life there. Even the older kids were beginning to drink. We heard about Siddy's death and then Margaret's. We heard that Dora might be sick. We kept working the same as always. We heard Lionel was doing well and winning bout after bout. That was about the only good news.

At the end of that bleak year, I received the remainder due to me for the property, although it didn't seem as much to me as I'd agreed on, since in the meantime our money had changed over from the English way of reckoning in pounds to the American way in dollars and cents. I couldn't quite get my head around it, and neither could I get my head around the fact that the land was no longer mine. Nothing seemed to change at first; that is, until three months later when the bulldozers came in to begin the clearing. Usually, when a property is cleared, it takes a long time, with the farmer clearing one paddock at a time, fencing it and seeding it, before going on to the next paddock. Usually a farmer does it on his own, farming as he goes. But the new owner was a rich man from Melbourne interested more in avoiding taxes than anything else. It was worth his while to spend lots of money quickly so he could claim it at the end of the financial year, rather than go slowly. He hired a team of people to clear the land as fast as they could.

They started on the easy end of the property where the trees had been cut years ago and the stumps were pretty rotten. They tore through two hundred acres in no time. I hadn't figured they would get through it so quickly. Even though it was only two hundred acres, the place felt altered and foreign. We could stand on the red hill and see all the way to the Track itself without anything in its way. The wind began to make itself felt in a way we had never noticed. I felt uneasy. But then all work stopped, and I began to breathe again.

He must have decided it would cost him too much, I thought. He'll never clear it. There's too much. This will always be bush.

But I was wrong. Six months later, the bulldozers were back. This time they tackled the thick of it, mowing down the saplings as if they were blades of grass; that is, grass that splinters and twists and makes terrible wrenching sounds as it goes down. When they came to the big trees, they were slowed down somewhat, but they didn't go around them as commonsense should have dictated. A couple of dozers at a time would worry the trees until they gave way and crashed to the ground.

I hadn't reckoned on how strange we would feel as the trees came splintering and twisting down around us. We felt like strangers on our own land. For months, the sound of bulldozers shattering and destroying trees was all round us, day after day. Once they falled one section, they would begin to push the fallen timber into long, heaped-up rows. And then we lived with the smell of wood fire and we worked in the haze of smoke as heap after heap of saplings and stumps was lit all around us. Once everything was burning they'd move on to the next section. Day after day. Month after month. Section after section. Each time we looked up from our work, the place was changed. If it had seemed like a plague had been through here before, now it seemed like a war was taking place. The wreckage lasted for eighteen months.

They were leaving nothing standing. Not even any wind breaks. They didn't seem to know what they were doing. They were being blindly destructive. They pushed down and dragged away all the trees along the creeks. Everyone knows a creek needs its trees. Then they went through and straightened the creeks so it would be easier to fence the place in rectangular paddocks. But everyone knows a straightened creek will wash out. It will cut deep down into the soil, eroding everything around it, carrying sand to adjoining properties. Turning a creek into a straight drain is a stupidity. Our part of Gipsy Creek began to silt up and the bottom near the mill began to turn into a boggy swamp. These people were criminals! But the rich don't care.

When I had agreed on the clearing, I had forgotten what it was like to live out in the open away from the protection of the trees. The wind blew and we felt its chill in our very bones. The rain beat down on the roof of the house, and the hail. As the season turned warmer, the unfiltered sun dried everything to dust. The earth cracked underneath our feet and grit ground in our teeth, our skin blistered and hardened. The birds disappeared. I had never dreamed it would go like this. I thought there would always be bush.

We were in the middle of something unnatural, in the middle of a place destroyed, in the middle of nothing. I know I was shocked, and I don't know if I've ever got over that shock. I know now that if Harry hadn't died, if Jimmy hadn't been killed, if Stewart and all the blackfellas had been left here, then I wouldn't have lost heart; I wouldn't have sold the property, and a mighty forest would still be standing today with creeks flowing through it and laughter in the air.

Grief

I AM EIGHTY YEARS OLD NOW and in all the years since the blackfellas were forced out and the forest was destroyed, I've never stopped thinking about it, never stopped missing the old times and the old people, the children. Gee, I miss the kids, so nice, warm, generous and laughing. I can hear them in my mind, spontaneous, playing, chattering away with their stories and games. They would come into our camp any time to make themselves a big sandwich, or clean a place on the ground to play hopscotch. It's all silence now, except for the wind.

What happened to everybody? I can't remember where all of

Daryl at seventy-nine years

them went: Anabelle Tregoning Kennedy didn't stay around long after the move into Drouin, but I don't know where she went, although I've heard she's still alive, a witness just like me.

Les and Nellie Stewart also disappeared, but others came to take their place.

After Roy Rose died, Euphie wanted Gina and the kids to move in with us instead of staying out in the bush paddock along the highway. Euphie is protective of her family and Gina is her closest sister. So Gina, the kids, and, of course, Jamby and Adelaide came out to stay with us in the crowded mill house while they waited for a house in Drouin. But with so many others gone, there was a sense of desolation for them. They went back and forth, going from Drouin to Jackson's Track trying to find the place where they belonged. Lionel worked for me, but he hitchhiked to Melbourne every single weekend to watch the fights.

Jamby died just before Gina got a house up near the school in Drouin. She and Adelaide moved in with all the children and stayed put. Adelaide was kept busy being a grandmother to the brood until she was finally placed in a home in Melbourne where she soon died. Gina had many children to raise on her own then, but they thrived and made her proud, especially Lionel, who became bantamweight boxing champion of the world. Gina is also still alive, another witness.

I kept in contact with many of the Austin children, who became a restless bunch and moved back and forth between Lake Tyers and Drouin, from house to house. They were still wonderful children, but tragedy dogged them. It is a shock to remember Lena's story. I'll never forget all the hope and love in her as she set off for Western Australia. She gave me a warm goodbye kiss and smiled and waved as she departed for her journey. We never saw her again. The next thing we heard was that some mongrel had poured petrol over her and set her alight. A beautiful girl like her! Out of all the stories, that one seems to break my heart. I weep. I've never seen a family go with so much grief and sadness. The Austins never should have left the Track.

Gene Mobourne took to the drink once he shifted to Drouin to be with Effie and their son, Sam. Gene died while he was visiting Lake Tyers. He drank himself to death, simple as that, as far as I'm concerned. But what a blow to think that I would never see my old friend again.

Dora and Stewart Hood never moved from their house, but Dora died of cancer in 1967 and Stewart died in 1970. Their son Ruben married Gloria and was shifted to the railway house in Rokeby where they lived with their growing number of toddlers and infants until they were moved to Warragul with their brood. There are many Hoods now in Warragul, keeping the place lively. The great-granddaughters are finishing school and receiving awards.

And Euphie and me? We stayed at the Track and raised our family. I continued to work the mill, but getting logs was difficult and I never did have easy access to the forest as I should have. The new owners made life difficult by putting too many gates along the easement to open and close, and they didn't like seeing black people around. They were trying to force me out.

They never got rid of me, for I am a stubborn man if I am anything, but I finally sold the mill itself in 1975. However, I didn't retire and it was not the end of my bush life. My boys were all reaching working age and as they finished school they came to work for me out in the bush, cutting poles to go to the treating works at Fischer's in Korumburra and Hickson's in Officer. They wanted poles instead of split posts for the treating and they had to be three to five inches thick for fence posts or eight to twelve inches thick for strainers. So we culled saplings, which were growing in over-abundance in the forest, and cut them into six- or eight-foot lengths for fence posts, and twelve-foot lengths for stays. We cut anything: wattle, messmate, stringy-bark, silver-top. We were doing the forest a favour, thinning it out, letting the strong growers find light and height instead of choking in the thick gloom.

It was enjoyable working with my sons, watching them grow in strength and confidence. All my children, the boys and the girls, learned to be workers. All they learned from their parents, year after year, were lessons about work, healthy living and achievement. They had two workers, Euphie and me, to look up to. I always thought Euphie worked harder than me in the long run. After all, she had twelve children and a husband to look after. Her work was always more perfect than mine, I think, although we were both skilled and both proud of our work. For one thing, Euphie knew how to keep a fire going, knew how to have the perfect burn for whatever she was cooking. She was a perfectionist and brought the kids up in the same way. They had it drummed into them to live decently. Euphie was the best mother alive. She was like a cow with her calf; she would turn and defend her young against any threat no matter how ferocious. To her the biggest threat to her kids was that they should lose hope. She insisted all her children went to school and never missed a day.

Euphie was fierce in her opinions and she always warned the children about no-hopers, which she thought many of the towns-people were turning into. To her credit, all the kids became great at sports, trying their best and succeeding. The five oldest won the Victorian state badminton singles and doubles championships over many years. We were so proud of those kids for their achievements. People never thought such triumph could have come out of the blackfellas' camp at Jackson's Track.

Euphie made sure our kids had a stable home life. Of course, we had visitors, people coming and going, but no drinking, never drinking. Drunks who turned up soon had to face Euphie and she let them know they weren't welcome. I've always been proud of Euphie and her strong spirit. I picked the right woman all right.

All my children – the Mullett kids – have found their place in the world: Dot, who has four children and looks after Buddy's two grandchildren, works in the public health system at a hospital; Mac (Philip) has always been a bushman like me and is living in far-east Gippsland, working at the mill at Cann River; Curly (Cheryl) has three fine children; Sandra was sensible and stayed single, but she has a job working on Native Title issues; Snag (Russell) is married with two children and works in Victorian Aboriginal Affairs as a Cultural Officer; Bic (Linda) has three children and works in the Department of Human Services (Health); Cat (Trevor), the smart one in the family – smart on trucks – has two kids and drives semitrailers all over this country; Haggie (Pauline) has three kids and works in arts and crafts; Ben (Howard) has one child and is living in Warrigal where he works as a labourer; and Valda is still young, living on my property. Chook (Gary) is single and lives in Drouin. Buddy is married, has two children and lives in East Gippsland. My kids are smart and they are using their knowledge in the best ways. I see bits of Euphie in each one of them.

When I finally gave the posts away in the early eighties, Euphie announced that she wanted to move into Drouin to help Dot with her children. I guess Euphie was feeling like she was out of a job now that most of the kids had moved on. I agreed to move to Drouin with her. But, of course, it didn't last long for me. I couldn't settle. Then we moved to Linda's place, but I couldn't settle there either. I was still doing work out at the Track, anything that was going: picking up spuds in season, handling cattle for Jimmy Robbo, cutting a bit of firewood, contract fencing. I couldn't stay away from the area. I went back and forth between the Track and Drouin.

I didn't like it in town. I didn't like seeing the blackfellas around me with nothing to do. I hated seeing them bored, getting dole money to drink with. To my mind they shouldn't have been in the town. They should have stayed in the bush where their skills and deep knowledge were useful. It's natural for the blackfellas to work for a fair wage, to build their own houses and to care for themselves. I hated knowing that what they were doing was unnatural. Towns are unnatural, all built up with brick and concrete. No house should ever be built that you cannot put a match to and get rid of when its usefulness is over.

Euphie could see that I was pining for a settled life in the bush, but she was happy anywhere there were kids and didn't want to move back to an empty mill house at Jackson's Track. Even old Dave Moore was gone. He had been coming and going for years. But one day, while he was on the coast of New South Wales, he had an accident and cut his leg on a rock. The next thing I heard, he had died in a hospital up there. Eighty years old. Another empty space that would never be filled on the Track. Euphie just didn't want to go back to a place full of ghosts, but she didn't want to stop me. Finally, once she got her own house in Drouin, she let me come back to the Track for good. I still cared for her, brought her firewood, cut the lawn, made a garden, supported her with money. She was happy and so was I.

Euphie became Ma to every grandchild, and there were lots of them in Drouin. They called me Pop and that's how it stayed. The friends and husbands and wives of my children began to call me D.A. I think it was Dave Proctor who started that, but don't ask me why, and I became Uncle to everyone else. But Euphie was Ma to everyone, a wise woman who demanded respect.

Euphie died only a few weeks ago. She called herself Euphemia Mullett Tonkin in the end. I know there's really nothing in a name, but that's how she called herself.

I still live here on the Track in the last of the mill houses. I spend my time gathering firewood for myself and the family if they want it. I keep the wood up to the fire in the main room that serves as kitchen, lounge room, dining room, office, workroom. I spend a fair amount of my time sitting directly in front of the fire watching the billy boil. The yarns people used to tell float around in my head as I tend the fire, throw a pinch of tea-leaves directly into my stained brown cup, pour some boiling water into it from the billy and let it brew. I remember the talk and laughter, the voices.

No use thinking about it.

I lift my cup of strong black tea and carry it outside. Now all I hear is the wind that whispers through the fine grasses growing in abundance on what used to be the forest floor. The creek is silent for it no longer runs but seeps through tussocks that come up through silt. Down where the creek used to be, all that remains of the mill itself is the concrete block the engine was bolted to and the rusted and corroded boiler standing witness. There are no trees. I lift my gaze and look off past naked, overgrazed paddocks to see the state forest. The boronia still grows there in spring and the currawong still keeps a man company if he's on his own and quiet about his work. I go there often, but I am sad to see that the forest is not being taken care of. There will be another burn there soon. In my opinion it will be worse than the last for the place is crowded with saplings that haven't had room to grow strong enough to survive a blast. Where's the sense in it? Who will remember what it was like?

The blackfellas will.

Jackson's Track for me and the blackfellas is now a dreamtime place. It was a place that was a paradise. The blackfellas hand down stories of their experiences on the Track to their young and to other blackfellas who were never there. It's the stories and the memories, the ghosts and spirits of the people who lived here that make the place belong to the blackfellas. It will never belong to anyone else for there was never so much love for the place as when the blackfellas were here. They are still here. I can sense them.

November 1997

AFTERWORD

Our kids were brought up without what most families take for granted. We carried our water up from the creek for drinking and used a forty-four-gallon drum cut in half to boil the water for washing and baths. We had no refrigerator or washing machine. The washing was done by hand and the ironing was done with a flat iron, heated up in front of the fire. For lighting we used kerosene lanterns.

But we gave our kids a good start in life. Their mother didn't have a lazy bone in her body and worked day and night for them. She made them attend school every day and taught them to be honest and good, and to respect their elders. She was responsible for their success

Left to right: Philip, Cheryl, Sandra, Russell and Linda Mullett
(Albert Park sports centre, Melbourne)

in life. When the kids went to school they were frightened and shy but their teacher believed all his students were equal and stood for no nonsense from them.

Not many people are aware of our children's achievements, or of their lifestyle and the conditions they grew up in. At Jackson's Track we managed to raise Aboriginal children who have really made successes of their lives.

I supplied timber to a man named Tom Hines and his family who had a dairy farm about four miles away from us situated at Labertouche North. Tom was in his nineties and had three sons who worked the farm. They were good, honest people, clean living and homely, who would share their meal with decent people. They were well respected in the district and took an interest in the neighbours.

They advocated that two tennis courts be built next to the Labertouche Hall for the local people to play on. When they got the approval from the shire they encouraged everyone in the district to play. They really got things moving. Dick Hines was keen to teach the Labertouche schoolchildren how to play, and he got them playing on the courts. Our children attended the Labertouche school and Dick told them that if they played he would give them a ride to our road in his car. So, of course, they started to play.

If it was dry they played tennis, but if it was raining he had them playing badminton in the hall. Our road was a mill road and was not owned by the shire. It was about half a mile long and used by trucks carrying heavy loads, which was hard on the roads and made deep holes in places that were too deep for motor cars. When it was wet, it was slippery on the hill, so Dick would only drive on the roads in the summertime.

Dick knew I had no time for sport as I spent all my time working in the bush. He also knew I would rather have the kids home working, so he knew if he didn't pick them up I wouldn't take them to sport. He loved taking the kids and they liked him. They also met a lot of people, which was good for them, and they were keen to play.

After they played for a couple of seasons in the local competitions he asked for our permission to take them down to Albert Park badminton stadium, where they played tournaments. Dick knew they were good enough to win championships.

We trusted Dick and knew he would take care of the children, for he was a sensible driver, so we said, 'All right.' Euphie made all the girls dresses for them to play in and Dick bought them a tracksuit each. He paid for fees, meals, accommodation and fares when they got good enough to travel interstate.

The kids would come home late at night after Dick dropped them off at our road. They were frightened of the dark and worried about mrartches, so their hair must have stood on end when the bush animals made noises as they rustled out of their way through the bush. They were always relieved to reach home, where our fire burnt all night in the fireplace that was six feet long and four feet wide. Euphie would have the lanterns alight. She always waited for her kids to come home. She was busy sewing clothes, ironing or cleaning up to fill in her time. They would arrive home laughing and joking about the fears they had had along the road.

All our children were successful in their badminton playing, and this was due to their dedication and the hard work they put in with Dick. They won every title in the state junior badminton competition in July 1968, while their cousin Lionel Rose won the world bantamweight boxing championship the same year.

Russell and his partner took the Victorian Under 17 Boys' Doubles Championship in 1967 and 1968. The City of Melbourne

Junior Schoolboy and Schoolgirl Championship Under 15 Boys'
Singles was won by Russell in 1968. Sandra won the Singles in 1969
and 1970. The Women's Doubles Championship was won by Cheryl
and her partner in 1969, and Sandra and her partner in 1970. Linda
won the Under 13 Girls' Singles in 1968. The Victorian Junior
Championship Men's Singles was won by Philip in 1966, 1967 and
1968, and Cheryl won the Women's Singles in 1965, 1966, 1967,
1968, 1969 and 1970. The Boys' Doubles was won by Philip and
Russell in 1968. Cheryl and her partner won the Girls' Doubles in
1967 and 1968, and Sandra and her partner won it in 1970. The
Under 15 Girls' Singles was won by Sandra in 1965, 1967, 1968 and
1970. The Mixed Doubles was won by Philip and his partner in
1968, and Cheryl won it with her partner in 1969.

The house was full of trophies. Euphie and I were proud of the
children.

It was a great achievement.

We felt it was necessary to write this chapter so readers could be aware of and understand the historical events and circumstances that have affected Aboriginal people in Victoria. We believe that life on Jackson's Track was a very important part of this history.

Europeans first made contact with Australian Aborigines in 1788. The natives in south-east Australia did not experience the invasion until 1834, but they felt the impact of introduced diseases before that. In 1789 and 1829 epidemics spread into central and western Victoria (probably from the Sydney region), killing more than half of the Aboriginal population, and severely weakening their culture.

The Hentys squatted at Portland in November 1834 and John Batman and John Pascoe Fawkner possessed Melbourne in August 1835. Within ten years of this, most of central and lower-western Victoria was overrun with sheep and cattle. One of the most unfortunate effects of the squatting movement was the tendency of white settlers to take up those areas that were the most important to the Aboriginal economy. Grasslands and woodlands near streams and rivers were most suitable for cattle and sheep grazing. The land was battered by these cloven-hoofed animals, ploughed and re-sown. This put native fauna under threat, particularly kangaroos and emus, which were dealt with ruthlessly and efficiently by the settlers. These animals began to grow thin because they were being hunted too much. A variety of plant food such as the daisy yam also suffered. Gradually the nutritious native plants disappeared. This all led to malnutrition and death amongst Aboriginal communities.

The Aboriginal population fell dramatically. In the western district and Gippsland areas of Victoria there were brutal massacres and individual killings. Much of the population decline was caused by the consequences of invasion and dispossession. Other deaths were caused by introduced diseases such as respiratory infections, dysentery and some European 'childhood' illnesses like measles. Venereal diseases caused sterility, and some people simply refused to have children because of the loss of their land and their culture. By 1850 alcohol abuse was also leading to further deaths.

In 1861 the Aborigines Protection Board created an Aboriginal reserve at Framlingham, outside Warrnambool. Four major church mission stations were also established. Ebenezer at Lake Hindmarsh near Dimboola (1859), Ramahyuck at Lake Wellington (1861), Lake Tyers in East Gippsland (1861), and Lake Condah (1867). In 1869 only a quarter of the Aboriginal people recorded in Victoria lived on these stations. The remainder lived independently until the Board succeeded in pushing them onto the stations by 1880. They did this by using various means of persuasion, which included withdrawal of rations, seizure of children (who were given over to the Department of Neglected Children) and forcible transfer under police escort.

Most reserves developed farming, which needed minimal financial help. Coranderrk reserve near Healesville, which was established by 1863, was the most prosperous. It became a showpiece for Aboriginal agricultural skill. John Green, the supervisor, allowed the people freedom of decision-making. They were expert hop-growers and wage earners, but were still guided by their own cultural principles. The Board increased its control over Framlingham and Coranderrk, removing Green in 1874 and selling Coranderrk in 1875.

In 1886 the Aborigines Protection Act was amended so that only those who were deemed as 'full-blood', or 'half-caste' over thirty-four years of age, and children were permitted to live on the reserves. People who didn't fall into these categories had to leave, fend for themselves, and eventually assimilate into the general community. The Act undermined the reserves and, in reducing numbers, split up families. The reserves were eventually closed altogether and sold, but a few defiant Framlingham people were allowed to stay on unsupervised. Everyone else was transferred to Lake Tyers. To this day, Aboriginal people are living in harmony with the land at both Framlingham and Lake Tyers.

Many Aboriginal people came to live at Jackson's Track in the 1940s, forming a large community. They came from all over Victoria and New South Wales, particularly from the Walaga Lake reserve, the Wimmera region and the western district. The Aborigines Protection Board knew about the settlement on Jackson's Track, but chose to turn a blind eye – the Aborigines were living scattered about in thick bush, without health problems, and were working and living independently. The local people complained to the police on the grounds of being afraid of black people. The police came out a few times to demand that the employment of Aborigines be stopped, but then just went back to where they had come from. When the employment continued, the police threatened charges of harbouring criminals, but these threats were ignored. The Aboriginal people made no trouble in the district so the police left them alone.

In July 1957, the Aborigines Protection Board, which had first been established by the Aborigines Protection Act of 1886, was dissolved. In its place a body corporate called the Aborigines Welfare

Board was established. The Aborigines Welfare Board consisted of education, housing and health ministers, and five other members, two of whom had to be Aborigines, and one an expert in anthropology or sociology. The function of the Aborigines Welfare Board was to: 'promote the moral, intellectual and physical welfare of Aborigines (which term for the purposes of the Act includes not only full-blooded Aboriginal natives of Australia but also any person of Aboriginal descent) with a view to their assimilation into the general community'. Most Aborigines around the state, and certainly the people at Jackson's Track, were not fully aware that the Protection Board had changed to the Welfare Board. To them, all 'whitefella' authority, whether it was the mission managers, the church people, the police or the social workers, was known as the 'Board' or the 'Welfare', and this perceived authority was impossible to resist.

In 1959 the Aborigines (Housing) Act made houses in towns available for the Aborigines Welfare Board to use. Towns like Drouin took advantage of the new policies to clean up 'eyesores'. The final tragedy that occurred in 1962 at Jackson's Track is mirrored in a long history of dispossessions and betrayals in Victoria.

Daryl Tonkin and Linda Mullett, September 1998

References

'The Aborigines of Port Phillip 1835–1839', *Historical Records of Victoria*, editor-in-chief Michael Cannon, vol. 2A, Victorian Public Record Office, Melbourne, 1982.

Aborigines Protection Act 1886 (Vic.).

'Aborigines and Protectors 1838–1839', *Historical Records of Victoria*, editor-in-chief Michael Cannon, vol. 2B, Victorian Public Record Office, Melbourne, 1983.

Anderson, Ian, *Koorie Health in Koorie Hands: An Orientation Manual in Aboriginal Health for Health-care Providers*, Koorie Health Unit, Health Department, Victoria, 1988.

Attwood, Bain, *The Making of the Aborigines*, Allen & Unwin, Sydney, 1989.

Gott, Beth, and Zola, Nelly, *Koorie Plants, Koorie People: Traditional Aboriginal Food, Fibre and Healing Plants of Victoria*, Koorie Heritage Trust, Melbourne, 1992.

Keen, Ian (ed.), *Being Black: Aboriginal Cultures in 'Settled' Australia*, Aboriginal Studies Press for Australian Institute of Aboriginal Studies, Canberra, 1988.

Koorie Creative Solutions, Information booklet of the Koorie Heritage Trust, Melbourne, 1991.

Massola, Aldo, *Aboriginal Mission Stations in Victoria: Yelta, Ebenezer, Ramahyuck, Lake Condah*, Hawthorn Press, Melbourne, 1970.

Pepper, Phillip, and De Araugo, Tess, *The Kurnai of Gippsland*, Hyland House, Melbourne, 1989.

—— *You Are What You Make Yourself To Be: The Story of a Victorian Aboriginal Family 1842–1980*, Hyland House, Melbourne, 1989.

Spreadborough, Robert, and Anderson, Hugh, *Victorian Squatters*, Red Rooster Press, Melbourne, 1983.